NEEDHAM

W9-CHD-602

2/5/72

OFFENSIVE MARKETING

or how to make your competitors followers

TO MY PARENTS

OFFENSIVE MARKETING

or how to make your competitors followers

J. H. DAVIDSON, M.A.
Foreword by Anthony J. F. O'Reilly

CASSELL · LONDON

CASSELL & COMPANY LTD
35 Red Lion Square, London WC1R 4SJ
Sydney, Auckland
Toronto, Johannesburg

First published 1972

I.S.B.N. 0 304 93772 X

Printed in Great Britain by
The Camelot Press Ltd, London and Southampton
F. 172

Foreword

by *ANTHONY J. F. O'REILLY*,
Senior Vice-President,
North America and Pacific, H. J. Heinz Company Inc.

Hugh Davidson is an iconoclast. He is also an immensely readable writer, with a strong commercial sense. The strategy of his book underlines the belief that offensive marketing or, in his view, successful marketing, comprises certain attitudes and practices towards marketing, competition and planning, which are, unfortunately, rare.

His definitions are refreshing and simple. He believes that professional marketing involves a determination to achieve all the major innovations in a given market, a freedom from the shackles of industry tradition or interruptive bureaucracy, and a view of marketing as a profit-oriented approach to business that permeates not just the marketing department, but the entire business.

Above all, he believes that offensive marketing requires a dedication to strategy and planning.

Hurrah! it has all been said before, but it has rarely been said so succinctly and so refreshingly. Not above employing popular gurus to bolster his case, he quotes Levitt tellingly: 'When it comes to the marketing concept today, a solid stone wall often seems to separate word from deed.' His answer: 'Kill the bureaucratic plague; dis-establish the maintenance men; stop talking about offensive marketing and *do* something about it.'

He observes, in my view accurately, that good marketing is not so much a matter of intelligence and ability (as good and bad companies seem to have an abundance of both) but much more a question of attitudes, organization and technique.

It is the age of mnemonics and Mr Davidson has a certain elegance in his choice of one. He says that offensive marketing is a matter of POISE, that it should be Profitable, Offensive, Integrated, Strategic (embracing short and long-term corporate plans) and Effectively executed.

The book unashamedly assumes that the right attitudes and organization structures have a profound effect on corporate profit, and essays only one real definition of marketing (and a very good one it is), that it 'involves balancing the company needs for profit against the benefits required by the consumer, so as to maximize long-term earnings per share'. In another way he is saying if you don't balance the short-term profit v consumer benefit equation against your long-term ambitions, you won't have a business to realize those long-term ambitions against.

I take issue with him on the assumption of the degree of control which the marketing man has in most organizations, or is likely to be able to experience in organizations in the future. There is the school of thought which says that the marketing man's responsibility ends at the contribution level, i.e. the difference between net sales value and the directly attributable marketing costs. The other school of thought, of which Mr Davidson is an archdeacon, if not a high priest, says that the marketing man is responsible right down to the net before tax stage.

I find myself in two minds about this. On the one hand I believe that the marketing man is clearly and definedly responsible to the contribution stage. On the other hand, I believe that he should have influence and concern further down the Profit & Loss account. In the final analysis, however, he is not responsible for the debt structure of the company, and items such as interest income and expenditure, which are a function of balance-sheet management rather than marketing skill, should not be his responsibility.

Being of a pragmatic disposition, I am prepared to compromise, and suggest that the responsibility of the Marketing Manager should extend to the operating income level (i.e. include all commercial expense, but exclude interest income and expense). This, therefore, takes the short-term management of the balance sheet and, in particular, the management of receivables and creditors, from his span of responsibilities. The counter argument is that it probably also takes the management of inventories, over which he has considerable responsibility, from his control. On balance, I feel this is a permissible compromise.

The author is at his best in describing marketing perverts. He instances five:

(1) The Consumer Worshippers—where the consumer is always right.
(2) The New Luddites—who view production men as an inferior form of human life.
(3) The Egotistic Employee—who panders to the Company President, knowing that the latter believes that sales volume is more important than profits.
(4) The Milker—who cuts everything, particularly above-the-line expenditure, and then runs for it,

and finally, a superb title:

(5) The Galloping Midget—whose exploits are worth the purchase price of the book.

What Davidson wants is integrated marketing, believing that it is an approach to business rather than a specific discipline. He states that the main benefits successful companies gain through offensive marketing are higher profits, a longer life-cycle on existing products, and a better success rate with new products and acquisitions. Could we ask for more?

My own experience suggests general accord with these principles, and great difficulty in implementing them. In particular, it is extremely difficult to graft policies of innovation and imagination on to big, successful organizations.

The entrepreneur is, by definition, almost a loner. Large businesses have a certain civil-service-like quality about them. Promotion in many instances is by non-mistake rather than by visible victory. Additionally, the gestation period required for new ideas to mature to profitability is often hampered by the internal accountancy disciplines of the organization. An idea, product concept or joint venture may take three to four years to mature to profitability. The normal reporting system of a business is the monthly account, followed by the quarterly report, the half yearly review and the annual assessment. Unless such systems are intelligently interpreted, they can sound the death-knell for a slowly maturing but potentially profitable idea.

One answer is the Venture Management team, free from the shackles of the system. Quite simply, a multi-discipline venture team can bypass much bureaucracy and operate on a discrete time frame, free from monthly interruption and quarterly execution. This is not to write a blank cheque for the Venture Manager, but it is an attempt to position him in a manner which allows imaginative distillation of new ideas, without the interference of systems which are appropriate to successful on-going business, rather than embryonic activity.

Additionally, New Business Development, which I define as any new product, concept, initiative or liaison which can create a new and viable profit centre for the company, should report direct to the chief executive. This does two things:

(1) It involves the chief planning officer of the corporation, the Managing Director/President, in that area where planning is most important, i.e. the development of new business.

(2) Secondly, it elevates the whole concept of new product/new business development on the corporate totem pole, and gives a thrust and vigour to this aspect of the company's activities which it will otherwise not achieve.

From practical experience in the Heinz Company in the United Kingdom, I can say that this structure has provided us with a rapid and apparently successful system of New Business and New Venture development.

The distaff side is that it is time-consuming, and for long periods of time sterile in terms of results achieved. Nevertheless, it remains among the most important responsibilities of any Chief Executive. The same is equally true of acquisitions, both in terms of the defining of the area of search, and participating in the negotiations for the acquisitions candidate.

Davidson analyses the product management system and asks some very blunt questions. For example, does the system justify its cost? Does the specialization lead to tunnel vision or enterprising decision-making? Is there a difference between the specification for the job and the actual powers enjoyed? He quotes an article in the *Harvard Business Review* by David Luck and Theodore Novak, under the heading: 'Product Management—Vision Unfulfilled'. They comment that product management is undoubtedly a difficult system to operate and has had indifferent success in many companies.

He summarizes that product management is no more and no less than a means for executing an integrated marketing approach, and adds that if this kind of approach is not accepted by top corporate management, product managers will be impotent.

The chapter on 'Offensive Strategy for Corporate Growth', with its heading 'The Three Stages of Battle' is sound and rather chilling. The book points out that there is good evidence that the majority of American companies do not use formal strategy to any great extent. It quotes a survey made of 195 American companies by the National Industrial Conference Board in the mid-1960s, which stated that half or more did not have formal policies for acquisition, trade deals, line withdrawals or private label manufacture. The major criticisms of long-term strategies by the participants in the survey were that the strategies tended to be too academic, inhibited flexibility and consumed too much time. He then effectively demolishes all three arguments, admittedly in certain cases with the aid of six/six hindsight vision.

His examination of planning and the product life-cycle is one of the most interesting chapters in the book, and he asserts that consumer tastes, distribution structures, economic and political conditions are today changing more rapidly than at any time in history. I believe he is correct in this assumption. The implications of it are profound. Bennett S. Chapple, Jr., Vice-President of the US Steel Corporation, says: 'Marketing planning is the starting point for all corporate planning. Whether your business involves a service or a product, it is based upon the existence of present and potential markets. Planning with respect to those markets is the basis for the extent and direction of all other corporate decisions.'

I don't operate in the same markets as Mr Chapple, but I agree wholeheartedly with his views in this regard.

Despite being an iconoclast, Davidson is old fashioned in some of his beliefs. He believes that consumers buy product benefits rather than advertising or promotions. He believes that the surest way to corporate growth is through product superiority. Additionally, he believes that all the other members of the marketing mix, such as advertising, promotions, pricing and packaging, respond most amiably to a superior product and will work hardest on its behalf. How many times have we all neglected this truism!

I found his book stimulating, provocative and original—or maybe it was that I was secretly flattered by his agreement with most of my pet prejudices.

22.12.71   *Tony O'Reilly*

Author's Preface

This book is aimed at the practising businessman, who has direct or indirect involvement with marketing. It should also be of interest to the advanced student, and for his benefit some background sections have been included. These are appropriately marked to enable more experienced readers to skip them. *Offensive Marketing* is a practical book, and if readers gain anything from it which enables them to do a better job the following working day, it will have served its purpose. Most good business ideas are simple, and jargon enlightens no one. I hope this book is relatively free of it, and that it will be as easily understood by accountants, sales managers and engineers as by professional marketing people.

Many people helped in the preparation of the book. Antony Carr, Peter Mitchell and Bruce Rowe all read the final draft and made a number of excellent suggestions, as well as providing case histories. I am most grateful to David Blunt and James Lamb of Cassell both for their open-mindedness, and for their informed comments on the first draft. Mr R. N. Wadsworth, Chairman of Cadbury Schweppes Foods, Mr B. Jenkins, Marketing Director of Carreras, Mr R. Gray, Marketing Director of Gibbs, and Mr L. Hardy, Marketing Director of Lever Brothers, were all kind enough to give me their views on assorted marketing subjects at quite short notice and these were most valuable.

Many other business or personal friends have commented on individual chapters or provided information, including Steve Wolloshin, Tom Meinhard, Tony Rogers, David Kearton, Mike Murphy, Jim Broom, Denzil Hughes, Jack Van Turnhout, Ewan Davidson, Jimmy Loughray and Frank Inglis. Others who have influenced the contents are Peter Gray, John Mann, Bob Beeby, Joel Smilow and Patrick Gallagher. Last, but not least, I am grateful to my wife Sandra for typing over a quarter of a million words in connection with this book, mainly between the hours of 8 p.m. and

1 a.m., for pouncing on jargon or pompous phrases whenever they appeared, and for making many common sense suggestions.

For permission to reproduce copyright material from the sources indicated, I am grateful to the following individuals and organizations:

Graham Turner and Eyre & Spottiswoode (Publishers) Ltd, for an extract from *Business in Britain*; and

Robert Jones and Oliver Marriott, and Jonathan Cape Ltd, for an extract from *Anatomy of a Merger: A History of G.E.C., A.E.I. and English Electric*, reprinted by permission of A. D. Peters & Co.

J. H. D.
Datchet, 25 April 1971

Contents

1: Introduction—Offensive Marketing

AN OFFENSIVE PREAMBLE

'Arnold Weinstock was a sceptic. He did not accept that the orthodox method of business was necessarily the most suitable. For example, all the television and radio makers brought out their new models each year in August to coincide with the Radio Show at Earl's Court. Weinstock threw aside this comfortable collective habit and brought out the first new model for which he was responsible in April 1955. It did not make Radio and Allied, or Weinstock, popular in the trade, but that did not worry Weinstock. He was not the clubbable type. The disapproval of the businessmen's cabals did not interest him in the very least. What the production of the new model in that spring of 1955, instead of in August, did do was to boost his sales considerably during the traditionally lean summer months when the public would be holding off ahead of the new models arriving at the Radio Show. While his competitors and even some of his colleagues at Radio and Allied confidently predicted that this ploy would put the company into bankruptcy, the retailers were delighted at the prospect of sales in the summer and pushed Weinstock's models hard. One of the benefits to them was that this new approach stopped the old trouble of all the orders coming in to manufacturers in a short space of time in the autumn and the retailers then not getting proper delivery. Weinstock did the same thing the following year, and the year after that the old system collapsed.

'What this and other unorthodoxies did was to make Radio and Allied phenomenally profitable.'*

You have just read an example of *offensive marketing*. It would have been easy for Weinstock to have considered and rejected the idea of

* Robert Jones and Oliver Marriott, *Anatomy of a Merger: a History of G.E.C., A.E.I. and English Electric* (Jonathan Cape, 1970).

introducing a model in the spring. He could have reasoned that if if it was a good idea, someone would have tried it before. No doubt there were gloomy historians who could point to another company which had done the same thing in 1945 without success. Or Weinstock could have become intimidated by his lack of experience in the industry. There was no reason to change and, as always, a string of arguments were available as to why the risk was not worth taking.

This book is about offensive marketing, which is merely a label for an attitude to business as old as the entrepreneur, combining the age-old virtues of risk-taking with the modern techniques of marketing. Offensive marketing is practised by only a handful of successful companies, and the phrase has been coined to differentiate the contents of this book from the sluggish and specialized concept that passed for marketing in many large companies. Before we describe offensive marketing in detail, let us first have a look at the background that makes it a relevant concept.

Marketing is still a new and relatively glamorous idea in business, and in the 1950s it seemed to be full of promise. It still is, although its performance in the 1960s has been disappointing. Marketing is potentially an enormously powerful booster for any company that uses it to the full. But in the 1960s it has been generally treated like a shiny foreign sports car driven only in built-up areas and never taken beyond second gear:

> The Midland Bank recently appointed a marketing manager— a man with good background and experience. However, he has no responsibility for either profit or revenue and is merely in a staff advisory role. He has no more chance of making the Midland 'marketing oriented' than the man in the moon because this would require a revolution in the attitudes of every company employee from the Board downwards.
>
> The Midland Bank has not adopted the marketing concept— it has merely taken a pep pill to reassure itself that it is keeping up with 'modern management techniques'.

THE PROMISING PLAYER TEN YEARS LATER

The signs that marketing has not fulfilled its pristine promise of the early 1960s are clear for all to see.

(1) One of the key roles of marketing is to accelerate company growth. New products are a part of this which depend primarily

on marketing skills for their success. And yet the failure rate of new products is still high—probably at least 70% of all products which are market-tested do not achieve financial success on a national scale. This might be acceptable if the majority of new products were highly innovative affairs, involving a fair risk of failure but also carrying the likelihood of major profits if successful. However, the sad thing is that many new products, often emanating from companies with marketing departments, are pimply little 'Me Too's' and 'Me Three's' that only create fleeting shadows in the market place.

(2) Acquisitions are the second major source of corporate growth, and they are a very proper area for involvement by marketing people. After all, companies buy franchises these days, not plants— whether they know it or not. But with a few notable exceptions, acquisitions are still the exclusive province of the financial people, who base the purchase price on past balance sheet performance rather than future potential.

(3) Many of the major American grocery companies closely associated with pioneering the marketing concept have had poor growth records in the 1960s. In a number of cases, their earnings per share have not increased even in line with increases in the cost of living index—a poor investment for shareholders and an unconvincing advertisement for marketing. Of course, most of these corporations operated in low growth areas like food and household cleaning products, but no company is entitled to make excuses about the nature of its markets over a ten-year period. It can always diversify as General Mills did into toys, and Procter & Gamble into paper.

(4) The application of marketing has only had limited success in UK companies during the 1960s. Appendix A shows an analysis of the profitability of 20 large companies with a reputation for 'marketing' and an established marketing department, chosen from the 200 companies in the *Management Today* 1970 British Business Growth League. The criteria used were degree of ten-year growth and the ratio between increase in profits and increase in capital employed, during the 1960–69 period. Even allowing for the limitations of any financial comparison between firms, the results were not impressive. Out of the 20 companies, 10 could be defined as fair to poor performers, 6 as good to high* and only 4 as outstanding (Rank, Carreras, Thorn Electrical and Smith & Nephew).

(5) Coming closer to home, most marketing men are employed

---

* And one of these firms—Spillers—had a disastrous year in 1970.

by larger companies. Whereas virtually every company has a sales manager, a factory manager and an accountant, only those with a certain level of sophistication in size and organization employ marketing people. Since the sole justification of marketing is that its practice adds to profitability, one would expect large companies to be more profitable than smaller ones, particularly since they have greater market power. That, however, is not the case in the UK. Based on '*The Times* 1000', the top 200 firms have a rather lower average percentage profit to capital employed than those below them in size (Table 1.1).*

TABLE 1.1 AVERAGE PERCENTAGE PROFIT TO CAPITAL EMPLOYED—FIRST 500

Rank in table	Average capital employed (£m)	% profit to capital employed
1–200	130·0	15·2
201–250	25·3	17·4
251–300	20·6	15·8
301–350	15·2	15·9
351–400	13·4	16·1
401–450	11·9	20·0
451–500	10·6	18·5

These are some of the more concrete indictments that can be made of marketing's contribution to date. These criticisms have been directed at results achieved, but there are also a number of mistaken attitudes to marketing, which cannot be quantified but certainly contribute to poor results. They dramatize how much of marketing's potential for profit remains unrealized.

(6) Many companies take too narrow and specialist a view of marketing. They fail to understand that it is a total approach to business, which places the consumer at the centre of things, and must permeate the whole company. To regard marketing merely

* 1970–71 edition. The fact that there may be other reasons for the un-impressive profit performance of large companies—in particular the problem of managing large and dispersed empires—does not invalidate this point. A truly marketing oriented company like Marks & Spencer (see case history on page 9) will relate its administrative procedures and management structure to the marketing task to be done and prevent the onset of bureaucratic plague.

as an amalgam of functional activities like advertising, promotions and market research is to miss its point. Theodore Levitt puts it as well as anyone: 'When it comes to the marketing concept today, a solid stone wall often seems to separate word from deed. In spite of the best intentions and energetic efforts of many highly able men, the effective implementation of the marketing concept has generally eluded them.'*

(7) Most marketing men today do a maintenance rather than a development job. This does not imply either lack of vision or misallocation of priorities on their part. It merely reflects a situation where they are hampered by such a bevy of day-to-day pressures that they are unable to find time for the really important longer term priorities like developing new products, innovating fresh distribution channels or thinking up breakthrough ideas. The recurring crises, the fires to be put out, continually force the attention of marketing men back into the present.

(8) The growing size of companies and the proliferation of information have too often produced caution rather than enlightenment. There is a tendency to seek areas of low risk rather than to maximize profit. While it is prudent to minimize risk, the greater profits often come to companies which actively seek out areas of high risk, but handle them better than their competitors. A corollary of this exaggerated sense of prudence is the tendency to concentrate on what competition is doing, and to be unduly influenced by its activities. It is desirable to keep an eye on competition, but not to the point of hypnosis. Examples of the 'flock factor', or the inclination to follow competition are described later on. The drive for security and the fear of making wrong decisions leads executives to copy competition, because that is a safe thing to do, for which a precedent has been established. Margaret Mead the anthropologist makes the point very shrewdly in an article called 'Must capitalism crawl?'†

'In his business activities, each administrator knows too much about all his competitors—what their market is, what changes they are making, how they are diversifying, retrenching and expanding. When knowledge of a field was very limited, the imaginative man made an informed guess and forged ahead, and his success or failure—in actual profit—gave him a measure

---

* *The Marketing Mode* (McGraw-Hill, 1969).
† *Harvard Business Review*.

of his achievement. But today when every field is researched, we have the spectacle of each company copying its competitors and, in so doing, limiting the profits of them all.'

THE PURSUIT OF INNOVATION

How does one tackle this dilemma? How does one realize the talents and energies of thousands of able but unexploited marketing men? How does one change the attitudes of top management so that it will see marketing as a dynamic approach which fundamentally affects the whole company? A few years of watching, listening and making mistakes in a variety of organizations have convinced me that there is a wide gap between the minority of companies, practising what I have chosen to call 'offensive marketing', and the majority, which do not. The difference is less a matter of intelligence and ability—since there is an abundance of people with plenty of both in every company—than of attitudes, organization and techniques.

Offensive marketing is not a neat concept, capable of instant encapsulation in an elegant one-liner. On the contrary, its boundaries are widely spread and ragged, because it describes particular attitudes and methods that cover the whole marketing spectrum. In essence, it involves aiming to innovate every major new development in a market, from the humdrum accomplishment of being first in with a new larger size to the heady success of launching a totally new brand. It obliges a company to innovate continually, to plan what is best for Number One, rather than following competition, and to respond to competitive moves by counter-attack, not by imitation.

This may sound like the kind of thing every company should be doing, and indeed it is. But the fact remains that few companies do follow this approach, and while a statement of objectives is easy, putting it into practice needs more than wish-fulfilment. It requires a hard, disciplined plan, since the road to marketing orientation is not easy. Offensive marketing is a five-finger exercise. In its ideal form, it is profitable, offensive, integrated, strategic and effectively executed. At the risk of gimmickry, but in the greater cause of good reader recall, these five aspects can be summmarized by the word P–O–I–S–E:

P for PROFITABLE: proper balance between firm's and
                                    consumer's needs;

O for OFFENSIVE: must lead market and make competitors followers;

I ,, INTEGRATED: marketing approach must permeate whole company;

S ,, STRATEGIC: action related to long and short-term strategic plan;

E ,, EFFECTIVELY EXECUTED: speaks for itself.

P–O–I–S–E SPELT SLOWLY

Let us take a look at the individual ingredients of offensive marketing in broad terms.

Profitable It is sometimes forgotten that the object of marketing is not just to increase brand share, or to make the consumer happy, but to increase profit. A company conscientiously applying the offensive marketing approach will often encounter conflicts between giving the consumer what he or she wants, and running the firm efficiently. And one of the skills of marketing is to reach the right balance between these opposing elements.

Offensive An offensive approach, as defined in this book, calls for an attitude of mind which decides independently what is best for a company, rather than waiting for competition to make the first move.

Integrated A company adopting the integrated marketing approach relates every one of its activities to the needs of the market. This contrasts with the view of marketing as a specialist activity restricted to advertising, promotions or market research.

Strategic The leadership in innovation, which is central to the offensive marketing concept, cannot be achieved without fore-thought and strategic planning. A business which is operated on a day-to-day basis, with no long-term marketing purpose, is more likely to be a follower than a leader.

Effectively executed No amount of intelligent approach work is of any use without effective execution. How many promising promotions have been spoiled due to faulty positioning on the pack, insufficient premiums to satisfy demand, or late delivery of a special pack? How many new brands have become stunted due to production shortages or weak selling? Effective execution is not just a matter of good administration by marketing people. It is also vitally dependent on the relationship between marketing and other departments, and how far common strategies and objectives exist.

CHECKING A COMPANY'S SCORE FOR OFFENSIVE MARKETING

If offensive marketing is as practical a concept as has been claimed, it should be possible to set up criteria by which the offensive marketing rating of a firm can be judged. Like any inter-firm comparison, the result will inevitably be biased and subjective, due to differences in definition and in market situations. The battery of offensive

TABLE 1.2   CRITERIA FOR RATING A COMPANY ON
OFFENSIVE MARKETING

No.	Criterion	Max. score	Profit/ growth	Company score
1	% of business in new products launched in past 5 years	40	G	....
2	Success rate of new products test-marketed	10	P	....
3	New markets entered in past 10 years	10	G	....
4	Earnings per share growth in past 5 years	40	P	....
5	Level of return on capital employed *v.* nearest competitor	20	P	....
6	10-year growth in net profit	20	Both	....
7	Whether led or followed latest innovations in major markets (new sizes, varieties/flavour, distribution channels)	20	G	....
8	Whether marketing dept has profit responsibility	10	P	....
9	Presence/absence of marketing profit improvement plan	10	P	....
10	Whether uses long-term plan as basis for current action	10	G	....
11	Whether takes marketing/financial approach to acquisitions	10	G	....
	TOTAL	200	{ 100 P 100 G	....

Note: In allocating scores, criteria 1, 2 and 5 should be measured against major competitors, and 3, 4 and 6 against the averages in the *Management Today* Profitability and Growth Leagues.

marketing yardsticks which has been constructed will not escape these criticisms, but they nevertheless contain sufficient objectivity to be useful.

The maximum number of marks, to which even IBM or Xerox could not aspire, is 200. Quite arbitrarily, 100 marks have been allocated to growth and 100 to profit factors. Under the growth heading, new product development and innovation in existing markets, two of the bastions of offensive marketing, are heavily weighted. Past ten-year profit growth is also a potentially high scorer, since it reflects the impact of acquisitions as well as the internal developments which are marked separately. Two other, primary yardsticks, firmly encamped under the profit umbrella, are return on capital compared with closest competition and earnings per share improvement over the past five years.

Some quite subjective criteria have been included—like the degree of long-term action planning, and the extent to which the marketing department has profit responsibility or involvement with acquisitions. Some people may question the desirability of these tenets or reject their relevance to profit and growth. Unless they are unusually open-minded, they should cut their losses and close this book, because it unashamedly assumes that the right attitudes and organization structures have a palpable effect on corporate results. Nevertheless, in recognition of the subjective nature of these criteria, relatively modest maximum scores have been allocated to them. Table 1.2 provides a basis for rating the degree to which a firm follows the offensive marketing concept, and a space is reserved on the far right for the company's score.

OFFENSIVE MARKETING IN ACTION— THE MARKS & SPENCER STORY*

Few firms exemplify the operation of the offensive marketing approach better than Marks & Spencer. Throughout its history it has innovated new forms of retailing and followed its own distinctive course. It has always had a clear purpose of providing good quality merchandise at the lowest possible price, and although

* This case study is freely adapted from Goronwy Rees, *St Michael: a History of Marks & Spencer* (Weidenfeld & Nicolson, 1969). This is an inspiring story for everyone interested in British industry—well written by an author of high literary abilities who also understands business.

the exact expression of this has varied through time as economic and social conditions have altered, the basic strategy has been consistently followed. From its inception, M & S has paid close attention to satisfying consumer needs and harnessed the effort of the whole organization, from sales assistant to buyer, from store manager to technologist, towards this end. At the same time, it has run its business very profitably, and the bulk of its post-war expansion of premises has been financed from internal sources. And yet to describe M & S's approach in purely business terms is to ignore an important part of the company's operating philosophy, which accepts a level of responsibility to the community and for the welfare of its employees that is well outside normal commercial limits. As Lord Sieff put it: 'Our whole business is built on the principle that as long as you put people—as human beings—first, you cannot go wrong, even about making money.' While this is outside the scope of a book on marketing, it is relevant to this study, because it has instilled in M & S a unique missionary spirit which is a key reason for the effectiveness of the organization.

Michael Marks was born in Russian Poland, and emigrated to England in the early 1880s. After spending some time as an itinerant pedlar in Yorkshire, he opened a stall in the open market at Kirkgate, Leeds, in 1884. Shortly afterwards, he moved to a covered stall in Leeds, and by then he had innovated a completely new approach to retailing, which was ideally tailored to the needs of his largely illiterate working class consumers. His retailing style had two unique features—he displayed all his goods in open baskets with the prices marked so that they could be seen and inspected, and he priced all his products at one penny. Above the stall was the slogan which was to become famous: 'Don't ask the price—it's a penny.'

The merchandising policy of open display and clear price marking was unique in those days, and it is by no means universal even today. And the strategy of concentrating on a single price point of one penny was also new, because although Woolworth independently conceived the same idea in America in the latter part of the nineteenth century, it did not open up in the UK until 1909. Even at this early stage in the history of the firm, Michael Marks equates the penny price with quality rather than cheapness, and did not attempt to sell scaled-down rubbishy versions of more expensive products.

M & S continued to trade as a 'penny bazaar' until 1914, and by then it already had 140 branches, mostly shops, and profits before tax in that year were £30000. But costs and prices had risen so much that it was not possible to maintain the penny price point after 1914. For a number of years the company was without a clear strategy, until in 1924 Simon Marks,* who was by then Chairman of the company, evolved a new trading concept. Following a visit to America, he decided that the company would market a range of products under the price of five shillings and pursue a policy of building larger stores—'super stores', as he called them.

This was a bold step. At the time, Woolworth was doing a thriving business based on threepenny and sixpenny points, and it would have been easy for M & S to have followed this example. And the new marketing strategy raised a host of problems. For a start, the cost of the 'super stores' envisaged by Simon Marks would require the company to raise new capital from outside sources. Much more important, a range of quality products which could be retailed profitably at five shillings just did not exist, and would have to be created. However, the reasoning behind this new strategy was sound. Simon Marks believed that the increased throughput of the 'super stores' would produce economies of large-scale production in goods made specially for M & S. This in turn would allow him to offer high quality products at under five shillings and to increase store turnover even more. It was very much a chicken and egg situation in which merchandising and production policy were closely intertwined. But marketing was the mainspring of the policy, because production, technology and store planning were all harnessed to the ultimate aim of giving good value to the consumer.

The primary responsibility for implementing the production side of this strategy fell upon Israel Sieff (later Lord Sieff), who became Vice-Chairman of the company in 1926. The product policy which he adopted had two aspects. Where goods under five shillings already existed, their quality would be upgraded in line with consumer needs. Where there were goods at present outside the five shilling price range, efforts would be made to reduce their cost without significant loss in quality, through the application of technology and the economies of large-scale production. The difficulties involved in carrying out this policy were immense. In asking manufacturers to produce tailor-made products for a retailer, which sometimes involved the installation of new machinery and always required the application of stringently unfamiliar quality control standards, Israel Sieff was postulating an entirely new relationship

* Later Lord Marks. He was the only son of Michael Marks, who died in 1907.

between manufacturer and retailer. And, to make life even more awkward, the world-famous manufacturers, to many of whom Sieff addressed himself, were not at all sure that they wanted to be associated with a retailer like M & S, which was still remembered for its 'penny bazaars'. The diplomacy of Israel Sieff and the large-scale buying power at M & S's command eventually won through, and from 1927 Simon Marks' new concept of the five shilling store was implemented, three years after its original inception.

Throughout the late 1920s and early 1930s, M & S increasingly concentrated on textile products. This was an area well suited to its product policy, because the textile industry was organized in small units and relatively unschooled in modern production techniques. This gave M & S the opportunity to apply its own technologies and production disciplines to the task of making better quality goods at lower prices. By 1936 a Merchandise Development Department had been set up, and this worked closely with the textile laboratory to check product quality, to set up specifications and process control systems, to keep up with basic research in universities, institutes and major suppliers, and generally to improve the value of M & S merchandise. At about the same time, a Design Department was established to develop designs for new M & S products and to advise suppliers. While textiles were certainly the area of greatest opportunity for M & S, they were also the one involving the greatest challenge. As every consultant knows, it is always most difficult to persuade a backward and conservative industry to adopt new techniques. Interestingly enough, Sears Roebuck, which was pioneering a similar approach in the USA in the 1930s, was either unwilling or unable to transform the woman's fashion industry to mass production methods—which is some measure of M & S's achievement.

Store policy reflected this trend in product policy. Counter space was progressively allocated to the fast-moving textile lines, and many other product categories were gradually eliminated. In 1926–32, hardware, cutlery, china, earthenware and boot and shoe accessories were cut out and in 1933–5, stationery and haberdashery were withdrawn. This was consistent with the company's marketing policy of concentrating on categories where they could give the consumer special value and move high volumes of goods. Furthermore M & S added to its number of stores and extended others, in line with its 'super store' policy, which was necessary to achieve the low-cost benefits of mass production. By 1939, M & S had 234 stores, and has not added many since.

Just before the start of the Second World War, about 70% of
M & S's turnover was in textiles and 20% in food, a proportion
not very different from that of today. The policy of the five shilling
price limit, the 'super store' and concentration on a limited line
proved very successful, and in 1939 M & S's profits were over
£1.1 million after tax, compared with only £40000 in 1925,
one of the last years prior to the application of the new strategy.
During this period, erstwhile competitors Woolworth and British
Home Stores (established in 1928) followed the traditional variety
store policy of a wide range of goods at rock bottom prices.

The M & S inter-war business strategy had followed the same
principle that Michael Marks laid down in his 'penny bazaars'—
value rather than low price alone—but had adapted it to the better
educated and more monied working class of the 1920s and 1930s,
and heightened its efficiency by pioneering a new relationship
between retailer and manufacturer. The post-war period involved
new challenges and required a new adaptation of M & S's policies
to the more affluent period of the 1950s and 1960s. Just as the 'penny
bazaar' had to be abandoned after 1914, so the rise in prices in the
1940s made the continuation of the five shilling price maximum
impracticable. In addition, a flood of new textile technology poured
out in the post-war years, with the development of man-made
fibres. This proved an opportunity rather than a problem for M & S,
because of the solid technical organization and knowledge it had
built up in the inter-war years.

M & S's marketing strategy in the 1950s and 1960s had a great
deal of continuity with the policies developed in the 1920s. True,
there was no longer a formal price maximum, although most
products cost under £5. But the 'super store' approach was taken
further and M & S has concentrated on modernizing and extending
stores rather than building new ones. Its total store area has almost
doubled between 1939 and 1968, from 0.20 to 0.37 million square
metres since the last war. It also refined and developed its relationship with suppliers, especially in food.

However, one of the most distinctive of its achievements in post-
war years, which demonstrates how every activity of the company
is geared to the market, has been its success in simplifying administration and preventing the creeping paralysis of paperwork bureaucracy which is apt to afflict any large organization. Michael Marks
was convinced that simplicity in business was essential, and from
the mid-1950s onwards, he personally led an attack on escalating
administrative costs. Characteristically, his eyes were fixed on the

market place: he was concerned that rising administrative costs would inhibit the company's ability to give value to the consumer. His campaign, named 'Operation Simplification' was a great success. An equivalent of 26 million pieces of administrative paper per year was cut out, and although turnover rose from £120 million in 1955-6 to £282 million in 1968, this increase was achieved with 2000 less staff. Sales per square metre in M & S are twice the national average for retailing and sales per employee are more than three times the national average. M & S's organization structure and attitude towards its employees are outside the scope of this book. However, in retailing more than any other business, the product is partly people, and M & S's success in motivating its counter staff is an important aspect in the quality of the total product it offers.

The spectacular progress of M & S over the years is evident from its profit and turnover figures. Apart from a short period after the First World War, its growth has continued uninterrupted since the 1880s through three different but connected business stages:

Year	Turnover (£m)	Profit after tax (£000)
1903	not available	7
1920	not available	28
1939	23·4	1 152
1956	119·4	4 955
1970	360·9	24 955

M & S must surely be one of the best run businesses in the world, and certainly among the most marketing oriented. No doubt it will continue to modify its marketing strategies to meet changing conditions, and will be faced with new problems as the 1970s roll on. While it still provides excellent value, its prices seem to be getting dangerously high, and clearly these cannot be allowed to rise to the point where M & S loses its mass market appeal. Since the last war virtually all M & S's expansion has been through extensions to existing stores, and in 1968 it was reputed to still have 0.17 million square metres of potential new development on its present properties. But how useful will this be, as town centres become more crowded and parking more difficult? How should M & S react to the posssibility of out-of-town shopping centres whose establishment just seems to be a matter of time? How long can the company continue to look to manufactured foods as a source of growth, when these continue to decline as a proportion of national expenditure? How far should M & S go towards stocking more youthful fashion goods, and can this be done without undermining the low costs of mass production which are the foundation of the excellent value it offers? It will be interesting to see how M & S adapts its marketing strategy to meet such challenges in the years to come.

SUMMARY

The record of marketing in the 1960s has been disappointing. The growth rate of the larger companies in which marketing people are concentrated has been below average, and new products, which depend primarily on marketing skills for their success, continue to have an alarmingly high failure rate. Many companies mistakenly regard marketing as an amalgam of specialist activities rather than as a total approach to business which should permeate the whole organization. The pressure of detailed routine has turned most marketing people today into maintenance men.

All this is the very opposite of offensive marketing, which is a set of attitudes and techniques designed to exploit the marketing approach fully. It requires a company to innovate every major new development in its markets and to respond to competitive moves by counter-attack, not by imitation. Offensive marketing is profitable, offensive, integrated, strategic, and effectively executed. These elements are conveniently summarized by the word P–O–I–S–E.

I INTEGRATING FOR THE
_____OFFENSIVE

Marketing cannot begin to be effective within a company unless it has the full support of general management and penetrates every nook and cranny of an organization.

Part I examines the advantages accruing from full acceptance of the marketing approach, and the means for developing it from a limp theory into a dynamic practice. It also (Chapter 4) outlines the basic principles of marketing at work.

2: *The Integrated Approach* *to Marketing*

WHO NEEDS MARKETING?

Although marketing has not fulfilled its golden prophecies, this is more through misapplication than lack of utility. The practice of marketing is almost as old as civilization, and its validity has been proved over and over again. The oldest profession in the world used classic marketing techniques—it identified and satisfied a need; it created a market where buyer and seller could meet, in the form of the brothel; and it turned a handsome profit on the operation. Buying a present for your wife is also a marketing operation. You try to establish what she would like through knowledge of her tastes, observation of her needs and subtle questioning. Then you sift through this mass of data and select an item which you believe she would like and which you can afford. The strength of marketing as an idea needs no justification. Its difficulties have arisen since it became known as 'marketing', and experienced the fashionable embrace of the large company. And the question which has been posed in Chapter 1 and will be answered in this book is how it can be successfully pumped into the bloodstream of the big organization.

Some companies need marketing more than others, and for a select few—which I hope governments are watching closely—marketing may be a waste of money. The organizations that most need marketing are in businesses where technology changes rapidly, competition is fierce and the number of consumers is large. If technology is changing rapidly, marketing can ensure that it moves in the direction that matches future consumer wants. The more competitive the market, the wider the choice of alternatives the consumer will have, and therefore the greater the importance of building a preferred product—one of the advertised skills of marketing people. And communication with many consumers usually requires heavy expenditure of money on advertising and promotion, which the marketing man is specially equipped to handle.

Consequently, marketing men have to date gravitated mainly to the fast-moving consumer goods companies, in markets like pet-foods, washing powders and human foods, where their efforts can have most impact. However, marketing can also be an important factor in slow-moving consumer products like washing machines or TV sets, or in competitive industrial markets, as IBM, Xerox and Caterpillar Tractor have so notably shown.

At the opposite extreme is the monopoly supplier, selling a product which has no good substitute. For such an operator, marketing is likely to be an unnecessary luxury, because his consumer franchise is guaranteed, and he can control prices. Companies of this kind are rare today in the western world, because governments look upon monopolies with disfavour, and with the increasing proliferation of products, every brand has some substitute—for instance, a house-holder can choose between gas, electricity, solid fuel or oil in pur-chasing a heating system, Before the Second World War, however, cartels were common, and one of the most famous was the world wide 'Phoebus' agreement for controlling prices and supply of electric light bulbs:

> The Phoebus agreement was signed in 1924 by all the world's largest electric lamp-makers, except General Electric of America, which co-operated in the agreement and in any case held a major shareholding in every one of the leading lamp producers in the middle of the inter-war period. 'Phoebus' companies controlled 80–90% of European production by 1939.
>
> Phoebus successfully imposed quotas in line with companies' existing shares of national markets, fixed prices by country and encouraged a complete interchange of patents. None of the companies concerned had any stimulus to use marketing tech-niques. Their price and market share was fixed, so there was no purpose in developing better products, and advertising or pro-motion would surely be a waste of money. The consumer had to buy the product because there was no substitute for it. And the only effective way to increase profits within the cartel was to reduce promotion and administrative costs, or to negotiate better terms from the cartel organization in Geneva.*

Marketing skills are of very limited importance in the highly regulated European airline industry. Most of the major companies

* Adapted from Robert Jones and Oliver Marriott, *Anatomy of a Merger*, a fascinating book that is well worth reading.

in this area operate 'pooling agreements' by which route capacity and revenue are shared on an agreed basis, usually 50:50. Prices are fixed through International Air Transport Association Agreements, and schedule planning, market research, advertising and promotions are often conducted jointly. The only incentive towards offensive marketing effort, and it is a slim one, is the danger that if one airline accounts for, say, only 45% of passengers with 50% of seat capacity, the revenue split may be re-negotiated on a less favourable basis.* Table 2.1 summarizes those characteristics of markets which determine how much marketing can influence them.

TABLE 2.1 IMPORTANCE OF MARKETING TO MARKETS	
Marketing less important	*Marketing very important*
Scarcity of goods or rationing	Free supply of goods
No price competition	Competitive conditions
Monopoly or cartel	Competition at distribution point
Tied distribution system (e.g. petrol, beer)	High margins for marketing and profit
Low margins for marketing or profit	Rapid changes in technology or consumer tastes
Limited competition	Frequent purchase by consumer
Low rate of product change	Good opportunities for product differentiation
Little chance to differentiate products	

WHAT IS THIS THING CALLED MARKETING?

Definitions usually sound pompous and are boring to read. But they cannot always be avoided, and so, with apologies, here is the only definition in this book:

MARKETING INVOLVES BALANCING THE COMPANY NEEDS FOR PROFIT AGAINST THE BENEFITS REQUIRED BY CONSUMERS, SO AS TO MAXIMIZE LONG-TERM EARNINGS PER SHARE.

* The purpose of this example is to show a category where marketing is not important, rather than to condemn pooling. Pooling is a complex subject, since airline operations involve a mixture of political and commercial considerations. It has certain advantages, like spreading flights more widely over the day, and avoiding excessive 'lumping' at peak hours. For a full discussion of pooling, see the Edwards Report, *British Air Transport in the Seventies*, pages 94–8.

Let us start with the purpose of the company, which has been defined as maximizing long-term earnings per share. A company exists for the benefit of a number of groups. It provides its employees with a living and, hopefully, an opportunity for self-development. Its obligation to the community is now increasingly being stressed, especially by people who can't see their beaches for oil sludge. But, most of all, it must provide an adequate return to its shareholders, who pay out the pocket money that companies need for expansion. A company has to keep its shareholders happy, to ensure that it can raise new capital on reasonable terms when this is needed in the future. And the minimum shareholders are looking for is a return that exceeds the yield on fixed interest investments and rises faster than the cost of living. Consequently, the majority of well-versed American corporate presidents frame their long-term objectives in terms of rising earnings per share. This concept seems at present to be severely under-exercised in the UK market.

Marketing is a philosophy and a method of achieving corporate financial objectives. It stands or falls according to how effectively it contributes to their accomplishment. And in a Utopian world it does this by arriving at a perfect balance between company needs for profit and consumer needs for benefits. Balance between these needs is important because they are often in conflict. Any fool can satisfy consumer needs at a loss. It would be a very simple matter to sell a large number of Jaguars at the price of an Austin Mini. The relevance of this balance is sometimes illustrated very dramatically.

John Bloom was a brilliant and daring innovator, who succeeded in building up a high volume of washing machine sales but was unable to maintain profitability in the long run. He began to import machine parts from Holland and carried out assembly in the UK from 1958 onwards. The machines were sold door to door by salesmen working entirely on commission, and backed by heavy advertising and promotion. The two major models sold were the Rolls Rapide at 39 guineas (£40·95) and the Rolls Rapide de luxe at 59 guineas (£61·95). The more expensive machine was profitable but the basic model was sold at a loss.

By contrast, Bloom's major competitors Hoover and Hotpoint had large teams of sales servicemen, but sold their machines via the retail appliance trade and spent much less on marketing. Their products were considerably more expensive than Bloom's. His share of market rose rapidly. He sold 101 000 machines in 1962, for a 12% market share, and in 1963 he doubled this figure to 201 400, for a 19·7% share. During this year he ousted Hotpoint from the Number Two position in the market and became one of the biggest advertisers in the UK, with a spending of £1·7 million.

In Autumn 1963 he rashly decided to set a target of 400 000 machines for 1964. To achieve this, manufacturing materials were ordered on the basis of production of 8000 machines a week, and advertising was planned at £3 million for the year. This target never looked like being achieved. Only 55 000 machines were sold in the first quarter, and advertising cost per machine rose from £9·62 in January to over £14 in March. Sales fell away steeply in the second quarter, and by mid-July 1964 the firm had gone into liquidation.

The firm failed for a number of reasons. One of them was the setting of unrealistic sales objectives and gearing production and marketing costs accordingly, so that when sales were not achieved, profits suffered. Another was the costing of the basic model, which gave consumers excellent value but failed to make a profit. Sales of this loss-making machine rose from 5% of total units sold in 1962 to 14% in 1963, and continued at a level above 11% in the first half of 1964. John Bloom had many of the characteristics of the offensive marketer, but failed to get his sums right.*

The effective resolution of the continuing tug of war between the firm's need for efficiency and the consumer's need for unique benefits is well illustrated by the dilemma that has always faced the motor car industry.

An automobile company can produce the cheapest possible car of the best quality by making just one model, and running it off by the hundred thousand. But cars are status symbols, and consumers have widely differing requirements. A single model would not satisfy the diversity of need of the total market and would have no appeal to consumers who wanted a different car from their neighbours. And a car tailored to the specific needs of each consumer would be prohibitively expensive to make. So where does one go from there?

Motor manufacturers have sought different solutions to this

* Adapted from John Bloom, *It's No Sin to Make a Profit* (W. H. Allen, 1971).

conflict between the cost efficiencies of mass production and the consumer's need for a tailored car. Volkswagen has followed the example of Henry Ford I with his Model 'T' Ford and gone for a highly functional model produced in enormous quantities at a competitive price. It has succeeded in Germany, where VW is regarded as the working man's car. However, VW is losing market share in Germany, and while it clearly has high appeal to people buying a car for the first time, one doubts whether it can continue to attract more than a minority of consumers in a 'mature' car market like the USA. VW indeed has a 5% share of the American market, but the total segment to which it is appealing in the USA accounts for less than 20%.

The VW approach is not attractive to a Ford or a General Motors, which need to produce a range of models appealing to the whole market, in order to retain their leading business positions. Ford of Britain, like others, has balanced the conflict of production efficiency versus individual consumer needs by manufacturing a small number of basic car bodies in large quantities, and offering them with a wide range of engine sizes and optional extras, which enables purchasers to buy a car tailored to their individual tastes. Ford has also altered the emphasis of its manufacturing objectives from mass production to large-scale flexible production.

This example from the car industry strikes at the very essence of marketing, and shows that it is a much more dynamic business tool than one would ever imagine from the flaccid definition of marketing as merely satisfying consumer needs.

Another battleground where profit and efficiency come into head-on conflict with consumer needs is the low volume brand. A product's volume can decline to a point where it is no longer profitable to sell, even at a premium retail price. For a large company with high overheads, a brand with a turnover of £100 000 may be unprofitable. True, on an artificial 'standard' costing, where its contribution to overheads is allocated in proportion to its share of company volume, such a brand can be made to appear profitable. But usually it eats up a slice of selling, distribution, marketing and management time out of all proportion to its volume, so that a *pro rata* allocation of overheads is unrealistic. If a brand of this kind is actually losing money on a proper costing, should it be withdrawn? After all, some consumers still want it and are continuing to buy, and isn't the purpose of marketing to satisfy the consumer? The answer is obvious: the brand should be withdrawn because it is unprofitable. And an offensive marketer would be the first to press for such a decision.

In a company applying offensive marketing, this conflict is being balanced in almost every decision, though its presence is usually less pervasive than in the clear-cut cases outlined above. Marketing always poses the question of what is best for the consumer. But offensive marketing asks two other questions as well: 'What is most efficient for the company from the cost angle?' and 'How do we balance consumer needs against company needs for low cost operation, in a way which will maximize our long-term profit? The offensive marketing man is as profit oriented as the accountant, but he does not share the latter's exclusive inward focus on the business. He is looking for ways to increase revenue as well as to reduce costs. He also gazes into the future and his spectacles have telescopic lenses.

MOST MARKETING MEN DON'T KNOW WHAT MARKETING IS

A somewhat obvious requirement for membership of the offensive marketing club is a clear understanding of what marketing is. Unfortunately, the majority of marketing men in the UK do not possess this desirable minimum qualification. The document which establishes this remarkable but not altogether surprising fact is published by the British Institute of Management, and housed in a sober green and white cover.* The universe of companies contacted by the BIM comprised all those with an annual turnover above £750 000. The majority of these were sent a mailed questionnaire, and the survey results were based on the 553 who filled it in. The question that concerns us here is the way firms defined marketing, and Table 2.2 summarizes the definitions offered.

58% of firms defined marketing incorrectly, and 17% did not answer the question. If the latter knew the answer, they were keeping quiet about it, because they responded to most of the other questions asked in the survey. Bear in mind that these were larger firms, and that the questionnaire was presumably filled in or at least supervised by the senior executive responsible for marketing. Then subtract those firms which can define marketing correctly but do not put their words into practice. Take a deep breath and consider how

* *Marketing Organisation in British Industry* (BIM, April 1970).

small and select must be the group of firms applying the offensive marketing concept.

TABLE 2.2 DEFINITIONS OF MARKETING	
Summary of definition	%
Satisfaction of consumer needs	14
Selling	13
Market research	5
Advertising and promotion	5
List of functions	9
Co-ordinative element in firm	4
Total business operation	8
SUB TOTAL OF WRONG DEFINITIONS	58
Satisfaction of consumer needs *profitably*	19
Having the right goods at the right time/place/price	3
'Textbook' definitions	3
SUB TOTAL OF ACCEPTABLE DEFINITIONS	25
Not answered	17
TOTAL	100

A PORTRAIT OF FIVE MARKETING PERVERTS

To continue with the theme of marketing misconceptions, there are a number of wrong attitudes towards the marketing approach, which prejudice both the understanding of its real nature and its effective application. These attitudes are most often held by marketing men, or their friends in the advertising agencies. Five have been picked out for demonstration purposes, and they are all enemies of offensive marketing.

The Consumer Worshippers

This group has already been referred to by implication above, but it is so influential that it deserves further treatment. The consumer worshippers believe that the consumer is always right, and seem to be under the impression that they are working for *Which?* or some such body, rather than a commercial organization. *Which?* does a fine job and fulfils a key role, but is non-profit making; businesses have to make money for their shareholders, and the reckless pursuit of consumer benefit irrespective of profit results in bankruptcy.

Only profitable firms can serve the consumer effectively. And it is in fact quite possible to satisfy consumer needs superbly well, while also returning above average profits. Few would deny that Marks & Spencer gives excellent value for money, and yet this firm makes a higher net profit on capital employed than any other UK retailer, with the exception of Tesco. Lesney Products sells well made toys at remarkably low prices, but still returned a post-tax profit of 29·1% on invested capital in 1969—its fall from grace in 1970 due to Mattel's innovation of 'hot wheels' in the USA is irrelevant to this discussion, but even in that poor year Lesney's return on capital was still well above average.

The fact that these companies are profit oriented does not mean that they lack interest in the consumer. On the contrary, anyone who shops regularly at M & S or John Lewis, or spends a few days talking to employees of companies like Heinz or United Biscuits, will recognize that they have a most genuine concern to provide the consumer with good value for money. The view that companies regard the consumer with Machiavellian cynicism is, I think, as outdated as that which objects to profit as an unmitigated evil.

The New Luddites

Once you have traced the traditional history of marketing, and acknowledged its emergence from an era of production orientation, where the machine's capacity rather than the consumer's need dictated the market, it is not too big a step to regard production as, in some undefined way, opposed to marketing. This sets the stage for the new Luddites, who view production as an outdated and inferior form of activity. They refer to 'production oriented' companies with a curl of the lip, and assume that the production department must always behave as a docile servant of the marketing group, to prevent a return to the dark ages of business.

This attitude is significantly responsible for the bickering and lack of co-operation that is so often a feature of the relationship between production and marketing departments. The posture of the new Luddite is of course totally unrealistic because marketing depends on good production for its effectiveness. Superb advertising, packaging and formula planning will be of no avail if the product that comes off the end of the line is of inferior or inconsistent quality. What is more, close co-operation between marketing and production can turn up excellent profit improvements through reductions in cost.

The Egotistical Employees

A great deal has been written in the past few decades about the widening gap between ownership and control of companies. The shareholders own the capital, but the management exercises practical control and, unless things go seriously wrong, the only communication between the one and the other is in the pages of the financial press or, less likely, at the annual general meeting. One little noticed aspect of the increasing separation between ownership and control is the inclination of some employees to run businesses for their own delectation and pleasure, rather than for the benefit of shareholders. This is particularly inimical to the operation of the offensive marketing approach, the purpose of which is to increase long-term profit.

Employee egotism starts right from the top, with the chief executive who is more interested in inflating his importance than in accelerating profit. Since size usually equals power, he is quite likely to pursue growth as opposed to profit, and to follow an aggressive acquisition programme. Company presidents who state their corporate objective as 'becoming a billion dollar corporation' are often egotistical employees. Why don't they talk about 'becoming a hundred million dollar net profit corporation'?

One type of egotist who regularly impedes the offensive marketing approach is the pseudo-professional. Now professionalism in its best sense, construed as job excellence, is clearly an admirable quality. But the pseudo-professional pursues irrelevant standards that do not relate to consumer needs, or which are calculated to be more rewarding to the employee than productive to the company. Let us take a few examples that will be easily spotted by those with an observant eye.

(1) It is generally accepted that research and development scientists are particularly prone to this disease. Being people of outstanding intellect, they naturally tend to be most interested in work that is technically challenging, irrespective of its likely commercial payoff. To counter this, marketing men have to take the lead in directing R & D effort to projects with profit potential.

(2) Copywriters at advertising agencies can also be difficult to motivate along offensive marketing lines. Some write advertisements to impress their peers or to draw attention to their skills, rather than to persuade the consumer. Such individuals care more about creative awards than sales graphs.

(3) Another not uncommon example of misplaced professionalism can still be found in the technical packaging expert. He may have a fixed idea of the minimum performance of a shipping container. Even though it can be demonstrated that a thinner cardboard only adds minutely to the level of breakage, and looks like a worthwhile profit improvement, he may still resist it on the grounds that a container involving any known risk of breakage is a bad container.

The Milker

The milker is just another instance of the egotistical employee, but because he is often a marketing man, and at the same time can do a great disservice to the offensive marketing approach, he is treated separately. The milker is the executive who thinks he will only spend a short time—perhaps a year or so—in his present job. He may be a rolling general manager with an international company, or a brand manager who moves quickly from job to job. The technique is to cut every cost in sight, including advertising spending, so that a vastly improved profit can be piled up over a short period. The degree to which the milker has mortgaged the company's or the brand's longer term prospects is not apparent at the time, and when revenue or profits turn down a year later, somebody else is in the hot seat to take the blame for yet another failure by marketing.

The Galloping Midget

He is twenty-five years old and has had four years' experience in marketing. He is among the 8% in the BIM survey who define marketing as the 'total business operation' (he hardly acknowledges the existence of labour relations or financial planning). Marketing is the only part of the business that matters, and every department exists just to provide a service to it. Time is the only thing standing between the galloping midget and the managing directorship and it won't be long now. This arrogant and naive type does great harm to the marketing approach.

INTEGRATED MARKETING

'Integrated' may sound like just another meaningless buzz word, but it isn't. When marketing is integrated, the whole company participates, not just the marketing department. Every part of the company combines to satisfy consumer needs at a profit. Howard Morgens, President of Procter & Gamble, puts the case for integrated marketing succinctly: 'There is no such thing as marketing skill by itself. For a company to be good at marketing, it must be good at everything else, from R & D to manufacturing, from quality controls to financial controls.'*

Marketing is an approach to business rather than a specialist discipline. It is no more the exclusive responsibility of the marketing department than profitability is the sole charge of the finance department. Unlike the more specialized roles of production, buying, selling, and research and development, marketing is the function of every employee. The marketing approach challenges every member of a company, whatever his specialist function, to relate his work to the needs of the market place and to balance it against the firm's own profit needs.

For example, in a marketing oriented company the works manager will ensure that his quality control standards evaluate those elements in the product which matter most to the consumer. He will also aim to meet the required product specification at minimum cost. The buyer will check that materials purchased meet consumer requirements at lowest possible cost. This will often involve moving away from materials whose cost is escalating, and substituting lower cost ingredients. But before authorizing such a change, the buyer will have checked any effect this substitution may have on consumer reaction, jointly with the marketing group.

Within the company, the marketing department should lead and catalyse the application of the marketing approach, just as the finance department will lead and monitor the application of the profit principle. *However, to be effective, the marketing approach requires the full belief and support of top management*—more about this later. The marketing department could no more apply an integrated marketing approach to a company on its own than could a football club manager win a match without a team. Integrated marketing is the first, and the most difficult step towards offensive marketing. Without it, marketing men operate in a vacuum, and their efforts are ineffective.

Let us close this section as we began it, with an example from Procter & Gamble.

Procter & Gamble was once more nominated as one of the ten best managed US companies, in 1970, based on a poll of 2300 top American executives, conducted by *Dun's Review*. Its ten-year growth in profits was 108% in 1960-69, and its post-tax

* *Dun's Review* (December 1970).

return on capital employed was 11% in 1969, both good results for a company operating exclusively in fast-moving consumer markets.

Although it is best known for its marketing people, the calibre of all its employees, whether in manufacturing, R & D or financial planning, is high. The quality of its sales force is outstanding. And every employee is, to varying degrees, marketing oriented.

P & G is successful because the whole company is geared to marketing and profit and because it has clear operating principles which it adheres to. The company believes strongly in product superiority and heavy marketing spending. It continually seeks innovation, but confines itself to new categories where its skills in the marketing of fast-moving consumer goods will be important.

Consequently P & G is continually updating its existing products. And when it launches a new brand, it usually has a superior formulation, supported by marketing spending of such weight that the product will be tried by a high proportion of its target consumers. The sales force achieves distribution and featuring, and the only consistent weakness in the mix is the mediocre quality of much P & G advertising.

The starting point for this successful approach is integrated marketing.

WHAT CAN OFFENSIVE MARKETING CONTRIBUTE?

Unless marketing is applied offensively as a way of doing business, its contribution to a company will inevitably be very limited. Perhaps little more will be achieved than a greater use of research, more efficient spending of advertising and promotion money, and a dim awareness on the part of top management that the company should be doing better than it is.

The application of the offensive marketing approach is neither easy nor achieved overnight. The embrace of marketing will not automatically turn a frog into a prince. And even companies that appear to have largely mastered the art, and absorbed the marketing approach into the corporate bloodstream, do not find offensive marketing an easy or automatic road to success. However, organizations like Avon Products, Marks & Spencer, Procter & Gamble, IBM and Mars Petfoods, which appear to practise most of the important elements of offensive marketing, do achieve an above average rate of corporate growth and return on capital. The main benefits they gain through offensive marketing are higher profits and a longer life cycle for existing products, plus a better success rate with new products and acquisitions.

SUMMARY

Marketing is most important in businesses where technology changes rapidly, where competition is fierce, and where the products are bought frequently by a large number of consumers. It matters least in monopoly situations.

Marketing involves balancing the company needs for profit against the benefits required by consumers so as to maximize long-term earnings per share. There is a continuing tug of war between the firm's need for efficiency, and the consumer's need for unique benefits.

Unfortunately, there are a number of wrong attitudes to the marketing approach, which hamper its proper application. The people holding some of these misguided views are described under the headings of 'the consumer worshippers', 'the new Luddites', 'the egotistical employees', 'the milkers' and 'the galloping midget'.

When marketing is integrated, as it always should be, it permeates the whole company. It is no more the exclusive responsibility of the marketing department than profitability is the sole charge of the financial group.

3: *Making Integration Work*

The task of getting a company to practise marketing on an integrated basis is largely one of changing the attitudes of people. Organization systems also help, but in the end a company is only truly marketing oriented if every employee relates his 'inside' work, whether in the office or the factory, to the 'outside' world of the market. The business decisions that control profit are made by the consumer at the point of purchase. The sequence of getting integrated marketing to work is not unique—the steps are understanding, acceptance and action. However, even the faithful pursuit of the three steps to integration will be of little value to a company unless its overall operation is competent. As Howard Morgens pointed out in the previous chapter, marketing relies for its success on the skills of other departments. All it can do is to apply these to the opportunities in the market place.

The purpose of this chapter is to illustrate some of the pitfalls on the road to integrated marketing, and to show what needs to be done to make integration work. To this end, you are invited to assume the mantle of managing director of a company which has in the past been dominated by the production and sales departments. You have just received a recommendation from a firm of consultants to become more 'marketing oriented'. Its specific proposal is that you should recruit a marketing director, and two group product managers. Job specifications for each of these posts are outlined in Appendix II of the consultant's report, the main body of which is replete with ideas for the new marketing men to get their teeth into. The packaging can be improved, say the consultants. More money should be spent on advertising and promotions. The sales force should be rationalized and improved in effectiveness. The plethora of profit building proposals evoke a land of corporate milk and honey, where the money will pour in. And the action steps necessary to achieve this? Just recruit a few marketing men and become 'marketing oriented'—whatever that means. Being a practical and successful businessman, you will first wish to ask a few questions before you commit yourself irrevocably to this new hot gospel called marketing.

ARE WE READY FOR MARKETING YET?

What a practical and relevant question for any managing director to ask! The disciplines which marketing imposes on a company are strict and demanding. It requires an innovative outlook and a quick response to change. Apply these extra burdens to a company which is struggling to carry out its normal tasks, and you may be faced with the temporary collapse of some important functions like selling or production. If your company is already trying to introduce a quality control system, or in the midst of closing down factories and transferring production to new units, or attempting to amalgamate two sales forces, you will be asking for trouble by imposing the additional pressures of marketing at the same time. Its introduction would just make things worse, and, as the new element in the mix, it would probably be made the scapegoat for many gaffes not truly attributable to it. Moreover, the potentially good moves made by marketing would stand a fair chance of being frustrated through production breakdowns, delivery delays or sales force inefficiencies.

An extreme picture has of course been painted, but it reflects the reality that too early an introduction of marketing can have a negative effect by making a difficult situation worse, or by wrongly branding marketing as a failure through no fault of its own—a gun cannot fire with faulty ammunition. Cavenham Foods is one of those companies which probably introduced marketing a year or so too early.

Cavenham Foods is a manufacturing group operating in the grocery field. It was put together quickly by acquisition, and many of the companies purchased had poor consumer franchises. Among the branded products in the group were Carr's biscuits, Procea and Nimble breads, Carsons chocolates, Hollands toffees and Parkinson's sweets.

At Cavenham, 'marketing' was introduced in 1965. Marketing men of high calibre were recruited from Procter & Gamble, Nabisco, Petfoods and Unilever. But unfortunately Cavenham thought marketing was a panacea and a solution to all problems. In fact, the problems were initially too fundamental to be solved by marketing, whose disciplines require a well established framework. For example, in the confectionery division, Cavenham had a large number of old-fashioned factories in the process of being rationalized. The production men were trying to change these at breakneck speed, and were closing down others. There was day-to-day financial pressure. The delivery system was creaking so badly that on occasion the salesman would arrive at a call and find that an order placed four weeks previously had not yet been delivered. The various sales forces were being integrated and developed. And on top of this, the new demands of marketing were being made.

Corporate management might have been much better advised to focus the effort of the marketing group on plans a year or two hence, which could then have been executed when the basic framework and organization of the company was completed. Or it could have waited till the bread and butter problems had shaken down before recruiting marketing men at all.

The decision on *when* to introduce marketing is a difficult one. But it must be made intelligently if offensive marketing is to have a chance of developing in a company. It can be tricky to decide whether the introduction of marketing into a changing or imperfect situation will catalyse the company into a more efficient operation or risk collapsing it. This was the quandary facing United Biscuits in late 1964:

United Biscuits was a combination of four biscuit companies in 1964. Macfarlane and McVitie had merged in the late 1940s, Crawford came into the camp in the early 1960s and Macdonald was acquired in 1964. Altogether the group commanded around 40% of the UK biscuit market. Until McKinsey reported in 1964, little integration had been carried out, and the various companies effectively operated as independent units with their own factories and sales forces. McKinsey recommended that the four companies should start to operate as a group, with rationalized production, personnel and selling, and that the group should introduce a marketing department.

Wisely, UB decided not to try to do everything at once in a rush. The sales and production rationalizations were spread over a number of years, and when the new marketing men took over their desks in early 1965, they found that the company did routine things quite well. The manufacturing operation was efficient and product quality was good; the sales force was conscientious and had wide coverage; and distribution was adequate, though rather too oriented to minimum cost.

The company operated efficiently as long as it ran on established lines. It had difficulty, however, in adjusting to the new demands of marketing for innovation. For instance, it was almost impossible in the first year or so of the integrated regime to make any headway with new products. There was no R & D department or pilot plant, and the factories were understandably reluctant to reduce their efficiency by running small-scale tests. The accountants were essentially book-keepers, and had little concept of how to cost new products or to make long-term cost forecasts. The sales force also had trouble in digesting the new consumer promotions being fed to it by marketing. Prior to 1964, it had just taken orders and the average call rate per man was 30 a day. Salesmen were unable to accommodate marketing's demands for merchandising and for selling consumer promotions because this wider concept of selling was incompatible with the number of calls they had to make.

The essential point here is that marketing entered a situation which was basically sound, but which was not geared to respond to innovation. Because it was operating within a competent basic framework, marketing's demands did not collapse the whole system. On the contrary, they revealed its flaws to general management and acted as a catalyst to change.

SPREADING THE MARKETING GOSPEL

Assuming that, as managing director, you have decided the time is ripe to introduce marketing, your first task is to ensure that you yourself fully understand what marketing is, and the kind of role you foresee it playing in your company. Of course you don't need to become familiar with the intimate details of marketing, any more than you have to know exactly how a computer works. But you cannot begin to adopt an offensive marketing approach until you have grasped its principles and limitations, and worked out what you expect of it and how you plan to handle the obvious difficulties which its introduction will entail. Certainly you could do much worse than go on a two-week course—it will probably teach you something, and the sight of the managing director going on a marketing course will emphasize to other directors that he is taking it seriously.

By now you will have grasped the basics of marketing, and the time has come for a marketing 'teach-in' attended by the whole Board. This could be a tailormade course consisting of two parts. Part I would simply get the principles of marketing across. Part II would involve a discussion between Board members, the leader of the course, and any other qualified person who could conceivably be useful, on how marketing could best be incorporated into the company. The problems of adjustment it will cause, the reallocation of power, and the real benefits it will bring should be examined frankly and openly. Hopefully, an intelligent concensus will arise from this debate, and a plan can be drawn up specifying the role of the marketing department, the way its results will be evaluated by the Board, and the methods proposed for training all key employees in marketing basics.

This is obviously only one way to introduce the concept of marketing. There are always a variety of means for achieving any business objective, and better routes to communicating an understanding and acceptance of marketing may be available. However, the point which has been illustrated is that for marketing to be effective in a company, its whole management must understand and accept it, and maintain a sympathetic attitude to the trials and pitfalls which will inevitably accompany the process of integration. This will avoid the hopeless type of situation epitomized by the half-serious comment of the chairman of a large German company, who was a noted connoisseur of fine paintings: 'I've just added an expensive new marketing man to my collection, but I'm still not sure where to hang him.' Are you surprised that the man he was describing soon moved on?

As managing director, you should underrate least of all the human implications of introducing marketing. Bear in mind that it will involve a reallocation of power within the company. Functions previously carried out by other departments will become the responsibility of marketing under the new set-up, and every part of the company will have to conform to a master plan drawn up by marketing in consultation with other departments. Let us examine an example of this, again from United Biscuits, which is probably not untypical of well-established UK food companies prior to the introduction of marketing.

Before 1965 McVitie, the brand leader in the UK biscuit market, operated autonomously like the other companies in the United Biscuits group. The centre of power was the three factories, situated in Harlesden (London), Manchester and Edinburgh. They were virtually independent fiefdoms. The factory directors who controlled them had their own accountants, buyers and personnel managers and the regional sales forces reported to them through one of the three sales managers. Neither buying nor quality control was centralized, and each factory produced a different recipe of Digestive, Ginger Nut, Chocolate Home Wheat, and so on. Although the factories had their exclusive sales territories, they were encouraged to follow independent policies and to compete against each other in quality. There were significant differences in packaging design by region; for example, until about 1966 the Jaffa Cake pack was blue in Scotland and white in the rest of the country.

When the whole group was integrated from 1965 onwards and marketing introduced, the factory directors' responsibilities were reduced. The sales force no longer reported to them; greater central control over buying was now exercised; and the marketing department led a programme to rationalize recipes, to set up standard product specifications, and to establish a single packaging design nationally for each brand.

The worst service marketing can do for a company is to demotivate personnel in other departments by creating confusion as to their role. That is why an organized programme to spread the marketing gospel should be adopted by general management before the arrival of marketing people. Understanding tends to banish fear of the unknown. And participation by the whole management group in planning the role of marketing within the company is most likely to lead to future co-operation. The sudden appearance of a marketing group without any prior preparation will force it to slug its own way in. This could result either in a dominance of the company by the marketing group, or in total company rejection of marketing, both undesirable alternatives.

In summary, you will now, as a managing director fortified by all these courses and discussions, clearly understand that marketing is a much more pervasive change than the introduction of a computer, because marketing is a total approach to business, not just a new management technique. The application of integrated marketing to a company will have as fundamental an impact on people as a merger, and it should be accompanied by a high degree of pre- and post-planning. The title to this section—'Spreading the Marketing Gospel'—was carefully chosen. Unless you, as managing director, understand and accept integrated marketing and can persuade your colleagues that its benefits outweigh its drawbacks, it will never take place in your company, however shrewdly you set up or staff your marketing department. Successful marketing is a mixture of business and straightforward evangelism.

ACTION 1: DETERMINING THE MARKETING DEPARTMENT'S ROLE

Presumably you will have already agreed this in outline in previous discussions with your fellow directors. It is facile to attempt to sketch an idealized standard role for the marketing department, because this will obviously differ from company to company. However, two basic principles of the offensive marketing approach, which apply irrespective of a company's situation, are that the marketing department should take primary responsibility for both corporate gross profit* and future growth. This is obviously subject to the overriding responsibility of general management and the Board, and does not remove the responsibility of every other department to maintain strict cost budgets.

The marketing department seems the obvious centre within the company in which to place gross profit responsibility. It is at the meeting of the waters, the only point where cost and revenue meet. This is a unique position. All other departments are involved in only one of these two streams. Manufacturing, buying, personnel and finance generate costs but produce no revenue. The sales department generates revenue and cost, but has no opportunity to observe or control any expenditure other than its own.

Gross profit involves the control of raw materials, packaging, factory operation, and advertising and promotion costs. The marketing department has direct authority for deploying the last two cost headings. And one of its tasks is continually to review expenditure on raw materials and packaging, to ensure that they are most productive. For example, after extensive testing, the marketing group might recommend adopting a less expensive formula involving no loss in consumer appeal, or the removal of one colour from the package design. Marketing has no control, of course, over

---

* Gross profit is defined as income less direct costs. The main direct costs are usually ingredients, packaging and factory operating costs. Overheads not deducted from the gross profit figure are selling, distribution, head office running expenses, depreciation and interest. It is normally the responsibility of individual directors, working to budget objectives, to control them.

the day-to-day efficiency of manufacturing, nor over its success in achieving standard cost targets. But if those targets are not met, it is logical to ask the marketing department what it intends to do in order to restore profits to their budgeted level. After all, marketing has the closest knowledge of the main short-term sources of extra profit—namely, changes in the price or weight of products or in the marketing budget.

Assuming that the Board has a policy making rather than an executive function, the only other department in the company which could claim responsibility for gross profit is the financial group. Its contention would presumably be based on its familiarity with what the company can afford, its impartiality, and its intimate knowledge of all company costs. These claims are valid, but they ignore the fact that profit is made up of two elements—cost and revenue. Cost is determinable and can usually be fixed with precision, and the marketing department is as capable as anyone of reading the figures on a cost sheet. Revenue is an infinite variable, constantly moving in response to market stimuli. In consumer categories, it comprises millions of small coins, reflecting the positive results of thousands of individual purchase decisions. To evaluate the likely revenue response to a given product stimulus, to a change in price, or a revision in packaging, it is essential to understand the consumer. This is the expertise of the marketing man.

If you have come this far in your consideration of the proper role for the marketing department, you will also be giving thought to the level of authority with which it should be vested. How can one give the department responsibility for gross profit without giving it authority over production and buying, and is this desirable? No, it is not desirable and the dichotomy between the marketing group's profit obligations and its obviously limited authority raises complex questions which are covered in Chapter 4. Briefly, the marketing department has authority, subject to general management approval, to determine what the manufacturing department should produce. Manufacturing, in its turn, has complete authority to decide how it will implement the agreed production plan, as well as the right to reject any plans proposed by marketing which it considers unfeasible. Thus marketing sets strategies and plans in consultation with the departments concerned but they retain the authority to execute the agreed programme in the way they think best. That, at least, is the way the offensive marketing approach views the position.

Marketing's second responsibility was defined earlier as creating corporate growth. This is more simple to justify. The main sources of revenue and profit are improvements in the marketing of existing products, the introduction of new products that make money, the identification of new markets which fit the company's expertise, and successful acquisitions. All of these are heavily dependent on the spirit of innovation and the knowledge of the market which a group of marketing people should possess. In saying this, I am not ignoring the potential of increased productivity as a source of extra profits; this is an area in which one would reasonably expect every department, including marketing, to be active.

ACTION 2: RECRUITING A MARKETING TEAM

It is evident that integrated marketing will be no more than an expression unless the marketing function is manned by qualified people. It is equally obvious that some companies genuinely believe they have become marketing oriented just by changing the title of their sales manager to 'marketing manager', and by bringing some of their best salesmen into head office with the title of 'product manager'. If the role of evangelist and catalyst of the offensive marketing approach is to be played by old faces wearing different hats and stumbling uncertainly over a new script, people are unlikely to be convinced that marketing is a dynamic new way of doing business.

To return to the situation facing you as managing director: you are probably best advised to recruit seasoned marketing professionals from other successful organizations to fill your senior positions. Promising younger men from within the company, or recruited straight from university, could then be trained up from the more junior positions in which they would start. An additional advantage of the time you, as managing director, have spent in 'understanding' the marketing process is that it will more easily enable you to recruit some outstanding marketing men. The proprietor of an old-established German firm, interviewing a young German general manager with a strong marketing background, was obviously not in that happy position.

    Manager: What are your latest year's sales?
    Proprietor: 500 million Deutschmarks [about £60 million].
    Manager: Are those sales to the trade?
    Proprietor: Yes, of course. Who else can you sell to?
    Manager: What were your sales to the consumer?

Proprietor: I've already told you. Whatever we sell to the trade
    moves through to the consumer.
Manager: I mean, what are your Nielsen sales and share?
Proprietor: Oh yes, we had those Nielsen people here last
    month. They tried to tell us that they could read our sales
    based on checking only 900 stores every other month by the
    application of some formula or other. I said to them that my
    salesmen call on 2200 stores every day, and they let me know
    daily what my sales are.

ACTION 3:   INTEGRATING CORPORATE STRATEGIES

Now we come to the moment of truth and hopefully the time of
benefit, which will determine whether all the enthusiastic talk
about marketing can be welded into action. This testing point will
indicate whether the corporate officers have been responding in a
token way to what they secretly regard either as a passing fashion
or a personal threat, or whether they are convinced that marketing
can improve the company's business efficiency and prepared to
re-direct strategies on that understanding. Now that you, as managing director, are a believer in marketing, probably the best you
can hope for is that your fellow directors will retain a sufficiently
open mind to give it a fair and extended trial. After all, businessmen are always more impressed by results than by theories, and
however eloquently you have put the marketing concept across,
your colleagues will not accept it completely until profits and
growth actually improve.

Both you and your new marketing director will be greatly
tempted to start with the big things, and speedily establish the
validity of the marketing concept with a series of thumping
boundary sixes—with the attendant risk that marketing will be
bowled out very quickly. You should listen patiently to your new
marketing director's desire to review 'the overall direction the
firm should be moving towards' or to discover 'what our business
really is', and then tell him to ponder these issues but take action
on smaller questions first. In any new context, action on immediate
issues involves faster profit payoffs and is more easily understood
by all concerned. Marketing, like any new employee, has to build
up a record of success on smaller issues before the company will
entrust it with big ones. So a new marketing department should
start by identifying some relatively sure opportunities for short-
term profit improvement, like upgrading product performance

or packaging, or developing some decent consumer promotions. And at the same time it should, with the support of general management, take its first important step towards integrated marketing by meeting with the heads of other departments, and drawing up agreed strategies affecting each one.

Many academics would rightly point out that this is a topsy-turvy way of going about things. Surely, they would argue, you must draw up a long-term corporate strategy and plan first, before individual departmental strategies can be discussed with any semblance of sense? Correct in theory, but in practice five-year plans take a long time to write. A new marketing director could very well spend his first six months doing nothing else. And at the end of that time people would be asking whether marketing people were being paid to write documents or to make money for the company. No, the marketing department must get off to a flying start, by quickly putting forward recommendations for improving short-term profit, in order to establish the credibility it needs to round the bigger corners down the road.

The series of meetings between the marketing director and other department heads should result in the agreement of *integrated* marketing strategies for every department. Each meeting will involve a fundamental review of the conflicting functions constituting the marketing approach, as far as that particular department is concerned. On each occasion, the costs and operating efficiencies of the department will be matched against its obligations to the consumer, and the marketing director and department head will attempt to forge a strategy at the median point between the two, where profit is maximized. The marketing director may very well find that his task is not to modify existing strategies, but to help create new ones from scratch. This does not reflect any lack of intelligence or efficiency on the part of other departments. Rather, it recognizes that the latter tend to think empirically, and that written strategic statements are uncommon outside marketing and corporate planning departments.

In developing these strategies, some very basic questions will arise and require resolution. For example, while the head of distribution will obviously recognize the trade's need for service, he will also be keen to run a minimum cost delivery operation. There is clearly a conflict between the two, which must be resolved. The agreed strategy should face up to such fundamental questions, and proposals that in any way resemble the inoffensive limpness of the typical diplomatic communiqué should be angrily torn up by general management. Returning to the distribution department example, the agreed strategy should lay down target lead times between order and delivery, guidelines to cover recurring situations like factory shortages or special demands from large customers, and a policy for delivery errors. Unpleasant facts must be faced. For example, it is inevitable that there will be a proportion of delivery errors. While it is easy to gloss this over, it is better to accept it, and to decide on a maximum level of error, above which red lights will begin to flash internally. Customers will accept an occasional delivery error, and it is usually uneconomic to build a distribution system which is 100% efficient. This basic quandary between cost efficiency and consumer benefit, which must be resolved in every departmental strategy, is well illustrated by the issue of airport baggage handling.

> Nearly all passenger baggage is handled by airlines which have automated systems for getting the luggage from the check-in desk to the plane, and back again on destination. These systems are for the most part very efficient, but errors take place. About one bag in 250 is temporarily lost, though the proportion which is never recovered is less than one in 2000.
>
> Baggage loss is mainly due to errors when transfers of luggage are made between airlines, especially when different terminal buildings are involved. A secondary reason, accounting for less than 25% of losses, is the fixing of incorrect labels to luggage by check-in staff.
>
> Although one loss in 250 may sound low, it is quite significant when the level of irritation to passengers is considered. In determining a specification for an 'acceptable' level of error, the airlines have to balance the extra cost of better systems or double checking against the estimated loss of revenue due to choleric passengers refusing to use their service again.

The marketing director will repeatedly find himself tackling the same basic conflicts in each departmental discussion. In the case of production, a balance must be struck between production department's desire for low cost long runs and marketing department's preference for short runs. A specific example of a strategy in this area may be illuminating. The one outlined below is probably not far from the practice of Petfoods, an integrated marketing company which does a particularly effective job in balancing production and marketing needs.

The factory specifications of products will be set up by production department and R & D, to reproduce exactly the performance and characteristics of the formulae successfully tested among consumers. A number of alternative approved specifications will be built up, all resulting in the same target level of product satisfaction to the consumer. Moves between these agreed specifications should be made in response to changing raw material prices, in order to minimize production costs.

Factory foremen can approve changes between agreed specifications. New specifications must be agreed with the marketing department before they can be authorized for production. Marketing may or may not require consumer tests on suggested new specifications before agreeing to their use.

Quality control procedures will ensure that all products meet necessary legal requirements, and will concentrate effort against those elements of the product which matter most to the consumer.

The production department will be run at the minimum possible cost, consistent with efficient working, and strict observance of specifications and quality control standards. Where the marketing department requires shorter than normal runs, to meet important marketing objectives like special promotions or market testing, the production department should co-operate fully. However, production should estimate the premium cost involved in such short runs, and the excess cost over normal will become a marketing department charge. Production should regard justifiable requests for short runs as a continuing necessity, and gear its system to handling them as efficiently and inexpensively as possible.

Our indefatigable marketing director will round out his series of meetings by seeing the heads of the buying, R & D, finance and sales departments. Clearly there should be a lot of give and take in developing departmental strategies, and some of these will not be to the total satisfaction of either party. Others may reach deadlock over an important issue, in which case general management should be called in to arbitrate. In any event, all the strategies should be put forward to the Board for approval. And because they involve crucial questions of corporate policy, the Board would be wise to do more than just rubber-stamp them.

The new marketing director will emerge from these talks a tired but very much wiser man. In determining well balanced departmental strategies, he will not only have set the stage for a truly integrated corporate approach to marketing, but will in the process have sketched out ground rules for co-operation between marketing and other departments. And, provided that his own people have by this time successfully made a few dramatic short-term profit improvements, he will be ready to scale the Parnassus of long-term corporate strategy and five-year plans. These, you will be relieved to hear, are reserved for another chapter.

SUMMARY

Marketing will not be accepted as an approach to the total business unless it has the enthusiastic understanding and support of general management. It relies for its success on the skills of other departments, and if these are seriously deficient, marketing's impact will be limited.

In companies previously unfamiliar with it, marketing should be introduced with care, and a clear plan as to its future role. Consideration should first be given to whether the basic structure of the company is strong enough to accept the strict and demanding disciplines which marketing imposes. Then the whole of the company's top management should be exposed to the marketing concept, and involved in planning the role of marketing in the organization. As a result, when qualified marketing people are recruited, a fair understanding of their function will exist, together with a readiness to adapt individual departmental strategies to the marketing approach. The two most important initial tasks of the new marketing director are quickly to demonstrate his ability to improve profit, and to set up integrated marketing strategies for each department.

4: *The Principles of Marketing*
in Action

(Advanced marketing practitioners are advised to skip this chapter.)

You will remember the 'teach-in' which you, as the notional managing director in the previous chapter, set up to give your fellow directors a basic understanding of marketing principles. This chapter will cover the same ground as Part I of that course. While it is not recommended for the advanced practitioner who is fully familiar with the marketing art, if what he has read so far has given him any reason to distrust this familiarity, or if he found himself among the majority who misdefined marketing in Chapter 1, he should congratulate himself on the honesty of his self-analysis and read on!

It is a truism that a clear understanding of how marketing works is necessary for anyone ultimately wishing to apply the offensive marketing approach, whether as a general manager or a marketing specialist. The principles of offensive marketing are very simply stated. You merely identify a profitable consumer need, design a better product, and then make certain everyone knows about it. Offensive marketing also looks simple to execute when it is carried out successfully. But looks are deceptive—consider the apparent simplicity of the Sydney suspension bridge or a Picasso painting.

THE BOOMERANG SEQUENCE

Offensive marketing follows a boomerang sequence to transform consumer needs into profitable products. The three steps in the sequence apply to the marketing of any products—from automobiles to magnetic tape. They are investigation, design and sale. Figure 1 shows our boomerang in action.

Investigation is necessary to discover what the consumer wants. Its object is to track down unsatisfied needs, of the kind that the company in question is equipped to fulfil.

Design is the process of developing a product and package that

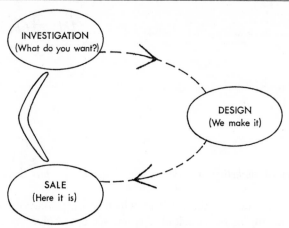

Figure 1   The boomerang sequence of marketing

meets the need which has been identified. It also includes the design
of the product financial plan, which ensures that the need can be
met profitably.

Selling is the finishing touch by which the consumer (and the
trade) is sold the product designated for during the investigation.
Advertising, promotions, merchandising, sales force effort and
packaging design are all part of the selling stage.

This description makes the transition from stage to stage of the
boomerang sequence sound smooth and assured. In practice, however, it is usually muffled and imperfect, pounded by all kinds of
distortion and interference. Misinterpretation and wishful thinking
are notable causes of this, so that when the boomerang finally
returns to the consumer in the form of a product, it is often rejected.

Each of the three boomerang stages involves a number of depart-

TABLE 4.1			
Name of department	*Investigation*	*Design*	*Sale*
Marketing	★	★	★
R & D	★	★	
Manufacturing		★	★
Advertising agency	★	★	★
Finance		★	★
Buying		★	★
Distribution		★	★
Sales		★	★

ments besides marketing, and Table 4.1 traces their participation. It shows that virtually every department plays a part in design and sale, but that investigation is usually handled by marketing, R & D and perhaps the advertising agency. Of course, the boomerang sequence of marketing refers equally to existing as to new products. Any reputable brand manager will be continually searching for ways to make his current brand more acceptable to the consumer or more profitable.

INVESTIGATION—THE FEMALE MIND

You may be wondering how you can ever hope to reveal the unsatisfied yearnings of, say, thousands of women all over the country, when you can't even choose the right kind of gift for your wife. The answer is that you have to listen to the consumer even more attentively than you listen to your wife. And observe her too. Research is the eyes and ears of the commercial firm. It is both a listening post and an observation tower. The marketing executive has to program the questions and interpret the results. As in the case of a computer, what comes out depends on the quality of the input. If you have a reasonably clear idea of what you are looking for, market research is a trusty aid in any investigation. But use it like a vacuum cleaner, to sweep over broad spaces, and the odds are that you will just pick up a load of rubbish.

Investigation of the market place involves two facets—finding out what the consumer thinks (consumer research) and observing her actions in the market place (market research).

Consumer research deals with attitudes and opinions towards existing products or hypothetical future ones. The techniques used vary, from simple structured interviews of large samples of consumers to elaborate three-hour depth interviews of small groups, conducted by a qualified psychologist.

Market research is more factual because it is concerned with action rather than opinion. It observes happenings in the market place, as reflected by trade or consumer purchases, and measures action based on money passing. These data are then projected into estimates of total market sizes and trends, brand shares, retail distribution, and pricing and stock levels.

Consumer and market research are complementary and act in unison. Consumer research is often used to check the reasons for purchase behaviour revealed by market research. And market research ultimately checks the market showing of products developed with the aid of consumer research. It is not difficult to identify the more obvious consumer needs if you think clearly and are not encumbered by the burden of industrial tradition. Straightforward research on consumer habits, product usages, and attitudes to brands and markets will normally pinpoint obvious needs. For instance, you do not have to be a particularly subtle investigator to conclude that improved taste or freshness in food products, better cleaning by household products, and greater speed or convenience of use for all brands are regarded by consumers as desirable attributes.

Paradoxically, comprehensive research is usually worth undertaking in any markets that seriously attract your interest. Admittedly the broad findings often merely confirm common sense, but at least they give a firm factual background, shorn of guesswork, from which to operate. And there's always a sporting chance that they will reveal new opportunities. To take a fictional example, a usage and attitude study involving 1000 interviews about a particular food market might indicate that existing products were considered too thick or too sweet, that the level of usage among families with children was high enough to justify the introduction of a child oriented product, or that most consumers added extra ingredients to existing commercial products, thereby making a more convenient 'all in one' brand a possibility.

Despite much clever talk in the marketing world about complicated and novel research techniques, it is apparent that most of the

TABLE 4.2		
New brand	Product category	Reason for success
Embassy	Cigarettes	First brand with a quality image to offer free coupon catalogue scheme
Clarksons	Packaged holidays	Low price holidays of good quality to desirable destinations, conveniently pre-packaged
Wilkinson Sword	Coated stainless steel blades	Closer shave, at higher price
Polaroid	Cameras	Good quality pictures developed almost instantly, at reasonable price
Ariel	Washing powder	Superior stain removal, at higher price

really successful new consumer products introduced in the past decade have fulfilled relatively obvious needs, which the simplest form of investigation would have revealed. The critical reason for their success was not shrewd investigation, but skilful design and selling. Most of the outstanding new products of the 1960s succeeded either by providing better performance at higher prices or by offering the same performance at a lower price. Table 4.2 gives some pretty representative examples of this. All the brands concerned were major successes.

INVESTIGATION—DON'T KNOCK THE OBVIOUS

Following the obvious is very productive if you can find a unique way to execute it, as we have just seen from the new product examples above. Ariel, Polaroid and Wilkinson utilized genuine technical breakthroughs to fulfil obvious consumer needs. Any fool could point out that men would pay more for a razor that gave a closer shave, but it took technical expertise of an outstanding quality to develop the stainless steel blade.

Embassy was successful because it saw the potential of coupons, and was prepared to commit major resources to producing a first class scheme. It also understood well that cigarettes were a status product, and that a quality image had to be established for a brand to succeed, irrespective of the strength of any other purchase incentive like low price or coupon schemes. The maker of Embassy (Imperial Tobacco) showed a much better understanding of the market than Gallaher, its major competitor, which already had a coupon brand, Kensitas, but had failed to give it a quality image. Embassy's superior understanding may have been based on deeper investigation or perhaps it was more a matter of plain old-fashioned business flair.

Clarksons came into the mass market for packaged tours quite late—in 1965. For the previous five years of its existence (it started up in 1959), it had concentrated on short tours, often day trips, abroad. In 1965 the leaders in the two-week packaged tour market were Sky Tours, Cosmos and Global. However, from this standing start, Clarksons rapidly caught up with and overhauled all the other tour operators, and for the past few years it has easily led the field. Its source of business was broadly 50% from competitors and 50% from expansion of the total market, and it succeeded simply by offering good quality holidays at a low price. Like Marks & Spencer, Clarksons aimed for value rather than cheapness, although its pricing was also extremely competitive. Almost two-thirds of Clarksons' tour volume in any one year is repeat business, which is a strong testimony to the value it offers. The company has recently been castigated, however, for a tendency to cut costs to the point where efficiency may be sacrificed—it is to be hoped that quality standards will continue to be maintained in the future.

An offensive marketer may also discover an obvious way to fulfil an obvious need which no one has yet thought of. Even if the product is easy to make and capable of speedy duplication by competition, he should still forge ahead, because the first company in with a new idea usually retains leadership provided it has the necessary financial resources.

You may well ask why you should find the obvious when others have missed it during their own market investigations. The answer is that what is obvious to one person may be wrapped in a blanket of obscurity for another. Much depends on the angle of vision. Take the case of Archimedes, for instance.* He had the pressing problem on his mind of finding out whether the crown of Hieron II of Syracuse was made of solid gold. If only he could determine the volume of the crown, he could easily check on its density, since the unit weight of gold was known. But there was no existing technology for calculating the size of irregular cubic shapes. He was thinking about this problem as he got into his bath and watched the familiar sight of the water rising. It then occurred to him that his own body was also an irregular cubic shape like the crown, and that he could measure its volume by calculating the amount of water displaced when it was put in a receptacle.

Generations of men for centuries past had possessed the same information as Archimedes but had failed to make his simple deduction. There is a lot of data of the same kind today, lying around in files, just waiting for an imaginative mind to light it up. Dominant companies in existing markets often fail to see the obvious, when it does not fit in with established tradition. Or they see it, but hesitate to act because of the possibly prejudicial effect of new brands on their current franchise. Or they may be lethargic or complacent. The outsider can often see opportunities which the insider looks right through. In the American frozen food market for instance, four of the major new ideas in the 1950s and 1960s were innovated by outsiders, not by General Food's Birds Eye division, the leading operator in the category. The case

* See Arthur Koestler, *The Act of Creation* (New York: Macmillan, 1964) for this and many other fascinating examples.

history below is a good example of offensive marketing in action.

The American frozen food market is divided into two major parts—commodity products like orange juice and vegetables, which remain in a form fairly close to nature, and recipe products which incorporate a considerable amount of processing by manufacturers. The commodity category is not expanding and there is very little profit in it (if any) for manufacturers. It is dominated by private label, with over 50% of some markets like frozen vegetables and orange juice, and by Birds Eye. The recipe side is profitable and growing, but Birds Eye has missed the opportunity to build a dominant position in it.

However, four new companies, all outsiders to frozen foods in 1950, have built strong franchises in the recipe sector of the market, all using approaches which were at the time novel, though the needs they fulfilled were fairly obvious, and the technology they used was presumably equally available to Birds Eye.

Kitchens of Sara Lee originally began distribution of high quality cakes within a 300 mile (480 km) radius of Chicago in the early 1950s. In 1953 it started to freeze its cakes so that it could ship them to the South without spoiling.* In the late 1950s Kitchens of Sara Lee began to distribute frozen cake nationally and built a large new market for premium priced frozen cakes of superior quality. It is now part of Consolidated Foods.

Swansons innovated 'TV dinners', which consisted of complete meals in foil trays. It was taken over by Campbell's in 1965 but remains the leader in the TV dinner segment.

Stouffer's developed the high priced luxury end of the complete meal market with dishes like Lobster Newburg and Chicken à la King. It is reputed to be a very profitable company and was acquired by Litton Industries in 1967.

The Green Giant Company, a relatively small canned vegetable packer, entered the frozen food market nationally in 1962, with the then revolutionary concept of boil-in-the-bag vegetables. Butter, seasoning and vegetables were all contained in a polythene bag, which the housewife just dropped into a pan and boiled. Green Giant's turnover and net profits almost trebled in the period 1960–69.

All of these innovations stemmed from the housewife's need

---

* These data on Kitchens of Sara Lee are derived from Ralph Westfall and Harper W. Boyd, *Cases in Marketing Management* (Richard D. Irwin, 1961).

c

for extra convenience, and the willingness of a substantial number of consumers to pay more for superior products. In each case, outsiders saw the opportunities more clearly than Birds Eye, the current market leader, which doubtless possessed reams of the most sophisticated research on every segment of the category.

To quote the words of Le Corbusier, the famous French architect: 'Our epoch is fixing its own style day by day. It is there under our eyes. Eyes which do not see.'*

INVESTIGATION—BEYOND THE OBVIOUS

Before we move into the deeper realms of research, a word of warning to the less experienced reader is in order. Some companies proudly parade their use of the latest techniques of depth research as a sign of their 'sophistication'. However, I am not aware of any correlation between an organization's degree of sophistication and its level of profitability. Indeed many of the top fifty companies in *Management Today's* Growth and Profitability Leagues are more notable for their adherence to no-nonsense common sense techniques than for the sophisticated methods used by their management. Conversely, there is a danger that the pursuit of sophistication will be seen as an end in its own right, and obvious profit opportunities will be missed because the mass of information collected prevents a true understanding of basics. This echoes Margaret Mead's words of wisdom in Chapter 1.

Effective use of advanced research tools is a proper weapon for the offensive marketer, since these tools may uncover hidden opportunities, and give him the chance to innovate. However, the emphasis is on the word 'effective'. A lot of money is wasted on sophisticated research, not through any incompetence on the part of the researchers, but because the marketing executives commissioning it lack a definite purpose. Depth research is, after all, no more than a technique for striking into the unknown, and unless it is properly directed, it is unlikely to yield much useful information. One could compare it to drilling new land for oil—for every good strike of rich new knowledge, there is a risk of finding a dry hole. So the simple message is that depth research should be used selectively and with finite objectives.

There are many imaginative and effective techniques of depth

* Le Corbusier, *Towards a New Architecture* (Architectural Press, 1946).

research, but I have neither the space nor the knowledge to list them all here. In most cases, relatively small numbers of people are used, and the object is usually to gain a clear understanding of how consumers think about or buy products, or how they react to new ideas. Depth research can be particularly useful in checking out experimental hypotheses, and in that sense has similarities to much of the bench work carried out in a laboratory. Depth research is not just a matter of sitting a woman down in front of a psychologist, and some of the methods used by System Three (Communications) Ltd give an idea of the variety of techniques available:

(1) dialogues between the users of different brands;
(2) intensive surveys of basic motivation, using packaging, visual and product props to draw out responses and fix the meaning of abstract answers;
(3) controlled brainstorming, using advertising/marketing personnel *and* consumers and depth researchers;
(4) creative sessions, using a creative visualizer to convert consumers' ideas into drawings to classify those ideas;
(5) acute and unobtrusive observation of the purchaser buying in the store: observation of grooming behaviour, examination of alternatives, degree of handling and speed of decision are made by trained psychologists.

THE FLOCK FACTOR

The offensive marketer carries out his own investigations, makes up his corporate mind about what the information means, and creates his own innovations. This book contrasts him favourably with the maintenance marketer, who is satisfied with the *status quo*, absorbed with the routine of keeping things going and always trailing his competitor in a sadly out of breath condition. He is very inclined to copy successful moves by others and is responsible for what we may term the flock factor.

The flock factor is a corollary of the well known principle of economics, that innovators who make super-normal profits will soon be joined by followers who will attempt to share in those profits. When an offensive marketer brings out a successful new idea, one can expect his competitors to scurry after him. Fortunately for justice and the free enterprise system, followers rarely do as well. A Nielsen study of fourteen pioneer products* showed that

* A. C. Nielsen Co., *How to Strengthen your New Product Plan* (1966).

the first follower only achieved 47% of the pioneer's volume three years later, and the second follower a mere 26%.

The psychology of the flock factor is not very clear. One would guess that it stems partly from fear of being left out of a possible bonanza and partly from the paucity of really new ideas in circulation at any one time. While a board of directors will recognize that its organization cannot realistically innovate every new development in its markets (although this should be the constant aim), it will be wise to conduct a searching self-examination if it always finds itself among the followers. Let us examine a couple of examples of the flock factor at work. They are worth looking at in detail because the flock factor is the complete opposite of offensive marketing and independent investigation. The first instance comes from hair colouring, the second from the packet meal sector.

In the early 1960s the hair colouring market was growing rapidly but was very quiet in marketing terms. The French company L'Oréal had the brand leader in Color Glo, and it was followed by Focus (Gillette) and Harmony (Gibbs). In 1963 Warner Lambert's Polycolor entered the market, and proved very successful because it offered a more natural-looking result, plus greater convenience.

Impressed by Polycolor's success, and by the buoyancy of the hair colouring market in the USA, a large number of new brands flooded on to the market. In 1965 alone there were at least nine national launches, including Sea Witch and Melody (both from Gibbs), Clairol Nice 'n Easy and Loving Care (both from Bristol-Myers), Toni Casual (Gillette), New Dawn (Alberto-Culver), Belle Color (L'Oréal) and Colorsilk (Revlon). Many of these new brands spent heavily on introduction, and some tallied up a level of advertising greater than the amount spent by all brands in the market during the previous year. None of the new products was particularly innovative—most were emulsified creamy liquids with a slight convenience advantage over the original Polycolor formulation.

When the dust settled a couple of years later, it was apparent that Harmony, the new brand leader, and Polycolor had weathered the storm well, and that none of the follower products had achieved a share of better than 5%. Most failed financially. And instead of doubling or trebling, the total market grew sedately from £3·6 million at manufacturer prices in 1965 to only £4·7 million in 1970.

The packet meal market was pioneered by Batchelors Vesta (Unilever), which was introduced in 1962 and still dominates the field. Vesta derived from Batchelors packet soup technology, and consisted of freeze-dried complete meals, with Beef Curry and Chicken Curry quickly becoming established as the leading varieties.

Between 1962 and 1967 Vesta was left almost completely unmolested. The only challenge came from Crosse & Blackwell's World Fair range, introduced in 1964 and withdrawn two years later. However, in the fifteen months from September 1968, no fewer than eight competitive new products were introduced either nationally or across most of the country. They were Harvey's Duo-Can (Cadbury Schweppes), Heinz-Erin, Presto (Reckitt & Colman), Sutherlands Secret (Quaker), Cerola (Ranks Hovis McDougall) and Knorr (Corn Products), Plumrose Danish dishes and Wall's 7 Star (Unilever).

One may again legitimately ask why all the activity took place in 1968-9 after such a long period of silence. True, the market was expanding quickly and had grown from £2·8 million at manufacturer prices in 1966 to £4·3 million in 1968. And manufacturer margins were high as food products go. But it was still an attractive market back in 1965.

To do justice to the new products, not all of them were 'Me-Too's'. Indeed, the Harvey's Duo-Can approach was completely new, Cerola was the first to introduce the boil-in-the-bag idea, and some of the other brands incorporated minor packaging improvements. However, none of them was able to offer a sufficiently important advantage over Vesta to persuade consumers to switch away from the entrenched leader, and Vesta's share of the market was again over the 80% mark in 1970.

THE COMPANY FITTING ROOM

Once the marketing executive has, through investigation, identified an unsatisfied consumer need, he then has to consider whether it is the kind of need his own company is well qualified to fulfil. Does the need exploit his company's skills, or do some of the companies already in the market possess strengths that it will be difficult to match?

This question of fit between company and market may not arise if the investigation concerns the improvement of existing products or concentrates on categories in which the firm is already represented. But even so close to home as this, the issue may come up. For instance, an opportunity may have been unearthed in the higher priced segment of a market when the company concerned only competes in the low price sector. Is the company equipped to market higher priced products successfully? This question should be considered very carefully before any decision is made to spend money on designing the new product. Another issue that can arise at this stage is that of technology. The investigation may reveal a need which can only be fulfilled by technology new to the company. Perhaps freeze-drying technology—a field in which the company has no experience—is necessary. Again, the company should ponder whether the potential of the unfulfilled need seems great enough to justify an ultimate move into the new technology. The answer may be an immediate 'No', or if the project appears promising, a final decision may be postponed until some initial design work has been carried out.

The issue of company fit is most important when radically new markets are being considered. It goes almost without saying that a company entering an entirely new category should not do so unless it has some definite point of superiority to counterbalance its lack of experience. However, in considering its suitability for new markets, a company is best advised to take an offensive approach and not to underestimate its skills. It is very easy to be intimidated by the apparent strength of the company in possession but, as the US frozen food example above showed, a determined competitor with a good idea usually has a sound chance of success even in unfamiliar markets. Objectivity is everything in these situations. A company should slightly, though only slightly, overestimate its strengths, while defining its weaknesses clearly—and honestly. Both strengths and weaknesses will obviously vary according to the market being considered.

The subject of the best fit between companies and markets is also reviewed in the sections of this book covering five-year planning, new products and acquisitions. Consequently, only a few brief examples will be given in this chapter. Let us take a look at two good fits between companies and markets, and one poor one.

During the early 1960s, General Mills was a marketer of cereals and cake mixes (Betty Crocker), among other things. In seeking new categories to enter, it defined its major skill as marketing.

Among the businesses it investigated was toys. Now toys may seem a long way from food, but General Mills observed that marketing skills were important in toys and that existing toy companies were not particularly advanced in this respect. It also noted that it possessed special skills in marketing to children, through its long-established position in the cereal market, and that toys were also a category bought by adults but used by children. So a decision was made by GM to enter the toy market, and a number of companies, including Parker Brothers (the makers of Monopoly) were purchased. GM became the world's second largest toy manufacturer after Mattel. The diversification proved very successful, but it had been preceded by a careful investigation of the market, and an objective examination of the skills GM could bring to it.

The second example of good corporate fit concerns Procter & Gamble's entry into the paper market in America.

Procter & Gamble's skills lie in marketing fast-moving consumer goods, sold to grocers. It has achieved its greatest success in product categories like soaps and detergents, where the quality of end result performance can be objectively assessed.

In the 1950s it investigated the market for consumer paper products (toilet and facial tissues largely), and liked what it saw. The market had reached a good size, was expanding fast, and offered sufficient margins to permit heavy advertising and promotion spending. What is more, the criteria by which consumers judged the performance of paper products—notably softness, absorbency and wet strength—could be assessed objectively, just like the whiteness result of a washing powder. There were only two snags—P & G knew nothing about paper technology, and the two entrenched competitors, Scott Paper and Kimberley Clark (Kleenex), were well managed companies.

P & G bought a small paper firm with a regional franchise, called the Charmin Company, in the late 1950s and used that as a base for learning about the business. The P & G people spent some years developing what they considered to be a superior product, and then moved slowly across the USA with it, placing all their marketing skills and resources behind it. By 1970 P & G had ousted Scott Paper as Number One in toilet tissues, and was Number Two behind Kimberley Clark in paper tissues.

One match that hasn't worked out at all well is that between tobacco and food companies.

Imperial Tobacco's acquisition of HP, Ross Foods and Smedley, and its development of Golden Wonder crisps has not yet proved very profitable. In 1970 Imperial only made a trading profit of £5·71 million on a £166·3 million turnover in foods. In retrospect, and it is always easy to be wise after the event, Imperial appeared to do a less good job than Procter & Gamble and General Mills, both in investigating its markets and in accurately assessing its strengths in relation to them.

For a start, it is rather difficult to understand why Imperial found manufactured food an attractive market. Following Engel's Law, spending on groceries is declining as a proportion of gross national expenditure in virtually every developed country, and certainly in both the UK and USA. While it provides a solid business base *from* which to diversify, for companies already in food, it is strange to find a firm choosing groceries as a category to diversify *into*.

Imperial presumably reasoned that its skills in marketing tobacco products were transferable to food, where marketing is also an important factor. This reasoning is very questionable, since tobacco marketing is very different in character from food marketing. In food, product performance and pricing are paramount, the trade is very strong and well organized, and most markets are extremely competitive. In cigarettes, packaging and advertising are the critical elements in the marketing mix, product performance is less important and the trade is relatively weak.

Although the record of Golden Wonder is outstanding in every aspect except profit, Imperial Tobacco in essence had no skills to bring to the grocery market which were in any way superior to those of entrenched competitors like Birds Eye, Bachelors and Heinz.

SO WHERE'S THE PROFIT?

To recap, thorough investigation of a business opportunity in the market involves answering three questions:

(a) Is there a genuine need which is not properly satisfied at present?

(*b*) Are we equipped as a company to fulfil it effectively?

(*c*) Does it look profitable?

We have covered the first two questions and now comes the third. One is tempted to give the answer: 'Let's first design a product and then cost it.' This may be in fact what one ultimately has to do in order to get a detailed picture of likely profitability. However, it should be possible to draw broad conclusions about probable profit from the results of the investigation. The key point is that a proper investigation involves not only the location of an unsatisfied need but also basic groundwork on likely profit. The sources may be rough but they are usually serviceable. You may be lucky and find companies with decipherable balance sheets in the market to which entry is proposed. More often than not, however, firms compete in a variety of markets, and the profit attributable to individual ones cannot be deduced. In any event, markets which are known to be turning up a nil or negligible profit—like crisps and ready-made cakes at present—are to be avoided like the plague, unless the investigating company has a sure-fire proposition which is unique and can be premium priced (or a revolutionary method for reducing production costs!). On a more hopeful note, it is possible to work out tentatively the desired kind of product, generate 'class B' estimates on the likely range of material costs, adding guesstimates for overheads, and thus see whether a viable marketing plan can be developed. If you find that you will have to price a product which is only marginally better than existing brands at 100% premium, you should drop the project there and then and look for something more promising. It will all be quite rough, and it won't pinpoint your likely profit with any accuracy, but it will safeguard you against sending the R & D department on a fool's errand that could not be commerically viable in any circumstances.

If the above description has given the impression of rough and ready practice, I have succeeded in my objective, because that is the way it usually is. Do not be deceived into thinking that marketing is a science. It is not now and probably never will be, because it deals with human beings called consumers, and with fragile ideas about the future that are hard to evaluate.

DESIGNING BENEFITS

We have completed our investigation, and have found an unful-filled need which is profitable, fits well with company capabilities and seems likely to excite the consumer. All we have to do now is to design a product to meet this identified need, and sell it!

The need pinpointed during investigation will resemble a police Identikit picture rather than a finished portrait. The profile of the need is pieced together from a range of differing consumer opinions, interwoven with clues as to their wants based on existing purchase behaviour in the market place. The role of design is to translate the Identikit into a product personality, which consumers will ultimately recognize as the thing they envisaged initially when they expressed a need. Investigation translates a bundle of information into a need, and design turns it into a commercially viable benefit. The working of this process in the improvement of existing products and the development of new ones is illustrated in Table 4.3 with a few real life examples.

TABLE 4.3	
Consumer need	*Consumer benefit designed*
Instant coffee looking and tasting more like real coffee	Freeze-dried coffee (Nescafé Gold Blend).
Fresher bread	Sunblest's identification of day bread was made on wrapper ('Happy Monday', etc.)
Potato in convenient form, with more natural taste	Cadbury's Smash
Purchase of cosmetics in the leisure and privacy of one's own home	Avon's 'in-home' sales technique
Non-drip, quicker drying paint	Magicote (Berger, Jenson & Nicholson)
Oil specially suited to front wheel drive cars (like the Mini)	Duckham's Q20/50 oil
Tyre with greater safety and better road-holding	Pirelli radial tyres (other brands subsequently followed).

The marketing department is responsible for defining relevant consumer needs, and for drawing up a design brief to guide the R & D department in its work; the tightness of this brief will depend on the extent of the technical challenge. If the consumer need is very specific, and the technical task a simple one—as in developing a cigarette to compete in a new pricing segment—the marketing brief for R & D would closely define the nature, quality and target cost of the product in detail. But if the research task is to achieve a major new invention, the marketing brief should leave the means for achieving the objective very open, and allow great latitude in time and expense.

So far, this section has concentrated on the technical aspects of design. The process has been made to sound rather mechanical: a need is identified, R & D is briefed, and a year later a superior product may—or may not—arrive on your desk. However, as any cosmetics marketer will tell you, consumers seek psychological satisfactions as well as performance benefits. They may have a need for reassurance, for status, or for a feeling of power. Investigation is designed to turn up *every* kind of consumer need, and where the benefit is primarily in the mind, the role of the advertising agency in designing the product benefit will be at least as important as that of the R & D group. Some very successful new brands in the UK have allied such a benefit with distinctive product characteristics that back them up. Daz is quite a good example of a product which originally had parity in performance but was regarded as superior by many of its users because of their touching faith in the magical properties of its blue colour. The 'better' whiteness was, and may still be, all in the mind.

Procter & Gamble introduced Tide, the first synthetic detergent in the UK, in about 1951. It did very well, achieving a high point of 33% of the total washing product market in its early days, but it was a pioneer formulation containing important 'bugs', including an alarming taste for eating through the rubber of washing machine rollers (this fault was rapidly rectified, but lived on in the memory of many consumers). Unilever's Surf was the second synthetic into the market, but has never achieved a major share.

P & G has always pursued the multi-brand approach, and wished to follow up the success of Tide with a second product. It was keen to introduce a new brand that was different from Tide and offered some new benefit. At the time, all washing powder contained white granules, and P & G's market investigations showed that a fair proportion of housewives put 'blue bags' in with their whites when they had completed the wash. These blue bags contained blue coloured perfumed particles which were reputed to give an effect of extra whiteness to the washing. The fact that women were actually prepared to pay money for a separate product to 'blue' the clothes convinced P & G that it was an important benefit. However, one suspects the benefit was more in the mind than real and that the efficacy of the blue bag was an old wives' tale.

This large group of women using the blue bag constituted the target for Daz, P & G's second synthetic detergent, launched in 1954. It was the first 'all blue' washing powder in the UK, which differentiated it from Tide, and provided the unique benefit of the 'blue whitener'. This was used as the reason-why for the superlative whiteness performance claimed by Daz, in common with every other washing powder launched before or since.

As stressed previously, investigation and design can be equally fruitful in recasting an existing brand as in launching a new one. The following case history on Chum dog food illustrates a variety of things. It shows the importance of psychological benefits. It is a classic example of market segmentation, which is covered separately (Chapter 17). And it demonstrates the principle we noticed in our observation of Archimedes in his bath—that the value of information depends on eyes that see and ears that hear.

Petfoods was the pioneer of the tinned dogfood market in the UK and established a strong early position with Lassie and Pal. However, by the early 1960s Spillers possessed a powerful brand in Kennomeat, acquired with Scottish Animal Products. Kennomeat was a second generation dogfood. Unlike Pal and Lassie, which were meat loaf products, and pink in colour, Kennomeat was dark brown and consisted of pieces of meat set in brown liquid. It was known in the trade as a meat-and-gravy as opposed to a loaf product. Petfoods introduced Chum to counter Kennomeat, but it was a parity product, and offered no significant point of superiority over Kennomeat. It achieved only moderate success, and by 1963, when a new brand manager was appointed, the Chum share was trending marginally downwards.

The new man, who had had no prior experience of the petfood market, picked up in conversation with some of the company vets that pedigree dogs had different nutrition requirements to other dogs. On checking available consumer research, he discovered that almost 50% of owners claimed their dogs were pedigree, and that this percentage was growing. Consequently, it was decided to reposition Chum as 'the food specially formulated for pedigree dogs'. The R & D department discovered that this claim could be legally validated by incorporating large doses of thiamin into the product, since pedigree dogs are more highly strung and sensitive than others. The product was improved in other ways—by stiffening up the consistency, putting in larger pieces of liver and making it look more like a meat stew. A quality package and new advertising were also developed to underline the new claim, and the brand's price was increased. Gradually Chum's share levelled out and began to climb. It gained brand leadership in the middle 1960s, a position it still holds.

The strength of the Chum approach was that it appealed not only to the owners of pedigree dogs, who saw it as a tailor-made product, but also to pet owners who regarded their dogs as of pedigree quality or wished to give their mongrels the 'best' food there was. Its positioning enabled Chum to establish itself as the quality product in the category. The benefits incorporated into its design were partly psychological and partly real.

IS THE PROFIT STILL THERE?

We established that only a rough estimate of likely profit for a planned new project could be made at the investigation stage. No such excuses are available once the benefit or, to take it more literally, the package and the product, have been designed. Now we have an entity that can be accurately costed. And the marketing plan can be drawn up in detail, to determine retail pricing, and advertising and promotion spending, all of which affect the profit on the bottom line.

The duty of the marketing man following the offensive approach is to design a profit for the company, as well as a new benefit for the consumer, and the two should proceed as far as possible in harness. The rough preliminary marketing plan, drawn up at the investigation stage as the basis for determining the product and package cost target in the design brief, should be gradually refined as the design reaches completion. The unexciting but essential work of drawing up alternative marketing plans should be undertaken, working on the principle that the retail price of the brand and the marketing support needed to launch and sustain it must be determined by the realities of the market place. Ignore this principle and you will have no choice but to price your brand on a 'cost plus' basis—the cost of the product and package that R & D produces, plus whatever you need for marketing funds and profit. It would be a remarkable coincidence if the resulting retail price happened to be one that the market would bear.

Profits on new product or redesign projects have an unendearing habit of disappearing without notice. The marketing man needs to watch them every scrap of the way, and one company with impeccable practices in this respect is Ford, as the case history on the launch of the Capri later in this chapter demonstrates. Profits have to be watched particularly closely during the initial R & D design stage, and when the transition is made from pilot plant to full-scale production. Consider the case of Lyons Harvest fruit pies. Like many good examples it illustrates more than one point, and the second one it demonstrates is how difficult it is for good marketing men to make an impact if other departments do not meet their objectives.

Marketing was introduced to Lyons in the early 1960s, and over the years, including the present, the company has housed some outstanding marketing men. This case concerns its bakery division. Lyons has been the brand leader in ready-made cakes throughout the 1960s, and is still well ahead of McVitie and Cadbury, the Number Two and Three brands. In common with its competitors, it has found profits in this market remarkably hard to come by.

One of the more dramatic of the marketing group's recommendations in the mid-1960s was the proposal to withdraw individual fruit pies, which had until then been the bedrock of the division. The turnover of individual pies was £1·8 million, but net profit before tax was only about £100 000. This proposal was the culmination of extensive investigation and market testing. Research showed that individual fruit pies were seen as a lorry driver's snack, and that they were not perceived as a product to be eaten at the table as a dessert. The quality image of the brand was not good, and indeed the product ingredients were oriented to minimum cost—'jam and cardboard' to use the words of one of the marketing men working on the brand at the time.

There were clear indications from the research that a much bigger market existed for a more expensive, higher priced product targeted at table use and 'all family' consumption. So Harvest pies were developed and tested in a small market area, using a modified pre-war machine as the pilot plant.

Harvest pies were round in shape (the previous product was square), contained fresh fruit filling, and were enveloped in best quality pastry. They were tested in six, four and single portions, and the alternatives of selling them on their own or alongside the previous product were evaluated in market situations.

Test market volume projected to £5 million nationally, and the withdrawal of individual fruit pies was proposed once Harvest pies were ready to go national. To its great credit, general management accepted this recommendation. Now things started to go wrong. The new plant necessary to produce Harvest pies nationally was costed at £875 000 plus or minus 10%, and it was estimated to be operational in two years. In the end, the plant cost £1·8 million and was not ready for four years. There was a failure in engineering design and financial control, and as a result Harvest pies are at best marginally profitable. They have been a notable success in volume terms, and represented a fine offensive effort of investigation and initial design, but they have ultimately proved to be a financial failure.

VALIDATE THE DESIGN OR CUT YOUR LOSSES

We mentioned earlier that the link-up between investigation and design was not usually particularly smooth and that misinterpretation of needs could occur. As soon as the product or package is completed, it should be checked back with the consumer via research. It is so much better to discover at this point that the design does not meet the consumer need, than a year later in test market, when capital equipment may have been irrevocably committed and tens of thousands of pounds spent on advertising and promotions.

If the product developed has no point of difference or superiority over existing brands, go back to Square One and start again, or discontinue the project. Which leads us to the question of sunk cost. Companies are often reluctant to drop projects on which large amounts of money have already been spent, because the executives are unwilling to admit that the expenditures have been unproductive. There is also a misconception that, in some strange way, heavy investment on a project automatically endows it with superior consumer appeal, or an above average chance of success. It is best to be honest and kill the project. If there's no oil below, it doesn't matter how deep a hole you dig. Some wastage is inevitable in trying to innovate new or improved products—all the checks and balances can hope to achieve is early identification of dead projects, and speedy action to minimize losses on them.

SELLING—THE RETURN OF THE BOOMERANG

When our boomerang completes its return journey to the consumer, the marketer always hopes it will receive a rapturous welcome, as indicated by that arbiter of men's careers, the brand share chart. Selling, in the broader sense intended here, embraces everything that influences the trade or the consumer to buy the product. It includes trade margins and merchandising, trade and consumer promotions, packaging and advertising.

This is, of course, a slight oversimplification because, as already noted, packaging development and advertising can also be a major factor in designing consumer benefits (remember Chum and Daz). At the selling stage, packaging will influence the product's convenience of use, and its impact on the supermarket shelf. It affects trade acceptance, since retailers want packages which are easy to store and move, and occupy the minimum amount of shelf space.

Advertising's role is to get across the product benefit, with the intention of creating favourable consumer attitudes towards it. Promotion and strong merchandising bring short-term purchase incentives to the housewife's attention, and are designed to convert favourable attitudes into money in the till. And, by no means least, the brand must have sufficient trade appeal to ensure widespread availability of the product at store level. It is very difficult to launch or maintain a successful brand in the face of trade hostility.

CASE HISTORY—THE FORD CAPRI

This case history not only illustrates the effective operation of the marketing approach; it is also an object lesson in skilful forward planning, and consistent cost and profit control. The Ford Capri was thoughtfully conceived, developed and introduced. It fully deserved the success it achieved.

Investigation

Long-range planning at Ford covers 4–10 years ahead, while tactical planning can be made up to four years in advance. Prior to the Capri, the last major development by Ford was the

Cortina, which was designed to offer big car benefits at small car prices.

At a relatively early stage, it was decided that the Capri would be planned on a multi-national basis, and introduced concurrently in all major European countries. Following extensive investigation of car-owners' attitudes and preferences, the initial objectives of the Ford Capri, which would ultimately be developed into a design brief, were as follows:

(1) The car should be very good-looking.
(2) It should be able to seat four or five people comfortably.
(3) It should offer good performance at low noise levels.
(4) It should be within reach of the average family budget.
(5) It should provide a choice of performance and equipment to meet individual needs.

Design

Following broad agreement in principle to these tentative objectives, a paper plan was drawn up, setting out detailed product requirements, volume expectations and profit implications/targets. This paper plan, which was approved in July 1966, covered the following areas:

(1) product outlines;	(7) sales volume;
(2) product objectives;	(8) capacity requirements;
(3) package dimensions;	(9) variable costs;
(4) performance requirements;	(10) fixed expenditure;
(5) features list;	(11) programme profit.
(6) final feasibility;	

Based on this plan, four clay models were developed by the stylists. One of these was rejected on aerodynamic grounds, and then another was discarded for appearance reasons. Consumer research was conducted on the remaining two models, and the preferred one was chosen for final development. A fibreglass and then a pilot metal car was built. At all points the model was checked to ensure that the actual forecast cost for each individual part was in line with objectives. At the same time, pricing, marketing spending, market share targets and introductory launch plans were developed and refined.

Following further consumer tests on final working pilot models, it was concluded that the original rear-window design was imperfect because it tended to induce a feeling of claustrophobia among back seat passengers. Consequently, the rear window was redesigned and elongated to eliminate this feeling. The car was manufactured in Hailwood and Cologne. The name 'Capri' had already been chosen in November 1967.

Selling

The final question was one of consumer positioning. Should the car be advertised as a sports car with space for the family or as a family car with sports appeal? Five hundred consumers were exposed to these alternative approaches, and the sports car positioning was most preferred.

It was proposed to launch the car across the whole of Europe simultaneously in February 1969. With this in mind, an English and a German agency worked together to develop the advertising. Various themes were developed and rejected—for instance, 'Capri, the unmistakable motor car', and 'Capri, the fast four from Ford'. Eventually the final claim—'Capri, the car you always promised yourself'—was agreed. Print was the major medium chosen for the launch and the photography was carried out in Portugal six months before the launch. All the photography was tailored to fit the individual requirements of each country around the common theme—for example, a blonde model was shot for the Scandinavian countries, a dark one for Spain and Italy, etc.

As part of the public relations plan, in December 1968, before the model had been publicly announced, the UK press was invited to Cyprus to try out the new Capri, and the German press was taken to the island of Capri. Motoring journalists were allowed to test the car as fully as they wished but agreed to make no press announcement until 24 January 1969. The level of press comment was so heavy and impactful that, one week after the first press announcements, 74% of motorists were aware of the Ford Capri, although no models were available for showing at that time and advertising had not yet started.

A few weeks after the start of advertising, consumer research indicated that 98% of motorists were aware of the Ford Capri. Sales exceeded the target significantly, and by November 1970, 20 months after launch, 304 000 Capri models had been sold.

SUMMARY

Offensive marketing follows a boomerang sequence of investigation, design and sale to transform consumer needs into profitable products. If this sequence is to be effective, the five elements of offensive marketing as summarized in P–O–I–S–E should be constantly applied.

Investigation is necessary to discover what the consumer wants, and market research is the eyes and ears of the commercial firm. Investigation may turn up obvious needs which other companies have missed because they were blinded by the traditional thinking of their industry. Alternatively, sophisticated techniques of depth research may be used. In either case, it is important for a company to create its own innovations through independent investigation, rather than resorting to the 'follow my leader' approach epitomized by the flock factor. Thorough investigation involves not only discovering an unsatisfied consumer need, but also checking that it can be profitable and that it fits the company's skills.

The role of design is to translate the need defined by the investigation into a product personality. The need may be for improved product performance or for psychological benefits, and the design may require years of basic R & D, or be very simple to accomplish. But the marketing man must design a profit for his company as well as a benefit for the consumer, and should constantly check back with the consumer that his design has correctly interpreted consumer need.

The return of the boomerang takes place with selling, which includes everything that influences the trade or the consumer to buy the product.

II ORGANIZING FOR THE
OFFENSIVE

It is not enough to believe in offensive marketing as an approach to business. One of the first steps towards making this approach a reality is the adoption of an organization which encourages innovation and risk-taking. Part II establishes the role of the marketing department and examines how it can best lead the application of the offensive philosophy. If the whole company is envisaged as a wheel, the marketing department is the hub while other departments are the spokes. Marketing holds the wheel together but, at the same time, is heavily dependent on the efficiency of other departments for its effectiveness. A lost or damaged spoke would adversely affect the operation of the whole wheel.

One of the unique characteristics of most marketing departments is the product management system and, because of its importance, this unusual organization mode is given a chapter to itself.

There are sensitive dividing lines between the authority and responsibility of marketing personnel, and a well framed organization can help to achieve the right balance between them. But in the end the authority of the marketing department depends as much on the personal capability of its members as on the organization structure adopted.

5: *Offensive Operation of* ____ *the Marketing Department*

The title of this part of the book is 'Organizing for the Offensive'. The previous part emphasized, perhaps to the point of laboriousness, that marketing cannot exist in a vacuum. To be really effective it must permeate the whole company. The term chosen to express this ideal situation was 'integrated marketing', which in itself is a cornerstone of the offensive marketing approach. But we haven't finished with integration yet. The degree to which a company integrates marketing into its total system depends significantly on how it is organized, especially in the marketing area. A quick glance at the organization chart and job specifications of a marketing department will usually reveal whether it is designed to do a broad management or a narrow specialist job, and how far it is likely to be a breeding ground for bureaucratic attitudes.

It would, of course, be naïve to pretend that organization alone can prevent complacency, defensive attitudes or a preoccupation with the routine. However, a good organization can create a climate where innovation, an independent approach, and measured risk-taking will be recognized and rewarded. It won't of its own volition make offensive marketing suddenly take off in a company, but it will provide a framework in which, with qualified people and the right attitudes, an offensive approach is most likely to flourish in the long run.

WHO NEEDS A MARKETING DEPARTMENT ANYWAY?

'Marks & Spencer haven't done so badly over the past few years without the help of a marketing department. And what about all the other firms mentioned in your introductory chapter, which succeeded without marketing men? Marketing is just a matter of common sense and keeping in touch with consumers—you don't need so called marketing men to do that. And in any case, the introduction of a bunch of young marketing turks will only complicate my organization and perhaps upset some of my senior employees, all of whom are doing a fine job at present. No I don't need a marketing department thank you.'

A reasoned rejection of the need for a marketing department, such as that summarized above, could justifiably be made by an entrepreneur running his own successful small business. Without knowing it, he is his own marketing department, as long as he has a clear concept of his business and a well based view of how to develop it. This may equally apply to a large organization. General Motors' concept of its business and its classic market segmentation policies were worked out in the first years of the 1920s by a group of men without any specialized marketing training. Even in those early times, General Motors was a substantial company with a turnover of over $500 million. And reverting to 1970, anyone suggesting that Marks & Spencer could improve its business by setting up a marketing department would have a very difficult case to establish.

M & S is a good example to examine in more detail, because it is a manufacturer (by proxy) as well as a retailer. Just look at its attitudes to the consumer, as manifested by its product design and quality control.

'To begin with, there are detailed specifications for everything —between two and three hundred altogether. Carrots must be straight and within half an inch [13 mm] of a certain size; for apples, the tolerance is only one eighth of an inch [3 mm]. Bananas must be entirely free of blemish. Marks' Food Technology Department, having isolated the breed of chicken which it wanted, specified exactly how the birds were to be killed, plucked, stored and packed.

'As for clothing, the specifications lay down types of thread, types and sizes of needle and stitch formation and density, not to mention the way in which the finished garment should be pressed and folded. Marks also insists on a specific number of quality inspection stations on every production line. In addition, there are minimum performance standards for every sort of garment: a Marks' shirt must be able to stand up to fifty launderings. Every part of every garment (including the thread) goes through the Marks' laboratory to be tested for strength, shrinkage, colour fastness and so on; three quarters of the testing is done before the merchandise goes into production. The result is a remarkable evenness of quality.'*

* Graham Turner, *Business in Britain* (Eyre & Spottiswoode, 1969).

But maybe M & S is too oriented to the consumer and is one of those organizations that lets profit look after itself? Wrong, as the description below, and M & S's ten-year profit record indicates.

'Nor will it offer any item on which it cannot make a contribution in terms of price and quality, or on which it cannot make a satisfactory return on capital (it likes a gross profit margin of 26%). Marks does not sell anything purely as a service to the public; if you have a $12\frac{1}{2}$ inch [32 cm] or $18\frac{1}{2}$ inch [47 cm] neck, that is your misfortune.'*

M & S does not need a marketing department because it already applies an offensive marketing approach. It would be no exaggeration to say that the Board of M & S *is* its marketing department. This underlies the essential point. The purpose of a marketing department is to catalyse the application of the offensive marketing approach. If a company already exercises this approach, it has no need of a marketing department.

Very few companies are in the enviable state of M & S, and for the vast majority, a marketing department is essential. Why? Well, starting at the most basic level, any organization spending substantial sums of money on advertising and promotions will usually find that marketing men can improve the efficiency of these expenditures. However, a marketing department should go well beyond this, and relate the strengths of a company to the best opportunities in the market place. In practice, this means developing improvements on existing products, launching successful new ones, and working closely with the financial department on any acquisition programmes.†

The marketing department is the link between the firm and the market place. It represents the views of consumers to the company, and works out, with other departments, how to transform these views into profitable products. To do this effectively, the marketing department must on the one hand understand consumers, the trade and the behaviour of markets, and on the other hand possess detailed knowledge of all costs affecting company products.

---

* *Ibid.*

† Unless a company has a diversification group such as that described later in this chapter, in which case, the marketing department would have a more limited role.

THEY SEEM TO DO NOTHING

The outsider often has difficulty in understanding exactly what a marketing man does, and I have never met with much success in attempting to describe my job to relatives making polite enquiries. It is quite easy to account for all the functions of a business without any reference to marketing. Production, sales, R & D, personnel, buying and finance are the major activities of companies and each has a department in its own right. Advertising is developed by outside agencies. So all that is left is promotions and market research, plus control of the advertising agency. But, as we have already seen, marketing has a wider role to play than this. As well as a direct line responsibility for advertising, promotions and market research, the marketing department has the broad task of *leading* the application of the marketing approach within a company, by setting strategies and plans for every aspect of the business affecting the consumer. The word 'leading' requires careful underlining, because there is a mistaken belief in some quarters that the role of the marketing group is to 'co-ordinate', as if it were an overpaid progress group. Mere co-ordination, with its suggestion of a passive communications centre, is inconsistent with the offensive marketing approach.

If we recall the boomerang sequence of the marketing process—investigation, design and sale—leadership will be seen as a perfectly logical role for the marketing department. The starting point of any action in the firm to improve revenue must spring from a market need, whether it be the humdrum requirement for a particular kind of promotion, or the more exciting diagnosis of a new product opportunity. As the group most expert in identifying and defining market needs, and most knowledgeable about company costs and skills, the marketing department is the obvious candidate for setting up a strategy and plan to meet the need in question. To move this into action, a detailed execution programme has to be set up in consultation with the departments concerned, and who better to do it than the marketing department? Beyond this, the marketing group will monitor the progress of the plan, take corrective action to keep it on target when unforeseen problems come up, and intervene drastically if any part of it is endangered by lack of priority or incompetence.

While stressing this leadership role, I wish to avoid giving the impression that the marketing department should dominate a company. This would be a highly undesirable state of affairs for at least two reasons. Firstly, it would relegate all other employees to the status of mere runners, with no influence on corporate policy. This would prevent them from fully utilizing their management skills, and in the long run act as a powerful demotivating force. Secondly, a dominant marketing department can have an adverse effect on profit because, left to its own devices, it is liable to over-emphasize market share at the expense of profit. One can frequently observe this Achilles heel in job interviews with senior marketing people, because, when asked to describe their best career achievements, the climax of the story is usually a large gain in brand share and one vainly strains to hear a single reference to profit. Aiming for major market share increases is only one of a number of possible strategies for maximizing profit.

The advantage of a balanced corporate structure, where the marketing department is strong but not dominant, is that the concentrated focus of other departments on internal costs and efficiencies will counterbalance marketing's tendency to bend over too far to meet market needs, and result in a better profit mix for the company as a whole. But while the marketing *department* should not be dominant, the integrated marketing *approach* should dominate the company's way of doing business.

This point has been stressed because it is easy to imply dominance in any theoretical description of a marketing department's role. In practice, the marketing department will never succeed by attempting to force its will on protesting employees from other departments. Some conflicts will occur, but the integrated marketing approach will only succeed if the marketing group enjoys the co-operation and confidence of other parts of the company. Equally, other departments retain the right to question marketing strategies (constructively!), to expose any production, buying or selling cost inefficiencies involved in marketing plans, and to wield overriding authority for the detailed *implementation* of programmes. We will probe the distribution of responsibility and authority between marketing and other departments later on in this chapter.

DAY-TO-DAY OPERATION OF MARKETING

There is no perfect analogy to illuminate the working of the marketing department. Opponents of the marketing approach might suggest that the movements of the octopus—with eight suckered arms around a mouth—provides a close likeness, but one hopes that they would not be taken too seriously. Probably the best analogy is the one that relates the marketing department to the orchestral conductor. But bear in mind that this is flattering to marketing, because the conductor's leadership position on the rostrum may give him a glamour and status out of all proportion to his authority or contribution.

What the marketing man and the conductor have in common is a programme whose execution depends on the combined efforts of a number of specialists. In the case of the conductor, these are instrumentalists, and for the marketing man, they are copywriters, chemists, production men, accountants, salesmen and researchers. Neither the symphony nor the marketing plans will succeed unless each specialist clearly understands his own role and how it relates to others. Equally, the failure of one specialist to perform effectively, whether he be an oboist who misses his entry, or a packaging development engineer who misses his agreed deadline, can sabotage the whole programme. It follows that, like the conductor, the marketing man must know his overall objectives, and brief, motivate and co-ordinate his specialists in order to achieve these.

The marketing department usually operates by briefing each department on its role in any marketing plan, by assessing the resulting proposal, and by recommending it to company management for approval if it meets the brief. In any decently run company, marketing briefs will precede the initiation of significant work by a member of another department. The rationale for this is obvious. Unless a pack designer knows the marketing objective behind a packaging change, he stands an excellent chance of producing an irrelevant design. A cost accountant can hardly be expected to make cost estimates for a new product if the marketing department is still guessing wildly about product formulation, expected sales or type of packaging. A production manager cannot work out a sound manufacturing plan unless he is briefed on required quantities, timings, type of formulation and variety of packaging.

A good marketing brief will be clear and unambiguous, and limit itself to a statement of objectives. It will not detail the technical means by which these are to be achieved since that is the task of the department concerned. When the appropriate department has responded to the brief, by putting forward either a production plan, a package design or a new product formulation, whatever the case may be, the marketing department will evaluate how far it meets the original brief.

And who do these marketing people think they are, deigning to criticize the proposals of a works manager or a package designer, when they've probably only seen the factory from the air and never been inside a design studio? A good question, because unless marketing men understand the answer to it clearly, they are set fair for a ruinous relationship with functional specialists. The golden rule is that the marketing man should never question the technical competence of an expert or attempt to tell him how to do his job. He should confine himself to checking whether the proposal meets the marketing brief and stop there.

Let us suppose that you are brand manager of a leading grocery product, whose packaging you have decided to facelift. It so happens that a brilliant but touchy designer is on retainer to your company and you decide to use him. The marketing brief is drawn up, setting out the objectives of the new pack. We'll keep it simple by saying that these are to provide an impression of greater modernity and higher quality than the existing pack design, while retaining a recognizable resemblance to it. Five weeks later the designer presents four alternative rough designs. They are very exciting, but represent much too great a departure from the existing design, and this is what you have to tell the designer. You are entitled to do this on the strength of your expert knowledge of the brand's consumers and your view that they would react adversely to a very radical change in design. But it would obviously be wrong to suggest exactly how the package design should be altered to meet the brief, because you are not an artist and have no technical expertise in this area. If the designer is a professional, he will start again, having ascertained as far as possible where you draw the line between a design which is too radical and one which retains an acceptable continuity with the existing pack.

Once the marketing department is satisfied with the response to a brief, it will authorize action, unless the issue is so important that it needs to be cleared with general management or the Board.

CARRYING THE CAN AND CALLING THE SHOTS

We have already pointed out that a marketing department should do more than just handle the advertising and promotion functions, but that it should not dominate the company; that it should be responsible for setting overall marketing policies, but that other departments will retain authority over much of the detailed implementation of plans. Are these just pious generalizations or can they truly be realized in practice? The question of the boundaries of the responsibilities and authority of the marketing department, and the degree to which they overlap, is a vexed one which has caused much controversy. In order to achieve any illumination of this subject, we need first to establish a very clear distinction between strategy and planning on the one hand and detailed implementation on the other.

Marketing strategy reflects the firm's best opinion as to how it can most profitably apply its skills and resources to the market place. A strategy is inevitably broad in scope, but the plan which stems from it will spell out action and timings, and the detailed contribution expected from each department. All this is the *responsibility* of the marketing department, with its knowledge of the trade and the consumer and its bird's eye view of the whole company. In practice, a strong marketing department will also have a good measure of *authority* over other departments in establishing strategies and plans. Obviously this authority is not absolute, because the marketing department requires Board approval for any major proposals, just like anybody else. But it is certainly false to imply that the marketing department, like the unestablished lance corporal, has all the responsibility but no authority, since it is difficult for other departments effectively to question strategies or plans which are based on appraisals of the market.

Detailed implementation of agreed plans is the responsibility of the functional departments concerned and they carry full line authority for this. The production director has complete control over the running of his factories. The sales director has control over the deployment of his sales force. This authority is obviously subject to the overriding power of the Board, but its strength is reflected in many companies by the proper convention that no head office executive whether of Board status or not, may visit a factory or accompany a salesman without first getting permission from the head of the department in question.

So where does this leave the marketing department? Must it just sit still and watch the implementation of its plans as a silent but perhaps agonized spectator? Fortunately, no. If the plans are implemented smoothly, there is no reason for the marketing group to become involved. But if they start to go badly, the department concerned is bound to let marketing know, and a way to handle the situation will have to be thrashed out. Maybe the marketing plan can be kept on schedule by some additional expenditure on overtime, or a reallocation of priorities; but perhaps it has to be changed.

If a particular department's consistently poor performance is sabotaging the proper implementation of marketing plans, the marketing department should bring this problem to the attention of general management and lobby for the changes needed. Typical situations where this can occur are repeated failure by production department to meet agreed schedules, inability of the sales force to get distribution for new products, or persistently late deliveries. But notice that the *action* to correct these basic faults in implementation cannot be initiated by marketing but only by general management.

In summary, the marketing people have no authority over implementation, but they have considerable opportunity to influence its effectiveness through the quality of their relationship with other departments and their power to lobby general management.

The distinction between strategy/planning and implementation is illustrated by a few examples in Table 5.1.

TABLE 5.1	
Strategy/Planning (*marketing has major authority*)	*Implementation* (*marketing has nil authority*)
1. Production schedule based on marketing dept's sales forecast	1. Physical production of agreed schedules
2. R & D brief based on marketing dept's assessment of market opportunities	2. Technical processes and lab. work involved in carrying out agreed briefs
3. Agreement with distribution dept that all deliveries should be completed 3 days after sales order placed	3. Purchase and routing of vehicles and siting of company warehouses necessary to fulfil agreed strategy

This discussion reveals the flaw in the role of the marketing department described above. It is a truism of management theory that authority and responsibility should be equal. You should not give a man responsibility for a function unless he has the necessary authority to carry it out. Otherwise, in the event of failure, he may say, often quite legitimately, 'Well, I wanted to do it a different way, but I wasn't allowed to.' If, as I strongly believe is right and proper, the marketing department is given responsibility for company gross profit, its responsibility will exceed its authority, since profit levels depend as much on good implementation as on the quality of plans. One just has to hope that corporate management is sufficiently enlightened to recognize this distinction, and to refrain from blaming the marketing people for weaknesses in implementation which they had no authority to influence. It would be unrealistic, for instance, to place primary blame on British Leyland's marketing group for its profit failure in 1970, when 15% of its planned production was lost through strikes, and various fundamental problems of plant location and payment methods made it a high cost producer compared with Ford. (British Leyland has 70 plants and a 40% market share; Ford has 11 plants and a share just under 30%).

Leaving the easiest subject till last, it is now rare to find a marketing department without line authority for advertising, promotions and market research. Table 5.2 outlines the levels of authority and res-

TABLE 5.2		
Function	*Authority*	*Responsibility*
Specialist marketing functions, like advertising, promotions, allocation of marketing funds, market research	Full	Full
Development and marketing of new products	Primary	Primary
Pricing, marketing budget, volume and profit forecasts; necessary revisions	Primary	Primary
Determination of strategies and plans for other departments	Major influence	Primary
Implementation of agreed plans by other departments	Minor	For corrective business action, also closely intertwined with responsibility for achieving company gross profit targets
Raising new capital for company	Nil	Nil
Acquisitions	Major influence	Primary

ponsibility considered appropriate for the marketing group, under the offensive marketing approach.★

★ This again assumes that a company does not have a diversification group, since such a group is a rarity at present.

Although ground-rules of authority and responsibility should be roughly set out, if only to place the role of the marketing department in proper perspective, the effective operation of the offensive marketing approach really depends on the spirit of the organization. If there is an obsession with procedures and a neurotic preoccupation with demarcation lines or levels of seniority, little progress will be made. The best results are achieved in an atmosphere of co-operation, where the quality of an idea matters more than the seniority or background of its originator. To this end, an effective marketing department will operate by persuasion even when it has ultimate authority. It is in a very strong position to persuade others since it possesses all the facts about the market place that underlie action plans, and has a clear picture of the total corporate operation. The brand manager should be the world's greatest expert on his own product—its history, its strengths and weaknesses, and its future plans. Persuasion is much more likely to result in enthusiastic co-operation and effective implementation. And it is very necessary in those many situations where the lines of authority between departments are fuzzy. After all, marketing men spend most of their time trying to get action out of people in other departments over whom they have no line authority.

AREAS OF CONFLICT

None of the above is intended to imply that a complete absence of conflict between departments is desirable. There will never be a perfect equilibrium in the relationship between marketing and other departments, and some level of conflict is proof that differing viewpoints are being brought to bear on the business. A total lack of conflict suggests either a dominant marketing department which has cowed the rest of the company into unquestioning submission, or one that is weak enough to be ignored. The only requirement for conflict is that it should be constructive, and genuinely designed to improve corporate efficiency. Conflicts which are caused by personal vendettas, attempts at empire building, or any other unworthy motivations, are of course worthless and damaging.

Conflicts occur most frequently between production and sales, on the one hand, and marketing on the other (Table 5.3, overleaf). If there are repeated conflicts between marketing and another department, the senior people concerned should get together and draw up a revised working strategy.

D

TABLE 5.3 POTENTIAL CONFLICT AREAS BETWEEN
MARKETING AND OTHER DEPARTMENTS

Marketing dept complaints	*Other depts' complaints*
SALES	
Failure to gain or improve distribution	Information on promotions comes too late
Inadequate level of merchandising	Too theoretical in approach
	Insufficient total marketing spending
Unreasonably high retail out-of-stock	Not enough money spent against trade
Extravagant expenditure on trade allowances	Promotions not tailored to special account needs
Inability to sell non-promoted product	Ineffective consumer promotion
	Merchandising material always delivered late
PRODUCTION	
Lack of flexibility for short or special runs	Uneconomically short lead times
	Inefficient use of productive capacity
Failure to meet agreed schedules	Late delivery of agreed new pack designs
Insufficient spare capacity	No attempt to reduce seasonal peaks/troughs
Poor quality control	
Long lead times required	Pressure to over-promise on production
R & D	
Too slow	Pressure to achieve impossible deadlines
Not creative enough	
	Too much focus on short-term problems
FINANCE	
Static and defensive attitude to profit	Not sufficiently profit-conscious
Financial data production too slow	Constant demands for detailed data of questionable value
Insufficient special cost breakdown	

ORGANIZING FOR THE OFFENSIVE

The organization of the marketing department should reflect the structure of the market place. If a company has a number of branded products with separate identities, like most consumer goods companies, it makes sense to have a conventional product management system. However, for a firm with only one or two very large brands marketed through a variety of distribution channels, like Coca-Cola, an organization by trade type is most logical. For example, one marketing group might be responsible for sales through grocery stores, another for vending machine sales and a third for all other outlets. The remaining type of marketing organization is the regional one, but this is rare in consumer goods marketing. It is, however, quite a good system for businesses like airlines, where the product can be isolated geographically. BEA, for instance, has product managers for key destinations like Glasgow, Belfast and Manchester.

The critical factor in any marketing organization structure is that it should be designed to encourage innovation, and to expose a maintenance approach. One of the keynotes of offensive marketing is the right organization for new product development and acquisitions. It seems to me that this function should be handled by a totally distinct group of people with specific profit and volume objectives, headed by a diversification director. He would be a Board member of equal status to the marketing director, and he may or may not have a marketing background. Reporting to him would be a small number of hand-picked marketing and financial men, plus a production and an R & D co-ordinator. (Please note that we are not talking about a corporate planning group. The latter typically exercises a staff function to facilitate good planning and has no profit responsibility.)

Heinz has recently set up an organization very close to this ideal, and it has many advantages. For a start, responsibility for new products and acquisitions can be pinned on one group, working full time on this activity and with clear targets to hit. Moreover, the fact that the diversification unit is headed up by a Board member helps overcome one of the bugbears of development projects— that other company personnel tend to give them low priority because they do not generate immediate profit and get in the way of pressing current problems. And thirdly, a diversification group would quite naturally regard new products as an alternative to acquisitions, and carry out 'make or buy' evaluations before undertaking any acquisition. This would be a great improvement on the present practice of most companies, which rarely consider the cost and profit of internal development versus acquisition. And even better, acquisitions would be looked at from a marketing as well as from a financial angle, whereas at present they are almost exclusively handled by 'balance sheet blimps' (see Chapter 18, The Marketing Approach to Acquisitions).

No organization system is perfect and this one, like any other, has drawbacks—two, in fact. The first danger is that the diversification group may become out of touch with the rest of the company and build its own ivory towers. This problem can be minimized by appointing as diversification director a rounded businessman with a strong taste for action, who has spent most of his business life battling it out in the market place. Don't give the job to a long-serving consultant or staff man. The diversification director we are envisaging would ensure that his subordinates didn't start to grow cobwebs, and would probably insist on a regular interchange of personnel between the day-to-day operating departments and the diversification group.

The second disadvantage of a separate diversification department has no easy solution, but knowing the sharpness of its teeth is half-way to taming it. No one likes to be handed an idea developed by someone else and told to 'get on and market it'. This applies even to the best ideas. So when the diversification group hands over a fully validated new product idea to the marketing department, it is apt to receive a less than rapturous reception. A close relationship between the marketing and diversification people helps a lot, of course, but the only way to overcome this particular problem is to avoid it altogether, by allowing the diversification group to take a new product right through to the end of its first year of national expansion. It can then hand over a going product to marketing. Some friction between Marketing Department and the Diversification Group is probably inevitable, but it is much better to have problems of how to handle dramatic company growth than to face the much bigger problem of a static business.

What are the alternatives to the offensive system just proposed? There are two others, and they are at present used by most companies. Both view new products in a narrower way, as the exclusive province of the marketing department, but make no provision for the handling of acquisitions otherwise than by the finance department. Perhaps the most common system, though I think declining rapidly in popularity, is that which gives managers of existing brands additional responsibility for new products. This has many weaknesses, and the greatest is that the manager in question will give first priority to the relentless day-to-day pressures of his existing product.

The other alternative is to set up a separate new products group under the marketing director. This is a halfway house to the diversification group approach. Its drawback is that it does not usually cover acquisitions, and since only part of the marketing director's effort is devoted to it, it is unlikely to receive the same level of overall company priority as a diversification director would gain. Furthermore, if the firm's current products are growing at a fast rate, the marketing director may be able to achieve his budget targets without bothering overmuch about new brands.

Appendix B summarizes the advantages and drawbacks of the various systems for organizing the growth function in a company.

THE FOUR HALLMARKS OF OFFENSIVE MARKETING ORGANIZATION

Each of these hallmarks has already been discussed. They are all important, and in combination they will create an atmosphere in which the offensive marketing approach can be developed. We summarize them below as a reminder, and as an opportunity for you to evaluate how far your own company matches them.

(1) The marketing department (and the diversification group where relevant) should have primary responsibility and authority for setting corporate marketing strategies and plans.

(2) The marketing department should be responsible for achieving gross profit budgets on all existing brands.

(3) The marketing department should lead the application of the offensive marketing approach but not dominate the company. The same applies to the diversification group as far as growth is concerned.

(4) The company should be organized for innovation and growth. We have proposed organizing the marketing department in response to the structure of the market, and giving profit responsibility for acquisitions and new products to a diversification group.

SUMMARY

Organization on its own cannot prevent complacency and pre-occupation with the *status quo*. But a good structure can create a climate where innovation, an independent approach, and measured risk-taking will be recognized and rewarded.

The purpose of a marketing department is to catalyse and lead the application of the offensive marketing approach. It represents the views of consumers to the company, and works out, with other departments, how to transform these into profitable products.

The marketing department has both authority and responsibility for determining marketing strategies and drawing up plans. It has no formal authority over their implementation, though in practice it will often influence this. Similarly, the marketing group is not liable for the failure of plans due to the poor implementation by other departments, although it is responsible for planning corrective action. Conflicts will usually occur between marketing and other departments, and these are useful if they centre round improvements in efficiency rather than struggles for personal power.

The critical requirement for any marketing organization structure is that it should be designed to encourage innovation and to expose a maintenance approach.

6: *Product Management—the Storm-Troopers of Marketing*

It is almost impossible to envisage a marketing department without product managers. General management and the marketing director can and should create the conditions in which offensive marketing can flourish by taking the various steps outlined in previous chapters. But there is a limit to the amount of action which they personally can undertake, if they are to see to their primary responsibilities of framing policies and forging positive attitudes to the marketing approach. Whether or not this favourable environment is exploited, to generate offensive marketing action at the grass roots level that counts most, depends on the proper deployment of product management.

THE WELL-KEPT SECRET

Almost incredibly, the product or brand management system has been in existence since the 1920s, although prior to the 1950s it was virtually unknown even in America except to a handful of firms. It has only been widely applied in the UK since the 1960s. Procter & Gamble is generally recognized as the originator of product management, through the agency of Neil McElroy, who is now Chairman of the company, as well as a former US Secretary of Defense. In the UK, P & G had product managers before the outbreak of the Second World War.

The system initially met a need for co-ordination on an individual product basis, as branding became common and communications within the firm more complex. Product management was very much a step-child of the marketing approach, because it enabled the company to view its brands from the same perspective as the consumer. And what was the product manager supposed to do? At minimum, he would plan and co-ordinate all marketing effort on a single brand. Theoretically, at least, if a product manager was off work through sickness for any length of time, operations on his brand would grind to a halt, because no one would be initiating any new action.

Unlike other employees, who apply a special expertise to *all* company brands, the product manager is concerned with *every* aspect of a *single* brand. It is his job to recommend an annual volume and profit budget, to propose marketing plans and strategies, and to monitor their implementation. The product manager is the representative of his brand within the company. If a strong new competitive brand suddenly loomed up in the market place, the reaction of a wise Board or marketing director would be to await the recommendation of the man managing the threatened product before taking action, because he would be expected to know more about the market in question than anyone else in the company. This deference would be less a tribute to his intellectual brilliance than a reflection of the fact that he spends all his time thinking about and working on the health of a single brand.

Before we leap into a detailed examiniation of this superman, let us take a quick look at his position within the marketing department. One of his problems is that he is some way down the hierarchy, which starts with the *marketing director*. Below him will be *marketing managers* or *group product managers** who look after whole markets or groups of products. They are managers of product managers, and may have anything from two to four reporting to them. The snag from the viewpoint of the product manager is that his group product manager and his marketing director also share responsibility for the running of each brand. This is usually regarded as a drawback by the product manager because it limits his authority, but his management sees this hierarchy as a necessary piece of insurance against the restricted business experience of the product manager, who is usually aged 25–30. We will see later that the tightness of the rein by which the product manager is held has an important effect on his performance. If it is too tight, it will stifle his authority and initiative and turn him into a pretty demoralized executive.

DOES THE SYSTEM JUSTIFY ITS COST?

As you will already have gathered, this book looks at marketing with a critical and realistic eye, and is by no means an unbroken paean of praise. In evaluating the product management concept, it

---

* Some of the larger companies have both levels. The marketing manager may have two or three group product managers reporting to him.

would therefore have been logical to have looked at both its *pros* and *cons*. This, indeed, was my starting point, but it is very difficult to find any serious drawbacks to the product management system, and I would heartily dislike leading a debating motion on its disadvantages—the only approach to adopt would be a humorous one, because the arguments are thin. The one possible ground on which to attack product management is that of cost. This is most telling when directed against a large marketing department, like Procter & Gamble's, which probably costs at least £400 000 a year to run. The question there is whether product management and its specialist supporting services within the company add £400 000 to net profit after tax by their presence. In the particular case we have chosen, my judgement would be a resounding 'Yes'. However, most companies have relatively small marketing departments, probably costing less than £100 000 to operate, and it is even easier to be positive about their value. All along, of course, I have made the bold and currently unrealistic assumption that all product management systems are effective, because one hopes this will become the norm in the 1970s.

The benefits of a strong product management team are numerous. They have been gathered up below under the headings of 'perspective', specialization', 'co-ordination', 'use of resources', 'accountability' and 'innovation'. Let us take them in that order.

Perspective

Every day of his working week, the product manager is putting himself in the shoes of his brand's consumer, and thinking about consumer reactions. He may start by asking who is the consumer of the brand. Is it the person who buys it, or the person who uses it, if the two are different? And what do consumers like or dislike about the brand? How do they rate it against competitors? How can it be improved? Nobody else in the company is thinking about the brand in that way except the product manager's superiors, and they certainly won't give the subject more than occasional attention. Most other employees regard the brand from a very different angle, which certainly has no relation to the way the consumer sees it.

As far as the works manager is concerned, it may be a confounded nuisance, because it has volatile raw materials, and the amount of waste they involve is constantly threatening his standard cost targets. The sales director doesn't find it very interesting because it is highly seasonal and only merchandisable in the spring. For the rest of the year it has a low demand, and he resists giving it any priority. By contrast, the product manager is looking at the brand as an outsider would. He is the eyes and ears of his brand and helps the company to see itself reflected in the mirror of the market place.

Specialization

Specialization has been a recognized feature of business for centuries. In the past its scope has been confined to specialization by function (e.g. production or buying) but the product management system extends its application to brands. If a man is responsible for only one product, he will rapidly acquire an expert knowledge of it. A good product manager has the same 'feel' for his brand and the way it will respond to different situations, as the racing driver has for his car. This intimacy can lead either to tunnel vision or to enterprising decision making, depending on the quality of the brand manager concerned.

Co-ordination

One of the original stimuli behind the product management system was the difficulty of keeping all the right people informed about pieces of action. The sales department would agree with the factory to produce a new product, but would forget to tell the accounting group about it, so that chaos arose when the time came to bill customers for the product. The product manager overcomes this problem by taking his brand as the centre of the universe, and relating the skills and resources of other departments to it. The responsibility for co-ordination is laid fairly and squarely on his shoulders. But just as the marketing department as a whole should exercise a leadership role, so should the product manager. Not for him the job of passive co-ordinator; on the contrary, he should transform the unrelated actions of various departments into an integrated circuit that propels his brand towards its chosen objectives. He needs to be a man of great energy and determination, because in any important programme, he will run up against bottlenecks that have to be resolved, and unforeseen difficulties that would try the patience of Job.

Use of Resources

One could almost rename the product manager as a resource manager. He is trying all the time to get the maximum share of company resources operating behind his brand. Every product manager would like more attention from the sales force and a greater proportion of the R & D department's time than he can command.

There are many common company resources, of which the sales force and money are the most obvious, and every brand group will be fighting hard to get an unfair share of these.

When management adds up all the requests for resources from the various product groups, these should always exceed what is available, and there has to be arbitration. But this is a very good way for a company to make the best use of its resources, because the product manager system ensures that every reasonable claim for priority is rationally presented, and fairly considered. One of the main jobs of middle and senior marketing management is to arbitrate between competing claims. In the absence of a product management system, resources are more likely to be allocated unfairly to the largest brands, or the individual favourites of top management. Small brands with bright future prospects may be ignored, together with low volume but highly profitable speciality products. The product management system does not provide any inbuilt guarantee that resources will be perfectly allocated, but it encourages their best use through fierce internal competition.

Accountability

The dream of every managing director is to delegate accountability for profit down the line to nominated individuals, both to give them a greater sense of participation and to enable him to put pressure on units trailing their targets. This is possible to a considerable degree under the product management system. Assuming that the marketing department is responsible for gross corporate profit, this total figure can then be split down accurately by brand, and individual product managers given profit targets.

Brand profitability is useful to general management as a means for pinpointing product groups which are doing poorly. However, it is not realistic to assess the performance of a brand manager by his profit results alone, without examining why the figures were poor. They may have been due to faulty implementation, over which the product manager had no control, or the product manager's preferred plan may have been rejected outright by his superiors. But if poor results appear to be due to faulty strategy, bad planning or lack of co-ordination, the product manager can expect to carry the can.

Innovation

The product manager knows that he is being evaluated largely on the volume and revenue his brand achieves. If he is smart, he will recognize that a couple of really strong new ideas will drive his brand ahead much more dramatically than the most dedicated attention to the minutiae of its day-to-day running. However, the gap between the thought and the deed is a wide one, and although product management does undoubtedly make innovations, its contribution on this score is often disappointing. This is because there is a mass of detailed routine and short-term pressure in just keeping a brand going, and most product mangers find themselves completely absorbed by this. The time to stand back and think up new approaches is often difficult to find, and a maintenance marketing operation may result.

GENERAL MANAGER OF HIS BRAND OR LEG-MAN?

I expect you have seen from time to time advertisements for product managers that run roughly like this:

> WANT TO BECOME A MANAGING DIRECTOR AT 26?
> Join the Zero company as a product manager, where you will have complete responsibility for the profits and results on a multi-million pound brand.
> If you have at least four years' experience in the marketing department of a company manufacturing fast-moving consumer goods or in a well known advertising agency, please write to Box 101. Degree preferred.

When the chosen candidate arrives to take up his new job and asks what his specific powers are, he may be told that he has the authority personally to approve projects involving an expenditure of less than £250, and to implement agreed recommendations. But any major proposals must receive the approval of the product group manager, the marketing director and in some cases the Board as well. What is more, our candidate has no line authority over the people in other departments responsible for implementing his plans—if he reaches deadlock with them, all he can do is to get his boss to take it up with their boss. Hardly the job for a power-hungry young autocrat of twenty-six!

The discrepancy between the prospects in the advertisement and the actual, as opposed to the formal, powers of the effective product manager is not as wide as it may seem. True, it is a gross exaggeration to compare the job of the product manager with a managing director, because the product manager has no line authority over other departments and cannot determine the allocation of resources to his brand except by persuasion. But he has much more *de facto* authority than the empty catalogue of his formal powers would indicate. His practical authority derives from his responsibility for the well-being of his brand, and his right to recommend to management how it should be run. If he can convince his superiors that he has the right answers, he has a lot of authority. Let us take an instance from the Scott Paper Company.

'Suppose, for example, that the product manager wants a shade between lilac and pink put in a roll of Scott tissue because he has evidence that this is the growing colour for toilet tissues. This may likely be a headache as far as the production department is concerned. Once this proposal is approved in concept by the marketing and executive committees, you may be assured that it will go into production. Thus the product manager is not operating without authority, even though the production department as such is not his responsibility.'*

In this way, the product manager derives his authority on important questions from his ultimate access to general management. He has a right to make a recommendation on any question affecting the gross profit of his brand. If he is respected by other departments, he will rapidly become the reference point for any decisions, problems or ideas affecting his brand. The factory manager may have a batch of product on his hands which marginally fails to meet specifications, but which he thinks is perfectly acceptable to the consumer. What does the product manager think—after all, he is the expert on consumer reaction? Can the product be sold or will it have to be scrapped? The product manager will decide. The sales department may feel that brand X needs a lightweight promotion in two months' time, since nothing is at present planned for the next four months and the brand is behind target. How do they proceed? They approach the product manager and tell him that if he will give them £20 000 extra to spend against the trade two months hence, they will guarantee to sell an extra 100 000 cases. The product manager again has to decide. Does he agree with the sales department's estimate of extra volume? How much of this will move through to the consumer, and how much will just add to trade stocks? Where in his budget can he divert the money from?

* Raymond J. Girvin, Marketing Manager for Scott consumer products, quoted in *The Product Manager System* (National Industrial Conference Board).

The reaction of any company employee to a scheme or problem affecting a particular brand, whether he be the managing director or the most junior shipping clerk should be 'Let's ask the product manager'.

'PRODUCT MANAGEMENT—VISION UNFULFILLED'

Such is the title of an article by David Luck and Theodore Novak in the *Harvard Business Review* of April/June 1965. They comment that product management is undoubtedly a difficult system to operate, and has had indifferent success in many companies. It seems to me that they are right on both counts. But if you agree with the strictures made earlier in this book on the disappointing application of the marketing approach, this conclusion should come as no surprise. After all, the product management system is no more and no less than a means for executing the integrated marketing approach. If this kind of approach is not accepted by top corporate management, product managers will be impotent. They will lack the informal powers that are such an important factor in their effectiveness, and find themselves locked in continual fruitless conflicts with other departments. Any product manager seeking a new job will, if he is sensible, look for a company that is successfully applying the integrated marketing approach.

THE OFFENSIVE APPROACH TO PRODUCT MANAGEMENT

But even if the climate for marketing is ideal, the product management system is still not easy to operate well. Its boundaries of authority and responsibility are vague, and there can be a world of difference between the theory and the practice of product management. In a company where it is working well, it will have gradually evolved its own code of practice, based on the experience of marketing and other departments as to what is most effective. It resembles the English constitution, which relies on the observance of the conventions, proved workable through time, rather than on the written rule of law. In essence, product management depends on the goodwill and common sense of all concerned. However, the observance of certain guidelines increases its prospects of forging an offensive marketing approach for the companies it serves. Here are three of them.

Profit Involvement

This has already been covered but it cannot be over-emphasized. A product manager is simply a marketing oriented businessman, and business concerns profit. Some companies, including ironically Procter & Gamble, the originators of the system, tell their product managers that they are responsible for hitting an agreed revenue target, while not exceeding the established marketing budget. They are instructed not to concern themselves with net or gross profit, since that is the task of higher management. The trouble with this kind of brief is that it gives the product manager no profit incentive to adjust his pricing, reduce the cost of his product or packaging or to challenge the level of trade margins. These are all important profit opportunities, which the product manager is well placed to exploit. Take away the profit responsibility from a product manager, and you may find yourself with no more than a sophisticated salesman striving to maximize revenue, and profits going by the board.

The Right to Recommend

The product manager knows that his authority is limited and that not all his recommendations will be accepted by company management. But since he is expected to take an important measure of responsibility for the profits of his brand, he must be granted an inalienable right to be heard on any important issue affecting it. If top management takes decisions on company brands without even canvassing the views of the product managers, they cannot expect the latter either to feel responsible for profit, or even to take much interest in their jobs. Sometimes Boards of directors in a profit squeeze unilaterally decide to raise the money by cutting advertising, without any formal reference to the marketing department, despite the anguished cries of the marketing director. This is a sure sign that a company is not following an integrated marketing approach. What a Board should do under these circumstances is to tell the marketing director that it needs £300 000 extra profit from him, and ask him to report back in seven days on how it can best be raised. He in turn would canvass his product managers, perhaps giving each one a target for extra profit. When the marketing director places his recommendation before the Board seven days later, he may very well conclude that a cut in advertising will acutally reduce profit because of its adverse effect on sales, and propose other ways of raising the extra profit needed, such as raising prices, reducing weight, or even cutting certain promotions.

Maximum Authority

We have already noted that the product manager has more responsibility than authority—he has been described as 'a general without an army'. But his own management can do quite a lot to bolster this authority. For a start, middle and senior marketing management can apply a bit of will power, and allow a product manager a wide degree of operating autonomy. The product manager will inevitably have to channel recommendations up the line on important issues; but as far as possible he should be allowed to run his own show. His superiors should resist the temptation to ask neurotic questions on every tiny detail. Some of them do not resist very well. Many will have been product managers themselves in the past, and learnt the lesson of attention to detail so well at that time that they never graduate to the art of delegation. They are always asking uneasily for status reports and probing for information in areas which, at their level, they should not even be thinking about. I call it molecule management, and few people respond to it so humorously as the product manager who said to me, 'I spend so much of my time telling people what we've done in the past and what we plan to do in the future that I never have time to do anything.'

In the end, it will all depend on the abilities of the product managers themselves. They will be given all the authority they earn if they have enlightened superiors.

SUMMARY

The proper deployment of the product management system will determine the success of the marketing department in leading the application of the integrated marketing approach.

Unlike other employees who apply a special expertise to most or all company brands, the product manager is concerned with every aspect of a single brand. The benefits of a strong product management team lie in perspective, specialization, co-ordination, use of resources, accountability and innovation.

The product manager has few formal powers, but his practical authority derives from his responsibility for the well-being of his brand, and his right to recommend to management how it should be run. In the last resort, the product manager's authority will depend largely on his own capability and persuasiveness.

III OFFENSIVE PREPARATION
—PLANNING FOR PROFIT
AND GROWTH

Offensive preparation is particularly concerned with the 'S' of 'P-O-I-S-E' Innovation creates leadership in a market and is usually the result of superior strategy. Strong strategies, in their turn, require a clear sense of direction, the selection of the best approach from a series of alternatives, and careful advance planning. A company which operates on a day-to-day basis is much more likely to follow than to lead its competitors. Part III focuses on the development of offensive strategies and the practical planning steps which can turn strategies into powerful action.

Efficiency should be distinguished from effectiveness. It is quite possible to do the wrong thing very efficiently, with a flawless quality of administration. Effectiveness, on the other hand, involves the pursuit of productive strategies which take a company in the right direction. Through the careful selection of innovative strategies, marketing helps to make efficiency effective.

7: *Offensive Strategy for Corporate Growth*

THE THREE STAGES OF BATTLE

Effective action is usually preceded by logical steps, which may be elaborately documented or followed intuitively, as the case may be. They are the objective, the strategy and the plan:

(1) *Objectives* describe desired destinations. They are usually stated in terms of revenue or profit.

(2) *Strategies* set out the route which has been chosen, or the means for achieving the objective. Often a number of alternative strategies are evaluated before a final one is chosen.

(3) *Plans* constitute the vehicle for getting to the destination along the chosen route.* They form the detailed execution of the strategy.

This threefold sequence provides a rational framework for decision-making directed towards a consistent end, and applies as much to chess and to warfare as to business. 'Chess is a . . . game in which drifting from move to move is sure to lead to disaster. It is vitally important to form a plan of campaign.'†

BMW's recovery effort in Germany provides a good example of the three stages of battle.

> In 1960, BMW was on the verge of bankruptcy. It was producing motor cycles for a dwindling market, and making a poor return on its bubble cars and six cylinder saloons. A takeover bid by Daimler-Benz, the makers of Mercedes, was narrowly avoided, and the group was rescued by a Bavarian investment group.
>
> Paul G. Hahnemann, Opel's top wholesale distributor, was

* Adapted from Philip Kotler, *Marketing Management* (Prentice-Hall 1967).
† H. Golombek, *The Game of Chess* (Penguin 1954).

appointed chief executive. His first objective was obviously to get BMW back on to an even keel, where it was sufficiently profitable to survive in the long term. He was convinced that there was an unexploited market for a sporty saloon car, which Mercedes was not tapping. As he pointed out, 'If you were a sporty driver and German, there was no car for you. The Mercedes is big, black and ponderous. It's for parking, not driving.' Consequently, he evolved a strategy of producing a range of high quality cars with better performance and a more sporty image than any other saloon. Mercedes was regarded as major competition.

This strategy was executed by first developing a 1500 cm³ car in 1961, but the breakthrough came when the 1800 model was introduced in 1963. This was the first year in which BMW made a profit under the new strategy. The 1600 and 2002 models were unveiled in 1966 and the 2500 and 2800 subsequently. In 1969 BMW overtook Mercedes in sales of petrol driven cars in Germany. By then its turnover was three times the 1963 level, and after tax profits stood at £6·28 million.

To put its achievement in perspective, it now sells about 145 000 cars annually, compared with Jaguar's total of under 30 000, and just fails to gain inclusion in the top 100 European companies in terms of turnover.*

AREN'T STRATEGIES RATHER ACADEMIC?

Although few people question the necessity for objectives and, at least to a limited extent, plans for action, many businessmen are sceptical about the value of strategies. Since the remainder of this chapter will appear irrelevant to anyone strongly entrenched in that camp, we will pause awhile and briefly examine the case for and against using strategies, in the hope of convincing any doubters.

To set the issue in a practical context, there is good evidence that the majority of American companies do not use formal strategies to any great extent. A survey of 195 American companies by the National Industrial Conference Board in the mid 1960s showed that half or more did not have formal policies for acquisition, trade deals, line withdrawals, and private label manufacture (Table 7.1). One is inclined to take the 'known and understood but not written' column with a pinch of salt, and would assume that if the

* Adapted from Doina Thomas, 'Second Bite at BMW' (*Management Today*, January 1971) and from an article in *Business Week* (20 May 1970).

TABLE 7.1			
	Formal written policy (%)	Known & understood but not written (%)	No fixed policy (%)	Total
Acquisition or merger	21	30	49	100
Trade deals	17	23	60	100
Product lines—slow-moving items withdrawn	11	37	52	100
Private label manufacture	9	31	60	100

majority of companies had no written policies on the relatively tangible questions shown in the table, they would be unlikely to have a formal strategy on the much more complex issue of future corporate growth. From personal observation, I would be surprised if the situation in the UK was very different from that in the USA, since outside the major international companies, strategy does not appear to get the priority it deserves.

The American survey showed that strategy was criticized on three main grounds—that it was too academic, inhibited flexibility, and consumed too much time. Let us examine these strictures.

The suggestion that strategies are too academic probably derives from the conviction among some businessmen that any discussion not related to immediate business action is theoretical and of no value. Strategies are academic in the sense that their development stems from a close analysis of all relevant facts, and the conclusions drawn from them. There was nothing theoretical about the results achieved by Procter & Gamble in the USA paper market, or by Haloid Xerox when it entered the office copying machine market in the late 1950s. But both succeeded through careful preparation of strategies for market entry.

Strategies may inhibit flexibility if they are too exact and encourage 'procedure book' management. But if they give clear direction as to general approach, and make considerable variety in execution possible, they do not place a manager in a straitjacket. For example, a company's product strategy may be to achieve and maintain performance and styling superiority over all brands in the same price bracket. The detailed ways in which this can be executed are infinite, and offer great flexibility. But there would be no flexibility to market a parity performance product. In that sense the strategy does limit freedom of manoeuvre, but that is its objective, since in this case product performance is an issue on which no compromise is to be allowed.

The criticism that strategies are too time-consuming is based on the difficulty of obtaining a consensus from the large number of people in many departments whose agreement has to be sought. One can feel some sympathy with this viewpoint, and there are times when it is best to let sleeping dogs lie. However, the fact that strategies are a source of controversy is itself a sound reason for giving them priority. It is much better to bring potential disagreements out into the open for resolution early in the life of a project than to let them fester on and slow down an action programme.

It would be naïve to dismiss criticism of strategies out of hand, because they can be misused, and many businessmen have obviously had poor experience with them. They can provide a platform for the hair-splitter or for the academically inclined who prefer the apparent safety of discussion to the risks of action. Sometimes strategies achieve a life of their own, and the action to which they are supposed to lead gets overlooked in the heat of debate. And there are undoubtedly many successful entrepreneurs who have an intuitive feel for strategy without the ability to rationalize it formally.

On balance, though, the benefits of strategy seem greatly to outweigh its disadvantages, provided it is used as a flexible means for deciding the right action rather than as an end in itself. A strategy forces management to be selective, and ruthlessly to prune the less vital goals of the business. If a strategy is painful to determine, it is likely to be a good one, because a clear identification of the non-priorities will have been made. A strategy also serves as a basis of agreement for all parties on the goals towards which the company or brand effort is to be directed, and helps ensure co-ordinated action. This is particularly important in any marketing effort, where a great many people of different disciplines are usually involved. If there is no agreed strategy, the action taken may reflect varying assumptions as to how the objective is to be achieved, and pursue a zigzag course. A third benefit of a strategy is that it directs marketing activity consistently towards a specific goal, and discourages management by expedient—or, to use the less elegant term, 'seat of the pants operations'.*

Those who still oppose strategy will, however, be encouraged by the fact that many of the world's greatest discoveries like penicillin and the law of gravity were discovered by accident—so any budding Flemings or Newtons may safely ignore this section!

* I am indebted for much of the thinking in this paragraph to George Modders, of European Marketing Consultants.

SETTING OFFENSIVE CORPORATE OBJECTIVES

Although corporate objective setting is the responsibility of the Board of directors, the marketing department will usually be asked for a viewpoint, because of its front line involvement in the achievement of these objectives. Objectives are usually expressed in financial terms. Although no measure is perfect, a projection of the desired future level of earnings per share seems to be the best starting point. At minimum, a company should aim for a rate of increase in earnings per share which will cover inflation, and give the shareholder sufficient growth beyond this to compensate for the risk of the investment.

The separation of objectives and strategies is a good intellectual discipline, but in practice there is considerable interaction between them. If the Board of directors knows that the company has a fully worked out strategy for entering a plump new market, it will be more inclined to set ambitious objectives. It would be purposeless for the Board to determine objectives without any reference to the company's present capabilities or known future strategies. Equally, a Board would be unwise to be unduly influenced by disappointing past results—this should make it even more determined to set and achieve tough objectives for the future.

It is difficult to discuss objective setting without lapsing into the platitudinous language of 'not too little, not too much'. But there is an undoubted psychological element in targets, as athletes have often shown. After standing as the pinnacle of track accomplishment for many years, the four-minute mile record was eventually broken by Roger Bannister, but his feat was rapidly emulated by many others, suggesting that the four-minute barrier was as much a psychological as a physical one. Charles Forte puts it well.

'It is amazing if one sets a target, how easily one hits that target. Unfortunately, I have learnt this at a very late age; I wish I had known it consciously before, instead of only subconsciously. If a manager says that this is the objective in two years time, and we want to reach that turnover or make that profit, it is quite amazing how one does it—given the possibility, of course. You must not say, we are going to jump 8 feet, because that is out of the question. You'll break your neck. But what is the record—6 feet 7 in? Try and jump that. And when you've succeeded, put it up another $\frac{1}{4}$ in. The art of reaching business targets is not to aim at the impossible, but to aim at the championship level—which you already know to be possible.'*

Objective setting is a good measure of a company's offensiveness. Unless ambitious objectives are established, there is little incentive for executives to apply the offensive marketing approach. Objectives are usually divided into 'short-term'—typically, the year ahead—and 'long-term' which is normally 3–5 years, but could be as long as 10 years for a company with long capital equipment lead times, like Ford.

OFFENSIVE STRATEGY

Offensive strategy involves the discovery and exploitation of distinctive advantages over competitors. It stands on the principle that a company or a brand should have its own concept of its business, and seek to achieve superiority over all contenders in at least one important aspect, whether it be product quality, method of distribution, packaging and advertising skills or whatever. Any commercial product or company without a reason for existence will soon cease to be.

But strong offensive strategies do not come easily. They are usually the result of prolonged and painstaking analysis of the market, competitors and the trend of change. While native wit is important, and there is certainly an element of creativity in many of the best strategies, the native grit to transform information into knowledge is the vital requirement. The most simple one line strategy may be the culmination of months of number-punching, and one should not be deceived by the simplicity of the result into thinking that the groundwork preceeding it was effortless.

This is by way of preparing you for the three bricks of strategy, each one of which requires considerable prior analysis. They can best be expressed in question form, and are:

(1) What is our business?
(2) Who are our competitors?
(3) What are our strengths and weaknesses?

Once these bricks have been firmly established, both for the company in total and for individual brands in particular, offensive

* Interview quoted in Robert Heller, 'The Making of Forte's' (*Management Today*, September 1969).

strategies can be developed. In marketing terms, the two most important strategy issues are:

(a) *Why should people buy our brands now and in the future?* This requires a strategy to establish a point of superiority for the company or its brands, which takes account of the present and the foreseeable future.

(b) *What will our business be in the future?* This question calls for a strategy to determine which types of market the company will serve in the future.

The remainder of this chapter will examine these strategy issues, which include the most important questions on which a marketing department is ever required to advise and guide a company. The quality of subsequent action will be greatly governed by the quality of the marketing strategies hammered out in the first place.

STRATEGY BRICK 1: WHAT IS OUR BUSINESS?

A deceptively simple question, but how easy it is to overlook, and how difficult to answer satisfactorily.

In the nineteenth century, the railway companies had all the glamour of the modern automobile or computer firms. They were go-go operations with apparently infinite growth potential. But they misdefined their market, and have been doing penance for that error through most of this century. Instead of seeing that they were in the transportation business, they wrongly assumed that they were in the railway business. Their mistake was to define their market in terms of a physical product—railways—rather than as the consumer benefit which they provided—convenient and speedy transportation. Airlines and cars were ultimately able to satisfy this need more effectively, but it was a long time before railways recognized that they were competing in the same market. Other examples of poor market definition abound. The motion picture companies failed to exploit the potential of TV, 'the commercial banks missed the significance of hire purchase and let the finance companies develop, shipping companies permitted containerization to be developed by the trucking companies.'*

Two good guidelines in market definition are first to discover the consumer benefit your products are satisfying, and then to frame it in terms which are wide enough to allow opportunities for

* From a speech by Mr E. Everett Smith, senior partner in McKinsey's New York office.

expansion, but not so broad as to be meaningless. Once more, we are in the realm of 'not too little, not too much', where the right balance is of the essence. And before we look at detailed examples, let us remind ourselves that companies sell benefits, not products. As Charles Revson, President of Revlon, is reputed to have said: 'In the factory we make cosmetics, in the drugstore we sell hope.' Or in the pithy words of Leo McGivena: 'Last year 1 million quarter-inch [6 mm] drills were sold, not because people wanted quarter-inch drills, but because they wanted quarter-inch holes.'*

A product-based definition of its business not only makes a firm vulnerable to innovations from outside technologies, but also restricts short-term opportunities for expansion.

> Although the 1960s were a bad period for all manufacturers of consumer durables, one reason for Hoover's poor profit performance in this decade (+ 2% increase in pre-tax profit in 1960–69), was its product-based and over-narrow definition of its business. It appears to have defined its business as all household products powered by electric motors or heated by electric elements. And within this definition it has been very successful, with a 38% share of washing machines, 60% of vacuum cleaners, as well as brand leadership in dishwashers and irons. The quality of these products is very good and they are well marketed.
>
> However, the company's definition of its business seems to have been product-based. Hoover's real business is to cater to the housewife's need for durable labour-saving devices. Electric power is not the only means for fulfilling this need, and indeed gas has enjoyed a remarkable recent upsurge. But it was only in 1969 that Hoover made its first successful sortie into gas appliances, and then in a very modest way, with a gas fire.†

By contrast, a company which has throughout the 1960s viewed its business increasingly broadly, and always from the standpoint of consumer benefit, is Xerox. This is despite the fact that it had a uniquely superior product, in the 914 copying machine and its successors, the 2400 and 3600.

* Quoted in Theodore Levitt, *The Marketing Mode* (McGraw-Hill, 1969).
† Basic data gained from Doina Thomas, 'The Hard Times of Hoover' (*Management Today*, March 1970).

The Xerox Corporation is one of the most spectacular growth companies of recent years. It markets its own products in the USA, but the company it owns jointly with the Rank Organisation—Rank Xerox—manufactures and markets them in all other parts of the world, including Japan. In 1970 Peter McColough, President of Xerox, defined his company's purpose as 'to find the best means to bring order and discipline to information.' This broad but clear market definition has characterized the expansion of the company.

Until the late 1950s, Xerox sold copying processes for the reproduction of engineering drawings, and for the making of offset masters. These employed xerography, an electrostatic process. Although Xerox's net profits tripled between 1949 and 1958, in the latter year they were only slightly over $£\frac{1}{4}$ million on sales of around $£11$ million.

The breakthrough came with the introduction of the 914 copier which brought Xerox for the first time into the general office copying field. Since then, Xerox has moved into educational publishing and computers, in line with its definition of its market. By 1969 its spending on R & D alone was more than three times its sales revenue twelve years earlier. Xerox had become the 84th largest American company, measured by sales, with a sales revenue of $£618$ million and net profit after tax of $£67$ million.*

Another company which has defined its business clearly in consumer terms is Gerber Products, whose statement of market definition is summed up in its slogan 'Babies are our business, our only business.' This has led the company to expand from its original business of baby foods, in which it has a dominant position in the USA, into baby clothes, tissues, washcloths and medicated disposable nappy liners.

A clear understanding by a company as to the nature of the market it is serving not only gives it a solid base from which to plan any future strategy; it can also, of its own volition, suggest new areas for market expansion, as we saw in the case of Xerox and Gerber. The fact that these may require new technology or involve new distribution channels is a challenge which the offensive marketer will overcome if the profit opportunity appears sufficiently attractive.

* Information from *Dun's Review* (December 1970) and from Ralph Westfall and Harper W. Boyd, *Cases in Marketing Management*.

STRATEGY BRICK 2:   WHO ARE OUR COMPETITORS?

In order to lead your competitors, you must know who they are and what they are doing, because competitive products represent the standard which you have to beat. The aim should be to learn as much as you can from observation and analysis of competitive effort, and to use this knowledge not to copy, but as a means of building superiority. There is, of course, a world of difference between keeping a watchful eye on competition and being hypnotized by it. A company which has an offensive long-term business strategy is unlikely to be more than marginally swayed by competitive activity, and is more liable to influence its competitors than the reverse. However, it is churlish to ignore competitors, since the appeal of their products in relation to your own is the best standard for judging the success of an offensive strategy.

The case of the Austin 1800, launched in 1965, is an example of the hazards run by companies which are so arrogant as to ignore their competitors. According to Graham Turner,★ Lord Lambury (the chairman of BMC until 1961) joked on one occasion that the initials 'BMC' stood for 'Blast My Competitors', but the handling of the Austin 1800 does not make very humorous reading.

> 'Alec Issigonis, BMC's chief designer, said in 1965 that he had never specifically thought about a competitor in creating the car, and Sir George Harriman (at that time, the chairman and managing director) added that they had not compared the 1800's performance and cost with that of the probable competition because they were so confident of the car's potential. The hope was that sales of the 1800 would steadily build up to perhaps 3,000 a week; on the eve of the Leyland merger in 1968, more than two years after its launching, it was running at about one thousand.'†

A brand's major competition consists of those products or services which the consumer regards as a viable alternative. This alternative may lie in products that, on any physical definition, are in different markets. For instance, British Rail recognizes that its major competitors are the private automobile and the airline companies. The newspapers compete against other newspapers, but also with magazines, television and ultimately commercial radio for both customers and advertising revenue.

★ Graham Turner, *Business in Britain*.   † *Ibid.*

The identity of a company or brand's major competition should be reviewed regularly becuase the situation may change. And the hazard to guard against is that of becoming so preoccupied with the activities of your traditional competitors that you overlook the emergence of a totally new rival from an unexpected source. There is a strong element of this in the complaisant attitude of the major American car makers towards imports.

The three large US auto makers—General Motors, Ford and Chrysler—have traditionally regarded each other as major competition. All three have large market shares, are American owned, and headquartered in Detroit, the long-standing centre of the car industry.

Each of the major car manufacturers is so obsessed with studying every move of the other two that, as a group, they fail to attach sufficient importance to activities outside their own magic circle. 'For years the auto men have been saying that the imports were of no consequence, that their share of market was too small to permit American manufacturers to participate in it profitably. They were saying that when the importer's share of market was less than 5%, when it was true, and they kept right on saying it as import sales topped 10%, when it was simply self-delusion.'* By 1970 imports accounted for 12% of all cars sold in the USA, with Volkswagen holding a 5·8% share and the Japanese coming up strongly on the outside. 'It is as if an invisible committee was running this industry. The feelers are always extended, sensing every internal movement and trend. Everybody is looking over everybody else's shoulder. They are responding to each other, and this is the primary reason why their products are all the same and why they take so long to recognize trends.'†

Detroit has at last responded strongly to these signs, and General Motors has introduced the Vega 2300 and Ford the Pinto, both of which are entirely new cars built to compete in the sub-compact market dominated by the imports.

STRATEGY BRICK 3:   WHAT ARE OUR STRENGTHS AND WEAKNESSES?

A careful catalogue of strengths and weaknesses is the third preliminary step that has to be taken before determining a final marketing

* *Car and Driver 1971 Yearbook.*   † *Ibid.*

strategy for either a company or a brand. Its value is that it enables a future strategy to be developed which builds on strengths and avoids exposing weaknesses to any degree. For example, General Mills' conclusion that one of its special strengths was its skill in marketing products to children was an important factor in the strategy it developed to exploit this, which eventually led to its entry into the toy market. However, it chose to enter the toy market by acquisition, and not by internal development, because it recognized that one of its weaknesses was a lack of knowledge about the technology of toys.

A company's strengths and weaknesses, or a brand's for that matter, must be probed with ruthless honesty. Outside consultants and agencies as well as middle management company executives are sometimes reluctant to identify genuine weaknesses in an operation for fear of offending top management or appearing disloyal. This shows a lack of maturity, since an over-rosy assessment of a company's strengths and weaknesses can lead to a strategy which is disastrously unsuitable. We have already seen that a tobacco company seriously over-estimated the relevance of its specialized marketing abilities to the particular conditions of the food market.

Any analysis of strengths and weaknesses at corporate level should differentiate between general strengths, which the company possesses in common with other firms, and unique ones, since it is on the latter that the most effective strategies can often be built. One example of a unique strength which does not yet seem to have been exploited to anything like its full potential is Nabisco's very large grocery sales force in the USA, which enables it to make good profits on biscuits while its competitors do not.*

> In the USA Nabisco has a unique strength in selling compared with its competitors in the biscuit market. Nabisco's market share of this £400 million category is about 55% and its major competitors (Burry, owned by Quaker, Keebler, owned by United Biscuits, and Sunshine, owned by American Tobacco) each have shares of 10% to 15%.
>
> The major skill in this market is the ability to obtain and hold in-store distribution. In almost every other grocery category in the USA, companies deliver their products to regional retail warehouses and the retail companies arrange distribution to their individual branches. However, because

---

* In the UK Nabisco sells Ritz, Ry-King, Premium crackers and Shredded Wheat, among other products.

historically biscuits were a perishable commodity, all US biscuit companies deliver their products direct to stores.

Nabisco has 3000 salesmen to maintain distribution of existing brands and to introduce new ones. The cost of this sales force will be around £12 million. Nabisco's competitors cannot afford such a massive sales force, since they have a much lower turnover across which to spread this overhead. Their sales forces each number about 1000 men. This gives them the dual disadvantage of higher selling costs than Nabisco as a percentage of turnover, and a less effective total sales operation.

Largely due to the efficiencies and economies yielded by its unique advantage in selling, Nabisco makes a reasonable return on its assets in the biscuit market. By contrast its competitors have either operated at minimal net profit levels or actually made a loss in biscuits in recent years. No doubt one of Nabisco's corporate strategies is to seek other limited life products for its sales force to carry.

OFFENSIVE STRATEGY IN EXISTING MARKETS

The scene is now set for the development of offensive strategies for all the major brands in the company. Let us assume that we have defined our market(s) in terms of the consumer benefit offered, have identified our major competitors and drawn up an inventory of strengths and weaknesses both for the company as a whole and for all our major brands.

As a basis for assessing the adequacy of our present strategy, whatever it is, we should now ask ourselves why consumers should buy our product(s) at present, and continue to buy in future, taking into account likely market conditions in the next few years. If no obvious answer comes through, and it is apparent that we have nothing better to offer than competition, the time for developing an offensive strategy is clearly overdue. No company or product can meander along indefinitely if its services are regarded as being more or less the same as any others. And even if a company has a clear point of superiority today, it may soon dissolve in the future, unless it keeps updating its strategy in line with changing market conditions, like Marks & Spencer.

Any company or brand has a wide range of possible offensive strategies at its disposal. It may base its offensive on a superior quality at higher prices—like Rover, Triumph and Jaguar. Triumph's strategy, for instance, was to produce cars that were 'a little bit more sophisticated' than Ford or BMC at a higher price and with larger profit margins.* An alternative strategy is to offer a product of parity quality to competitors, at a lower price. The inclusive tour market offers an interesting contrast in the approaches of Horizon and Clarksons, both applying offensive strategies while aiming for different sections of the market.

A former Reuter correspondent, Vladimir Raitz, was the founder of Horizon Holidays and is reputed to have been the first person to apply the inclusive tour principle of low prices through the use of air charter in the UK. His first tour, just after the war, involved a charter flight to Corsica, and a few days there under canvas.†

Horizon's current strategy is to concentrate on the top end of the inclusive tour market and to offer a wide range of destinations with superior quality accommodation at higher prices than Thomsons, Blue Sky or Clarksons tours. For instance, Horizon has over 100 aircraft destinations compared with Clarksons, which has under 30. A Horizon holiday for 15 days in Palma Nova (Majorca) at peak season rates cost £64–81 in 1971, while a Clarksons one cost £51–54. Horizon's stated strategy, as expressed in their brochure, is 'to provide an effective, fully inclusive service which embodies the principle of maximum value for money, consistent with the highest standards of hotel accommodation in every price range and transportation in the most up-to-date jet aircraft of the leading air companies'.

Clarksons, by contrast, aims for the volume sector of the inclusive tour market. It offers good though not luxury accommodation at very low prices. All flights are by jet, and every bedroom has a private bath or shower. Clarksons sold over 300 000 tours in 1968, making it easily the brand leader, and its strategy of a limited number of destinations plus high volume enable it to negotiate low prices with hotel operators.

Both Horizon and Clarksons are highly successful companies because they each have a strategy for maintaining product superiority in their chosen market sectors.‡

Although this example involved strategies aimed at different sectors of a market, Horizon and Clarksons successfully compete

* Information from Graham Turner, *Business in Britain.*

† Data from Peter M. Kraushar, *New Products and Diversifications* (Business Books, 1969).

‡ In 1969 Horizon launched a new subsidiary, 4S, to cater for the lower priced segment of the market.

against other firms in the same segment, and manage to differentiate themselves clearly from these direct competitors. This leads to another important strategy question. There are two ways of approaching a market. Either one can aim for the same slice of business as close competitors and gain a profitable share of it by offering the same kind of benefit as existing brands, in broadly the same way, but doing it better. Or one can aim to sidestep competition and carve out an unoccupied market niche of one's own by aiming for a slightly different type of benefit. For the sake of clarity, we will call the first approach the 'head-on' strategy and the second the 'blind side' strategy* (using the rugger analogy). They can both be effective approaches.

Procter & Gamble normally uses the head-on strategy. For example, as we have already seen, in entering the USA paper market, it decided to gain a strong market position by developing superior products to Scott and Kimberley Clark and marketing them more effectively. Golden Wonder also used the head-on strategy in the UK crisp market, by introducing a product with better crispness than Smiths through superior packaging, and by concentrating on the wholesale grocery sector of the market which until then had not been strongly developed (there's obviously an element of blind side in the latter).

By contrast, Marks & Spencer has invariably used the blind side strategy, since it has consistently innovated new forms of retailing. From the 'penny bazaar' to the inter-war 'super store' to its highly integrated operation today, Marks & Spencer has run a totally unique business. Hoover used the blind side approach when it entered the household iron market, by introducing the first ever steam iron.

Moving on to another strategy issue, a company must decide whether it wishes to build large brands in mass markets or develop lower volume high profit brands in speciality markets. The latter strategy has substantial advantages or smaller companies with low overheads, and no inclination to indulge in an expensive face-to-face spending contest with a large competitor. Some companies have in fact grown quite large by following such a strategy. In the USA, the American Home Products Company (the majority shareholder in Prestige, the UK household product company) has a number of very profitable brands in speciality market segments like ammonia,

---

* There is a very good exposition of this by Mr J. Phillips, President of R. J. Reynolds Foods, under the title 'The End Run', in *Plotting Marketing Strategy*, edited by Lee Adler (Business Books, 1967).

silver polish, corn removers, nylon whiteners and wart removers, which are not large enough to justify the high marketing costs of entry for Procter & Gamble, Colgate-Palmolive or Bristol-Myers. The Reckitt & Colman household division, with such products as Cherry Blossom shoe polish, Brasso, Silvo, and the Mansion and Goddard's lines, appears to have built its business on a similar approach. Since the object of business is to make money rather than to enjoy the fierce atmosphere of hand-to-hand fighting, a strategy which deliberately seeks markets that are unlikely to attract the heavy spenders can be very shrewd for certain companies.

There are clearly numerous alternative offensive strategies available, and a company or brand must choose the strategy which best fits both its strengths and the specific market situation facing it. Within the limited confines of this book, only a few of these strategies can be covered, but one other which is worth a close look is that based on superiority of distribution. Take Coca-Cola, for instance.

> 'The company's great leader, Robert Woodruff, laid down the policy in the 1920's of putting Coca-Cola 'within an arm's length of desire'. Today, Coca-Cola is distributed in 1,600,000 outlets, more than any other product in the world. Every kind of retail outlet carries the brand. It is put into these outlets by over 1,000 local franchised bottlers in the United States. Because these bottlers, guided by the parent company, have created this extraordinary distribution, it is easier for the company to market new brands. So, with increasing competition on all sides, the heart of this success is the means of achieving widespread availability.'*

Another example on the same theme, but closer to home, is the story of McVitie & Price's rise to leadership of the UK biscuit market.

> McVitie's success in the biscuit market is primarily due to superior product quality, and competitive pricing made possible by low cost production. However, another significant factor in its success was the widespread availability of its products. This was a result of the company's policy to call direct on virtually any store in the country which stocked biscuits, and its refusal to deal through wholesalers. Even in the mid 1960s,

* *Plotting Marketing Strategy*, edited by Lee Adler (Business Books, 1967).

the McVitie sales force called on about 200 000 stores at least once every eight weeks. By contrast, its competitors dealt through wholesalers and called on less than 100 000 stores direct.

The outcome of this was that McVitie built up a special relationship with the small end of the trade, and some of the smaller stores stocked McVitie products exclusively. With the increasing concentration of the grocery trade, it is doubtful whether this strategy would be economic in the 1970s, but it was certainly well suited to the conditions of the 1950s and early 1960s.

It is all very well discussing techniques for offensive strategy development, as we have in this section, but in the end the most exhaustive knowledge of the best techniques will not necessarily result in an offensive approach. Without the right attitude, all the techniques in the world are so much wasted knowledge. If the attitudes are right, distinctive and superior strategies will usually follow. Two companies with strong attitudes are Xerox and Tesco. Peter McColough, the President of Xerox, recently said, 'We are working very hard to obsolete our present equipment, because if we don't somebody else will.'* In the 1969 *Annual Report* of Tesco, its Chairman Jack Cohen remarked, 'The pattern of growth is directly attributable to a management team which is constantly seeking new and improved methods in every department of operation, new fields of activity in anticipation of the consumer's changing requirements, and new trading techniques which will enable the company to sell profitably at the most competitive price.' In the case of many companies, this would be rightly ignored as so much chairman's 'blab'. In the case of Tesco, whose net profits after tax rose from £441 000 in 1960 to £5·5 million in 1969, it is a statement of reality.

OFFENSIVE STRATEGY FOR ENTRY TO NEW MARKETS

Perhaps the most important question on which the marketing department has to guide the company is whether it should attempt to enter entirely new markets, and if so, which ones. Although the hammering received in America by many conglomerates has reduced the corporate appetite for diversification, expansion into new markets is still fashionable, because it contains a touch of adventure.

* Quoted in *Dun's Review* (December 1970).

But there may be very good reasons why a company should remain in its current market and not direct its resources to a new and un-familiar one. The company's present markets may be profitable and fast-growing, so as to absorb all its financial and management resources fully. It would not, for instance, make much sense for Ford to diversify strongly out of cars.

On the other hand, if a company's major markets are stagnant or declining, there is an urgent incentive to diversify either by acquisition or by internal development. Esquire is a case in point, as Stephen L. Bogardo, Assistant to the President of Esquire, describes.

> 'Six years ago, our company was in magazine publishing almost exclusively. . . . Today, Esquire is a highly diversified operation. We get only 30% of our volume from magazine publishing; the rest comes from such completely unrelated businesses as education, lighting and stamp publications. . . .
>
> Esquire has grown as much in the last two years as it did during its previous 34 years of operation. A compounded growth rate, in profits, of more than 80% annually over the past five years has given us a ranking with the country's fastest growing companies.'*

Assuming it is decided to enter markets new to a company, the question is which ones. The answer is really quite simple. A company should enter those new markets which best match its strengths—'best' in this sense meaning most profitably.

The process of defining the three strategy bricks dealt with earlier may in itself reveal suitable new markets for a company. Any com-pany working out a consumer benefit definition of its curent mar-kets for the first time is often surprised to discover that they are much wider in scope than it ever imagined, and that the company's brands only cover part of them. And the very act of identifying a company's strengths often sparks off ideas for new ways of exploit-ing them. But the venture into new markets is always risky because new knowledge is involved. Let us assume that you are marketing director of a company with a pressing requirement to move into new markets. We will further take it that you have enough common sense to realize the need to start from solid ground. First of all, the new market should offer a better long-term profit opportunity

---

* *The Business of Acquisitions and Mergers*, edited by G. Scott Hutchison (Presidents Publishing Houses, 1968).

than existing markets, since if it doesn't, it is not worth the risk and effort of entry. And secondly, in entering a new market, you must have something better to offer than existing competitors, otherwise you will never break in successfully.

So, armed with a list of your company strengths, you then beam it against potential new markets. What you are secretly hoping for, but are, of course, unlikely to find, is a small highly profitable market, growing at a phenomenal rate, which perfectly fits your company strengths, and has not yet been spotted by any of the large corporations. With your strengths of consumer goods marketing and sophisticated financial control, you could no doubt build a major position in such a market. But life is not usually as easy as that, and you will find that you have to lower your sights and become more realistic. Some companies with sophisticated new market strategies never make a move because they are continually seeking ideals which do not exist—they grow old seeking the Golden Fleece.

International Playtex Corporation has built a substantial world-wide business by matching its existing strengths to new market opportunities and by persistently applying an offensive marketing approach:

The company was founded before the Second World War by Mr A. N. Spanel, a vigorously entrepreneurial individual. Its expertise was latex technology, and the original product was a shower cap, but this was soon joined by baby pants and rubber household gloves.

Soon after the end of the War, Playtex entered the girdle market for the first time, with a latex product. At this time, other girdles were still 'trussing mechanisms', and extremely uncomfortable to wear. Playtex's product achieved good figure control with much improved comfort, and was at the same time unique in appearance and texture.

Latex girdles proved to be extremely successful, and in the early 1950's, the company entered the brassiere market. Within three or four years, elastic stretch straps were introduced by Warners, and this major innovation was followed by other manufacturers. However, there was considerable consumer disappointment with these elastic straps, since they were uncomfortable and had a limited life. Using its expertise in rubber technology, Playtex introduced a stretch strap product of greatly improved performance and called it the 'living' bra, which 'lives and breathes with you'.

In successfully entering the girdle and bra market, Playtex effectively applied its technological strengths to product categories new to the company. However, it also utilized strengths in selling and marketing against competitors who were weak in these areas. A key to Playtex's success was that it approached the girdle/bra business not as a fashion category, but as a packaged goods market, responsive to packaging, advertising and display. While existing competitors sold their products 'loose', via a counter clerk, Playtex packaged all its products in attractive cardboard boxes, and merchandized them, in self-service style, from special display fixtures, which it placed in stores. Playtex had an aggressive and highly professional sales force to carry out this merchandizing policy. It backed its products with heavy TV advertising, whereas other girdle/bra companies advertised much less and rarely used TV. And it developed products with superior performance and mass appeal, which generated the high volume and long product life necessary to make heavy TV advertising economic.

Playtex's important strengths were unique in the bra/girdle market. These and its offensive approach have made it the unchallenged market leader in the USA and in many of the highly developed countries of the world.

Some companies set out quite detailed criteria for new market entry. One useful technique is the 'New Market Selection Grid'. This uses certain criteria like size and trend of markets, estimated profitability, fit with existing company strengths and competitive factors, and provides a rating system by which the total score for each possible new market can be totted up. The method is not unlike some of the more thorough techniques for evaluating personnel. An example is given in Appendix C.

Since the whole subject of strategy for new market entry can best be illuminated by demonstration, we will examine some other shorter examples of successful strategies. Let us take a look at the strategy behind the diversification of Esquire, the excellent results of which have already been referred to.

Esquire considered its greatest strength to be in marketing, particularly in distribution, sales promotion and advertising. In looking at new markets, the first thing Esquire seeks is a 50–60% gross margin, which will enable it to spend heavily on marketing (thereby exploiting its strengths) and still make good profits. It is also particularly interested in categories where the level of current marketing skill is not very high—for example, it was able to develop a strong distribution network for some of the companies it acquired in the lighting business.*

You will incidentally notice that I am deliberately not distinguishing in this section between new market entry by internal new product development and entry by acquisition. There is often an artificial separation between these two functions in a company, new products being the job of marketing while acquisitions are looked after by finance department. In fact, they are merely alternative means for executing whatever strategy for new markets is decided upon.

A very interesting new market strategy was followed by Carnation in the USA, although some over-conventional marketing men might frown upon it as being production oriented (which it wasn't).

Carnation started off the 1960s with a rather 'square' image as a staid milk producer, most of whose profits lay in liquid, powdered and condensed milk. By the end of the decade, it had established a well deserved reputation as an imaginative and effective product innovator. Its sales more than doubled between 1962 and 1969, and earnings per share rose from $1·69 to $5·18 over this eight-year period.

It appears† to have reasoned that its main strengths were excellent technology in milk-based and granular food products, together with a strong consumer franchise, through the Carnation name, for any product related to milk. Its strategy was to scan the market for any new uses to which this technology could be put, and it did in fact come up with three very successful ones.

The most dramatic success was Instant Breakfast, launched in 1965. Carnation discovered that a high proportion of Americans never ate any breakfast at all because they had no time. There was a need for a high nutrition product that could be consumed quickly, and this was the need that Carnation Instant Breakfast supplied. It was a flavoured milk based powder, fortified with vitamins and protein which, mixed with milk, provided 375 calories and all the protein of a normal

* Data from *The Business of Acquisitions and Mergers*, edited by G. Scott Hutchison.

† I am making deductions from observation of events, rather than from any inside knowledge of the workings of Carnation.

breakfast. It could then be mixed and consumed in about
1 minute. This brand's volume is now running at about £20
million.

Another new product type invented by Carnation, following
the same overall strategy, was powdered dietary supplements.
From about 1960 onwards, the dietary market had been
dominated by Metrecal with a canned *liquid* drink. This was
based on milk, with vitamin and protein additives, and could
be taken as a replacement for a meal. Since it contained only
225 calories, while the average main meal generates between
500 and 1000 calories, a dedicated Metrecal user could lose
weight. The only trouble was that Metrecal did not taste
very good because the milk had to be sterilized before it was
put in the can. Carnation saw the opportunity for a better
tasting dietary product and, again using its technological
strengths, weighed in with Slender, a powdered product
which, when mixed with *fresh* milk, produced 225 calories.
Of course it tasted better, because fresh milk does taste good.
Slender immediately became brand leader in the dietary market,
which is still much larger in the USA than in the UK.

The other entry by Carnation was Coffee Mate, a white
granular product in a glass jar, for adding to coffee instead
of milk or cream. Its advantages are that it is low in calories,
unlike milk, and can be mixed easily without cooling down a
piping hot cup of black coffee (as milk does). Coffee Mate has
also been successful.

So out of some milk and granule technology, Carnation was
able to develop three entirely new products, each in different
sectors of the grocery market. This is a story not only of clear
strategy, but also of brilliant execution, and a true application of the offensive marketing approach.

BRAND MARKETING STRATEGY

Although the examples so far in this chapter have centred round
corporate marketing objectives and strategies, exactly the same
principles apply to brands. A brand needs to set overall objectives,
and develop offensive strategies. It is customary to set an overall
strategy for the total brand and, stemming from this, to draw
up sub-strategies for each key activity—like advertising, product
development, promotions and packaging.

The following case history on Heinz ketchup in the USA illustrates the application of offensive strategies. It is a classic example of how superior marketing strategy and implementation can outgun a competitor with much greater spending power. In case you react to this case by saying 'We wouldn't have time to do all those things—they must have had scores of marketing assistants on Heinz ketchup', let me point out that there was only a Brand Manager and one assistant on Heinz ketchup throughout the duration of this case.

Heinz had installed a product management system in the USA in 1955, but most of the personnel had been recruited from the field and the system had not worked well. In late 1963 a new chief executive was appointed. He brought in a marketing director from outside, who in turn recruited a number of experienced marketing executives from other companies, including a new Brand Manager for Heinz ketchup, in early 1964.

Ketchup was Heinz's largest and most profitable brand, and its turnover was about £12 million at trade prices. In 1962 Heinz had been clear brand leader with 28%; Del Monte (19%) and Hunt (15%) lagged far behind But in early 1964, Heinz was struggling to retain market leadership. Its share, at 24%, was only slightly ahead of Hunt (22%) and Del Monte (21%).

Heinz ketchup's two major strengths were the superiority of its product's performance and its high reputation on a branded basis among housewives. The ketchup brand group undertook a careful analysis of the market and as a result Heinz made a number of critical changes in strategy in 1964 and 1965. It concluded that the major reason for its fall in share in 1962–64 was its widening price premium over competition—this had risen from about 15% above Del Monte and Hunt in June–December 1962 to around 30% higher in January–April 1964. Based on correlation analyses over a number of years between Heinz share of market and its price premium versus competition, the brand group decided that a 15% premium was the most profitable pricing level for Heinz. Consequently, when Hunt and Del Monte increased their prices following rises in the costs of tomato solids, Heinz made no change, and reached its target price differential (+15%) by mid-1965.

Although Heinz expected to finance the cost of its new pricing strategy through increases in volume, this was an untested proposition and it had to cut back its marketing budget in 1965 as a precaution. This was despite the fact that Hunt had outspent Heinz on marketing by almost 2:1 in 1964

and was known to have ambitious plans for 1965. Key spending
figures in 1964 and 1965 turned out to be as follows:*

| | HUNT | | HEINZ | |
	1964	*1965*	*1964*	*1965*
Advertising (£000)	2400	2700	900	800
Promotion (£000)	100	400	500	400
Total Marketing (£000)	2500	3100	1400	1200

Heinz had appointed a new advertising agency in early 1964—
Doyle Dane & Bernbach. Previous advertising had used 'run
of the mill' ingredient and taste appeals and was thought
to have lacked impact. A new advertising strategy was agreed—
that Heinz tasted best because it was thicker and richer than
any other ketchup. The product could clearly deliver this
claim, and, in order to minimize the effect of Hunt's spending
dominance, Heinz sought an arresting new campaign from the
agency. This eventually took the form of a ketchup race, in
which Heinz ketchup was poured out on a timed basis against
a competitor. Heinz lost the race because 'It's too thick, too
rich to win a ketchup race'. Other executions, emphasizing
Heinz's unique thickness and richness, were developed on
the theme of 'Heinz, the slow ketchup'. The advertising researched well, and had an evident effect on the market place.

At the same time, Heinz was reviewing its trade promotion
strategy. Until 1964, Heinz ketchup had run trade buying
allowances for twelve weeks on both its sizes and paid the trade
off invoice at the time the product was sold. In August 1964
Heinz tested out a promotion on one size only, for just five
weeks. It insisted that the trade furnished written proof of
compliance with the promotion conditions (advertising,
display or price reduction) and only credited the trade with the
allowance money *after* performance was proved. This promotion sold through the same weekly volume as the old type,
at less than one-third of the cost. As a result, a new strategy of
running promotions on individual sizes for short periods, and
insisting on proof of performance, was adopted nationally.

Heinz undertook market tests of alternative strategies which

* All the years referred to are Heinz financial years (1 May to 30 April) not
calendar years.

were not expanded—tests of parity pricing to Hunt and Del Monte, and of higher advertising spending levels. It also conducted tests of different trade allowance values, some of which were applied nationally. There was little consumer promotion in the ketchup market, because ketchup was a favourite 'retail feature' item, and as a result trade promotion was usually productive. Heinz also consciously adopted a strategy of being first in the market with any new innovation, and therefore carefully examined every promising development opportunity it could find.

In the packaging area, it examined but rejected plastic and aerosol containers on the grounds of cost and size impression (in the case of plastic). However, it spotted a need for a larger size of ketchup for families with children and also for a ketchup bottle with a wider mouth which the consumer could either spoon or pour from. As a result the 'ketchup lovers' size was introduced nationally in 1965 and 'widemouth' in 1966. Both had been tested previously in Baltimore district and were entirely new to the market. The net amount of extra business produced by the 'ketchup lovers' size was rather disappointing, because it gained the large majority of its volume from other Heinz sizes. 'Widemouth', however, produced a useful total increment.

Despite being heavily outspent by Hunt,* which had unsuccessfully tried to introduce Pizza and Hickory flavoured ketchups from the end of 1965, Heinz gained share steadily in 1964–68 and is now the dominant brand in the American ketchup market:

USA KETCHUP % BRAND SHARES—1964 TO 1968					
	1964	*1965*	*1966*	*1967*	*1968*
Heinz	25·4	27·1	31·2	32·6	34·9
Hunt	20·3	20·7	21·6	22·5	20·8
Del Monte	20·1	20·1	19·1	19·6	20·2

The importance of right attitudes as the basis for offensive marketing strategy has already been stressed in this chapter, but

---

*Hunt has shown great strength in new product development in recent years, especially with its new Snack-Packs, and appears dramatically better at marketing today than it was in the middle 1960s.

one attitude which has not been emphasized sufficiently is that however well you may be doing now, you can always do better. It is very easy for a dominant brand or company to rest on its laurels and lose its offensive edge. Our final case history illustrates an offensive approach by a brand with a leading share, which had just fought off a determined competitive attack, and might well have sat back on its haunches in an orgy of self-congratulation.

By 1965 Procter & Gamble's Crest was easily the leading toothpaste in the USA, with a 33% share of a market worth £96 million at manufacturer selling prices. It contained a unique stannous fluoride ingredient, was the only toothpaste whose effectiveness was endorsed by the American Dental Association and had no fluoride competition.

In 1965 and 1966 two new fluoride toothpastes—Cue (Colgate-Palmolive) and Fact (Bristol-Myers)—were introduced nationally, supported by over £5 million in marketing funds during their first year. Although Crest did not even increase its share of total category advertising spending, both competitive brands failed.*

However, while fighting off these competitive efforts in 1965–6, Crest was planning a major development move. Its flavour had always been wintergreen, whereas all other major brands used the more generally popular spearmint/peppermint flavour. Although the wintergreen flavour was acceptable to current Crest users, Crest's management felt it was inhibiting the brand's future growth prospects, since many people who might otherwise have bought Crest strongly disliked its flavour.

This was the background to the development of a new flavour strategy by Crest. Its aim was to improve the flavour appeal of Crest to non-users, while retaining the loyalty of the large body of existing users. But how was this to be achieved? In fact, Crest introduced a companion flavour, coloured green, and tasting of mint. This approach also executed another Crest strategy, which was to expand its share of facings on supermarket shelves.

Crest's second flavour was expanded nationally in July 1967, and drove the brand's market share up by about 15% at rela-

---

* These two expensive new product failures are analysed in more detail in Chapter 15, 'New Products—the Difference between Success and Failure'.

tively low cost. Share grew from a plateau of about 33% in the five years ending in 1966 to 38% in 1970.*

SUMMARY

Objectives describe desired destination, strategies set out the routes chosen for achieving the objective; and plans constitute the vehicle for getting to the destination along the chosen route. Objectives are usually expressed in financial terms, and a company should aim at minimum for a rate of increase in earnings per share which will cover inflation and give the shareholder sufficient growth beyond this to justify the risk of the investment.

Offensive strategy involves the discovery and exploitation of distinctive advantages over competitors. This requires considerable analysis, and the three bricks on which successful strategies are often built can be expressed in question form:

What is our business?
Who are our competitors?
What are our strengths and weaknesses?

An offensive strategy should be built on a company's strengths. In its present markets, a firm can usually choose from a wide range of alternative strategies. In determining which new markets to enter, a company should seek those with attractive profit opportunities, which also exploit its corporate strengths. A new market selection grid may be built for this purpose.† But in the end, all the knowledge of the best techniques will not result in an offensive approach unless it is allied to the right attitudes.

---

* It is also believed that the introduction of mint-flavoured Crest accelerated the total market growth.   † See Appendix C.

8:   Marketing Planning to meet
_____Corporate Objectives

'*The truth is that planning is a victim of lip-service, far more so even than the pursuit of profitability.*'*

'*Marketing planning is the starting point for all corporate planning. Whether your business involves a service or a product, it is based upon the existence of present and potential markets. Planning with respect to those markets is the basis for the extent and direction of all other corporate decisions.*'†

We now have clear objectives, and have re-evaluated our corporate and brand marketing strategies. This heart-searching has enabled us to decide whether our current strategies are effective and likely to continue to be so for the foreseeable future. And we also know whether we wish to enter new markets and, if so, which ones. This represents good progress towards offensive marketing action, but so far we only have words on paper and ideas for the future. There is a strong element of vision and conceptual thinking in formulating strategy, because it scans new paths which may never have been followed before. But planning is much more down-to-earth, and transforms the broad ideas of strategy into hard-nosed action plans which are feasible and designed to meet company profit objectives.

Before we delve into the details of marketing planning, let us first blow away some major misconceptions about it. An impression seems to have got abroad, fostered no doubt by the spread of cor-porate planning departments, that planning is a specialized activity carried out mainly by economists, statisticians and suchlike. This is of course incorrect, since planning for the future is one of the primary responsibilities of every manager, especially if he is in the

* Robert Heller and Geoffrey Foster, '*Management Today* Revisited' (*Management Today*, June 1970).
† Bennett S. Chapple Jr, Vice-President of US Steel, quoted in *Formulating the Company's Marketing Policies* (National Industrial Conference Board).

marketing department. In a company with a corporate planning department, the planning staff will indeed provide useful future forecasts and advice on the planning process. But individual line managers should still develop their own plans, because they are the people on the battlefront with the obligation to transform the plans into reality.

Another misconception about planning is that it is an astrological exercise for attempting to foretell the future. Obviously, any plan has to make assumptions about future trends, and indeed it will be concerned to exploit them in the company's favour. But one certainty which good planners recognize is that no forecast will ever turn out to be 100% accurate, whether it concerns broad economic trends or specific brands. That is inevitable, but it does not invalidate the planning process one little bit, because the purpose of planning is to make enlightened guesses about the future and to take action today in order to reach a desired objective tomorrow.

WHY MARKETING PLANNING MATTERS

Anyone who reads proverbs will be impressed by the number which deal with planning and emphasize its importance. Two of the better known ones are 'A stitch in time saves nine' and 'Look before you leap'. If planning was important in the days when those phrases were coined, it is even more so in the second half of the twentieth century. There are two main reasons why this is so in business today—the tyranny of lead times and the accelerating rate of change.

The Tyranny of Lead Times

I suppose there was a day, perhaps even within living memory, when you could think up a new product idea in the morning, manufacture it on the plant in the afternoon and sell it the following week. Things are different now, and not just in relation to new products. The initiation of any business action involves lead times, whether the event is a simple one like setting up a promotion, or a more difficult one like moving a company into entirely new markets. With the increasingly complicated nature of modern business, lead times exert their own tyranny and place a premium on planning. The gap between the idea or the strategy and its performance is an ever-widening one. Planning links the two and attempts to narrow the gap.

Examples of the tyranny of lead times abound. There is typically a four-year gestation period from conception of the first fragile idea for a new grocery product to the date at which it starts to show a profit.* The lead time between the draft paper plan for a new car and its emergence on the market is 3–4 years. In advanced technology businesses like computers, electronic equipment for military systems, new aircraft, etc., the lead times can stretch beyond ten years. So the profit performance of your company today will depend significantly on what you or your predecessors were doing 4–10 years ago. If a particular change in consumer tastes or a specific need for new products was not foreseen then, and action initiated at the time, there may be little you can do to remedy the situation for the next year or so. Action now to create profits for tomorrow is what planning is all about, and the two instances below, from the car industry, demonstrate the dire effects of its absence.

We have already observed the slowness of response by the big three American car manufacturers to the challenge of imports and the sub-compact segment. However, in the race to enter this market, Chrysler has been left far behind by General Motors and Ford, and even by the baby of the industry—American Motors—which only has about 2% of sales, compared with Chrysler's 15% or so.

Ford was first in with a compact, the Maverick, in 1970. By 1971 Ford (the Pinto), General Motors (the Vega 2300) and American Motors (the Gremlin) all had their own sub-compact cars, manufactured in the USA and costing hundreds of millions of dollars to tool up for. Only Chrysler is left out in the cold, and for 1971 it is attempting a holding action by importing the Hillman Avenger (renamed the Plymouth Cricket) and the Dodge Colt, made in Japan by Mitsubishi. When Chrysler's own sub-compact eventually comes out, probably in 1972, the Pinto and the Vega 2300 will be strongly entrenched.

Chrysler has been slower than Ford or GM to read the signs of the market and to make plans for action based on them. If this can happen to Chrysler, the eighth largest American company in 1969, it can happen to anyone.

It certainly happened at British Motor Corporation, where

*The time lag is often more than four years. The four-year figure is made up of one year from idea to test market, another year to national expansion, and a further two years before the initial launch investment costs of advertising and promotion are recouped by profits.

there appeared to be a complete absence of effective market planning for new cars. At the time of the Leyland takeover in 1968, there were no new car products in the pipeline for the mass market. Even though British Leyland rapidly gave high priority to a new model for the high volume sector, and broke records by developing it in three years flat, it has only appeared on the market in spring 1971.

So far we have been looking at lead times for major development projects. But even the more mundane tasks of keeping a business moving on established lines involve significant time lags. A new package design may take up to eight months between start date and completion; almost any promotion in the grocery market now has to be planned at least six months ahead; and a new advertising campaign usually takes some months to develop. If the need is not seen far enough ahead and planned for, the result may suffer through shortage of time. Anyone can develop a new advertising or promotion campaign in an afternoon, but with such little thought the quality is unlikely to be good. Too many marketing plans today bear the tell-tale signs of rush, resulting from patchwork planning.

The Accelerating Rate of Change, and Product Life Cycles

Consumer tastes, distribution structures and economic or political conditions are today changing very rapidly. The rate of change seems to be progressing geometrically, with each decade showing more change than the one before. A glance at any table showing ten-year trends will give even the most hardened observer a sense of shock, and perhaps bewilderment. The proportion of homes with refrigerators has doubled in the past six years, from 30% in 1963 to 61% today. Ownership of portable radios has more than doubled over the same period to 65% of homes in 1969. And certain industries have been through massive changes of taste in the past few years.

Take ladies' hosiery. The 1960s opened with seamed stockings still dominant. As the decade progressed, seamless stockings took over, and increased their share of market from 33% in 1962 to 95% in 1969. At the same time, just to complicate matters, panti-hose followed behind the mini from the middle 1960s and began to make stockings obsolete. And as trousers gained in popularity, women were prepared to wear hosiery in very poor condition or to dispense with it altogether.

This rapidity of change has led to the theory of the product life cycle, which is relevant to marketing planning. Unlike some theories, the product life cycle theory is useful in practice, though it does not apply equally to every market category. According to the theory, products are compared to human beings and life divided into three stages:

EXAMPLES

Youth	Embassy Regal, Jaguar XJ6
Maturity	Guinness, Johnnie Walker, Nescafé
Decline	Crosse and Blackwell soups, Tide

In its youth a product has novelty, and gains in market share and profitability, once it has got over its expensive launch period. During maturity its sales and share begin to level out or decline, and profits probably start to fall as other 'youthful' brands with better ideas enter the market. The sad period of decline takes place when sales begin to fall more rapidly, the brand loses retail distribution and sterling profit falls.

The theory is that unless the marketing people in a company continually update a product in line with changes in market conditions, it will eventually disappear. Updating should, according to the theory, be done before maturity sets in, and some new brands apparently plan their first relaunch even before they are introduced to the market. The rash of packages containing 'new improved' messages, which you will see in any supermarket, represent attempts at relaunch or recycling by manufacturers eager to postpone the grim ravages of the ageing process. The operation of the life cycle can be seen dramatically in the case of cars. A new model comes out and may remain unchanged for the first year or so, when sales are booming. In the next few years, minor modifications may be made to the body, a GT or more powerful version introduced, and various knick-knacks added as 'improvements'. Eventually, unless it is the VW Beetle, the model becomes obsolete and is withdrawn.

The theory of the product life cycle is very useful if it is not always taken too literally. It certainly has a strong application in markets where fashion is important or where technology develops rapidly— cars, aircraft, computers, footwear and clothing are prime examples. It is less important, though certainly not to be ignored, in food and drink, and its inevitable ageing effect can be seen in most markets. There are, however, a number of consumer products which, either through static conditions or through shrewd recycling, have survived for scores of years—like Bisto, Bovril, Guinness, Ovaltine, Horlicks, Johnnie Walker ('still going strong' from 1820), Persil, Dettol and the VW Beetle (over thirty years old and still accounting for 70% of VW sales in the world's most developed market).

The contribution of the life cycle theory is to dramatize the importance of constantly improving products in order even to stay still. And it brings home the fact that fast growth can usually only be achieved through new products or acquisitions. A Nielsen study of 454 grocery brands from 35 product categories in the UK and USA showed that only 13% continued to gain share of market after their first three years of existence.*

What conclusions for action should the wise marketing planner draw from all this? Well, first of all, he should make specific plans to relaunch each of his major brands every couple of years with improvements that keep them ahead of changes in market conditions—through formulation or styling improvements, line extensions, new sizes and so on. Unless those are planned at least a year ahead, they will be very hard to implement effectively. Secondly, he should aim for most of his future growth through new products because there is pretty strong evidence that existing products will have to work hard even to hold share in the future. And thirdly, he should take a close look at all his products and divide them into the three categories of the life cycle. Those in an advanced state of maturity or in decline should be given especially close scrutiny.† Can the miracles of modern marketing surgery save the brand, or is it beyond recall? If the brand is too far gone to recover, it should be milked—in other words, marketing support spending should be minimized or cut off altogether and short-term profits maximized. Anticipating future trends and planning to capitalize on them before anyone else is one of the hallmarks of offensive marketing. Change is the ally of the offensive marketer because it rewards the innovator and penalizes those who vainly try to retain the *status quo*.

DEFINING THE PROFIT GAP

The profit gap is a standard tool of long-term marketing planning, and is a very simple concept. It represents the difference, over a

---

* *The Nielsen Researcher* (May–June 1967).

† For an interesting consideration of this question in case history form, see A. T. Wright, 'Quaker Puffed Wheat', in *British Cases in Marketing*, edited by J. S. Bingham (Business Books, 1969).

3–5 year period ahead, between the profits you expect to gain from existing products, and the profits you need to achieve in order to hit corporate objectives. The profit gap can only be filled by new products* and constitutes the company's new product targets.

Figure 2 and Table 8.1 show a profit gap from a fictional five-year marketing plan. The objectives are ambitious and require the company to generate $27\frac{1}{2}\%$ of its 1976 profit from new products not on the market in 1971. Let us hope that this particular company already had some successful new products in test market at the time of drawing up the plan!

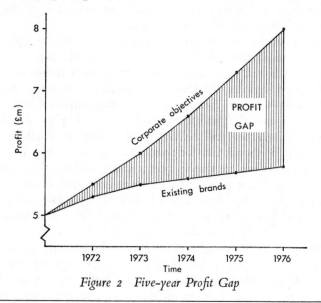

Figure 2   Five-year Profit Gap

TABLE 8.1 FIVE-YEAR PROFIT GAP						
NET PROFIT BEFORE TAX (£m)						
	Current year 1971	*Yr 1 1972*	*Yr 2 1973*	*Yr 3 1974*	*Yr 4 1975*	*Yr 5 1976*
Corporate objectives	5·0	5·5	6·0	6·6	7·3	8·0
Existing brands	5·0	5·3	5·5	5·6	5·7	5·8
Annual profit gap	—	0·2	0·5	1·0	1·6	2·2
Cum. profit gap	—	0·2	0·7	1·7	3·3	5·5

* If a company makes an acquisition, it should raise its overall profit targets to reflect a reasonable return on the new capital assets it has just taken over.

In working out a plan like the one in the table, a vital decision for the marketing department is how much to spend on developing existing brands and how much on new brands. Only a limited amount of money is available, and the kind of question a marketing department might well face is whether to relaunch two of its major existing brands in 1973 or whether to introduce a major new brand. One cannot generalize on this (if one could then marketing men would not be needed—a computer could do the job). But the answer will obviously depend on a comparison of the relative short-term and long-term profitability of the two alternatives. This kind of conflict can be very real, and for companies with little in the new product larder, existing brands may have to go short in order to finance an ambitious new product programme.

FILLING THE PRODUCT GAP WITH NEW PRODUCTS

The profit gap is just a lump of money that doesn't yet exist, and cannot lead to action in that unrefined form. To make the objective a reality, the profit gap has to be subdivided into a number of separate new product projects. Let us take Figure 2 as an example. The profit gap, or target for new products, is £5·5 million at the end of the fifth year. In theory this figure could be achieved by one major new product, launched in 1972, breaking even by the end of 1974 and generating £2·8 million per year net profit in 1975 or 1976. Or it might take fifteen new products, launched at various points in the five-year period, to hit the £5·5 million target. Just how is one to cut this large profit cake?

I know of only one satisfactory way, and that is to set minimum figures for new product volume and profit, and to use these as a starting point. To begin with, we have some useful given information—a short list of new markets which the company plans to enter in the next five years, which was worked out as part of the corporate marketing strategy. Based on this, we can build some assumptions about the minimum acceptable sales volume for a new brand. It should be large enough to make the effort of preparation worthwhile, and to gain a sufficiently high share of market to justify continuing marketing support. For example, it would be pointless to spend heavily to gain a target 5% share in a strongly advertised category, only to find that this share was too small either to support an effective advertising campaign or to retain retail distribution in the long term. The minimum volume for a new brand will vary greatly, according to factors like the size of the company and

the nature of the markets it plans to compete in. A car manufacturer may have a minimum target of £50 million annual sales for
any new model in the high volume sector while for a UK toiletry
or cosmetic company the figure may be as low as £200 000.

As for profit targets, the minimum is normally expressed in net
profit, both as a percentage of sales and of capital employed. The
profit on sales targets should be higher than the company's past
average, because new products should at least plan to upgrade
existing profit percentages. If the company's historical return on
sales was 14% before tax, maybe the minimum for any new product
should be 16%. The return on capital should, at the very least, be
greater than the cost of borrowing.★

Finally, a maximum period of new product payback has to be
established. This is the time it takes to recoup the heavy initial
marketing costs of introduction by means of profits from the new
product. A typical major new entry in the grocery market will
be heavily in the red for the first year, and only reach a profit
breakeven in the second or third year, if it is successful. What
constitutes a reasonable payout length, depends on the average
life cycle for products in the chosen market. I was stunned to see,
fairly recently, a new brand marketing plan based on a ten-year
payout in a category where the average product was usually stone
dead in five years.

In the marketing department of a food manufacturer, the
minimum new product criteria established could be as follows:

NEW PRODUCTS—MINIMUM FIGURES FOR PLANNING	
Sales volume	£500 000
Pre-tax return on sales	16%
Pre-tax return on capital employed	14%
Maximum payout period	2 years

These minimum figures would be used to screen out any budding
new product projects which failed to meet them.

Now that we have these agreed minimum criteria, we are in a
position to fill in the profit gap which has to be satisfied by new

★ An article by Robert Heller in the *Observer* (28 February 1971) states
that a company in the 1960s needed to make 15% on capital employed to do
the minimum job of covering the replacement of assets at inflating costs and
to reward shareholders at going rates of interest after tax. But the median
return averaged over the whole of the 1960s by 185 large companies surveyed
by *Management Today* was only 14½%.

products. In markets where the opportunity for entry seems good, or where the company has special strengths or an exciting new idea, volume and profit figures well above the minimum should be planned. Applying these criteria to the five-year profit gap table on page 136, our new product requirements might be as in Table 8.2 (for those who are gluttons for punishment, Appendix D shows the detailed workings behind this table).

TABLE 8.2 NUMBER OF NEW PRODUCTS REQUIRED 1972–6						
Size of brand (sales volume)	1972	1973	1974	1975	1976	*Total*
Major new brands (£5m+)	1			1		2
Medium new brands (£1–2m)	1	1	2		1	5
Small new brands (£0·5m)	1	1				2
Line extensions* (£0·5–1m)	1			2	1	4
TOTAL NEW PRODUCTS	4	2	2	3	2	13

Armed with this blueprint for new products, we at last know quite specifically what we have to do to fill that yawning gap. And now the action begins. The first step is to decide whether the company has the people and the know-how to achieve this plan and, if not, to make certain that it gets them. The marketing department should be asking basic questions like: Are we as a department properly equipped and organized to meet this programme? Does the R & D dept have enough people with the technological skills we will need in the future? Are we generating enough good ideas and, if not, how can we do better? How many new ideas will have to be drummed up, and how many new formulae developed commercially to a stage where they can be consumer tested, in order to reach our new product targets—bearing in mind the known high mortality rate for new product ideas†—and how do we best handle this work load? Having got the right people organized in the right way to achieve the new product plan, the hard grind of initiating and developing ideas for each of the thirteen new products required can begin, working to a strict timetable designed to bring the bacon home on time.

* E.g. new varieties or sizes of existing brands; a Heinz pheasant soup would be a line extension, not a new brand.

† For detailed discussion of this, see Chapter 15, 'New Products—the Difference between Success and Failure'.

DOES PLANNING WORK?

Any reader of this chapter will recognize that marketing planning as described here is an elaborate process taking up considerable time. He may well be constrained to ask whether the time could not be more profitably spent on other more immediate projects.

Marketing planning does not 'work' any more than marketing or computers work. It is merely a management tool which may be well or poorly used. The mere fact of planning will not drive a company's business forward one iota. But if a company uses planning as a precursor of action, and judges its managers on their performance against agreed plans and targets, planning should work. Equally, it is obvious that where planning is merely a paper exercise to which line management feels no serious sense of commitment, the whole exercise is a shameful waste of money.

I cannot personally envisage any company achieving ambitious future profit objectives without some form of long-term marketing planning, even though it may not necessarily be as formalized as the mode described in this chapter. And one of the major reasons for the high failure rate of new products is poor planning.

SUMMARY

Planning transforms the broad ideas of strategy into hard-nosed action plans which are both feasible and designed to meet company profit objectives.

The tyranny of lead times and the accelerating rate of change make planning increasingly important. Anticipating future trends and planning to capitalize on them before anyone else is one of the hallmarks of offensive marketing.

The profit gap is a standard tool of long-term marketing planning. It can only be filled by new products and constitutes the company's new brand targets. However, taken on its own, the profit gap is just a lump of money that doesn't yet exist, and it must be divided down into a number of separate new product projects.

Planning is a useful management technique, but it will not drive a company's business forward of its own accord. To be effective, it should be used as a precursor of action and a yardstick for judging management performance.

IV ON THE OFFENSIVE— EFFECTIVE EXECUTION

Effective execution is the final step in the operation of effective marketing. It is the 'E' of 'P-O-I-S-E'. Execution stems from strategy, and the two are interdependent. A fine execution of a poor strategy is just as ineffective as a poor execution of a great one. Marks & Spencer was very successful between the wars, not only because its strategy of excellent value at under five shillings was well suited to contemporary consumer needs, but also because it was able to execute it well, due to a unique relationship developed with suppliers.

Part IV covers the various marketing tools for executing strategies. Chapter 9 deals with product development, Chapter 10 with market research, Chapter 11 with pricing, Chapter 12 with sales promotion and packaging, Chapter 13 with advertising and Chapter 14 with distribution channels. Each main topic in Chapters 11–14 is divided into two sections. A very brief outline of each marketing function is given in the first part, in cases where it has not been covered earlier. This is designed for advanced students and is intended as a short background rather than as a comprehensive treatment, since this is not a textbook. The second part, which should interest all readers, describes a number of attitudes which characterize the offensive marketing approach towards execution.

9:   Product Development

'*It is difficult, if not impossible, to find anyone who doubts the prime importance of product appeal. The need for top product quality is a universally acknowledged truism among companies in the consumer packaged goods field. However, the fact remains that there are vast differences in the extent to which individual companies actually do something about this belief. It is also a fact that the largest profits generally go to those companies which most devotedly follow a policy of insisting on a competitive advantage, no matter how small, for every product they market.*'*

The most important principle of product development, beside which all others pale, is that no other corporate activity matters more. Consumers buy product benefits, not advertising and promotions. And the surest, and sometimes the easiest, route to corporate growth is through product superiority. All the other members of the marketing mix—advertising, promotions, pricing and packaging—respond most amiably to a superior product, and will work hardest on its behalf.

With this track to an Eldorado set out so clearly, one would expect it to be as crowded as the M4, jammed with companies accelerating in powerful vehicles to the promised destination. But few companies follow it with full dedication. Marks & Spencer does, and we have seen where it got them. Procter & Gamble pursues the simple policy of developing superior products and backing them with heavy marketing support—and this usually works. IBM and Xerox rate the priority they give to research as a major factor in their success. IBM spends 5–6% of its sales on R & D, and Xerox has averaged 5% on sales over the past decade. Many other fine companies also give high priority to R & D, but they are certainly outnumbered by those who do not.

Half measures in R & D are unlikely to produce any results. The key to success is substantial expenditure, backed by right

* Unpublished statement by Mr R. H. Beeby, President of Glendinning Associates Consulting Division (U.S.A.).

attitudes. R & D costs money and does not come cheaply. Some companies are reluctant to spend heavily on it, because of the waste involved. There is no question that the size of this waste is alarming. However, companies probably waste more money on advertising than they do on R & D. The difference is that they can measure waste in R & D reasonably precisely, while there are no workable tools for assessing how much advertising money is wasted. A company that really believes in building product superiority will always find the resources to back an effective development programme, even if it means skimping or cutting back in other business areas.

> The Xerox Corporation was very small when it developed its major breakthrough in office copying technology. And yet it spent £15 million of borrowed money in perfecting the process. The size of the subsequent rewards was gigantic.*

But, as in most things, money alone is not enough. It must be combined with the right attitudes. For every small company which overcomes barriers through *right* attitudes, there are larger companies with great technical and financial resources which rarely develop even minor product innovations, because they have the *wrong* attitudes. So let's examine five principles of offensive product development and probe their application.

1. GIVE PRIORITY TO PRIORITY SETTING

The majority of R & D work does not result in commercial appplications. *Business Week* reports that out of the 100 000 patents applied for annually in the USA, only 3% see the light of day as commercial products. A study by the management consultants Booz, Allen & Hamilton based primarily on 800 client assignments conducted in the few years up to 1965, showed that '4 out of every 5 hours devoted by scientists and engineers to technical development of new products are spent on projects that do not reach commercial success.'†

The first decision on priority setting, and it is very much in the province of the marketing department, is how much time to spend on genuinely innovative work, and how much on maintenance

---

* Derived from Peter F Drucker, *Managing for Results* (Heinemann, 1964; Pan, 1970).

† *The Management of New Products* (1968).

work, like making minor improvements or cost savings on existing products. The pressure of the immediate is as strong in the R &
D area as in any other, and unless a clear priority is set, short-term
projects with a low potential payoff are likely to clamour for attention, and receive it. The results of an investigation by Unilever's
Special Committee in 1959 typify this problem, which requires
as much vigilance today as it did twelve years ago.

'It was pointed out in 1959 in reply to some searching questions
from the Special Committee that well over half of the research
endeavour of Unilever went on what was called "protective
research", that is research that was designed to maintain existing
products in a competitive position. Another quarter went on
"service" work, mainly designed to assess the performance of
competing products and giving advice to various users and
consumers. 10 to 15 per cent could be said to be concentrated
on genuinely novel developments which would bring new and
additional business to Unilever. This (said the then Head of
Research Division, Dr Woodroofe) was, for a company of
Unilever's size, "woefully inadequate but it is sad that I have to
assure you that we in research are under no pressure from
marketing to increase this part of our work".'[*]

Once a division between genuinely new work and maintenance
or replacement effort has been determined, priorities should be set
for individual projects. This is a continuous process and is very much
a matter of judgement. Obviously the highest priority should be
given to those projects with the best profit potential, and this is
affected by marketing, technical and cost variables. The three
questions that should be asked about any product development
project are:

(*a*) Assuming technical success, what is its profit potential
in the market place?
(*b*) What is the chance of technical success?
(*c*) How much R & D time and cost is it likely to absorb,
from start to completion?

The answers will obviously be quite rough, but each question should
be considered and an eventual priority arrived at based on a balance
between them.

A useful device for bringing some order to these generalities

[*] Charles Wilson, *The History of Unilever*, Vol. III (Cassell, 1970).

is the product development priority table, which is shown in Table 9.1. Scores are allocated for market potential and likelihood of technical success, and based on these, plus likely cost and time-scale, a priority is set. Six fictional projects are included in the table for the purpose of illustration.

TABLE 9.1 PRODUCT DEVELOPMENT PRIORITY TABLE						
	Project no.					
	1	2	3	4	5	6
Market potential (max. 100)[1]	90	25	40	20	60	95
% chance of technical success	55	100	70	40	20	10
Likely time-scale (years)	5	$\frac{1}{4}$	2	1	4	4
Estimated cost (£000)[2]	65	1	15	2	80	50
PRIORITY RATING (A–D)[3]	A	A	B	C	D	D

Notes:

[1] The score ranges from 0 to 100. 0–25 is a marginal improvement in consumer benefit. 26–50 is a significant improvement. 51–100 is a major breakthrough.

[2] This column refers to R & D department cost.

[3] Priority rating A is best, D worst.

Analysing this table, project 1, which offers a breakthrough opportunity with an above average even chance of success, gets priority A, even though gestation time is five years. Project 2 also gains top priority because, despite its marginal market potential, it involves no technical challenge and can be developed very quickly. Project 3 is also worth pursuing, but projects 4, 5 and 6 would be dropped.

An orderly approach to priority setting will reduce waste, but it will not eliminate it because research is a creative rather than a mechanical process. Risk and reward are often interrelated, as in business itself, and the most difficult technical project may also hold the highest market potential. However, throughout this section we are focusing on products as a means to consumer benefits, rather than as ends in themselves, and it is often possible to identify a major new benefit which involves little technical challenge. The Carnation Instant Breakfast case in Chapter 7 was one example, and a number of others are given in Chapter 15, 'New Products— the Difference between Success and Failure'. This principle can apply to industrial markets as well as to consumer products, as Scaffolding Great Britain discovered.

The SGB group of companies now operates in a number of diversified markets, but it originated as the innovator of the steel scaffold.

In the early 1900s, all scaffolds were made of timber lashed together. This was neither particularly efficient nor economic as a scaffolding method. An improvement over lashing as a means of joining the timber was made in 1909, when the scaffixer tie, a friction fitting method, was invented. However, scaffolds continued to be made of wood.

A few years later, the founder of SGB noticed some tubular steel gas pipes and decided to try them out as scaffolds. They proved much more efficient than wood, which rapidly became obsolete. To this day, steel scaffolds and gas pipes are almost identical in specification—the main difference being that steel scaffolding is not pressure-tested.

In this case, an innovator picked up a product which had been around for a long time, and his stroke of inspiration was to use it as a structural member rather than as a pressure vessel.

2. PRODUCTS ARE PATHWAYS TO CONSUMER BENEFITS

A technical success may be of no interest to the consumer, and the Booz, Allen & Hamilton study already referred to concluded that for every three products emerging from R & D departments as technical successes, only one was a commercial success. Technical performance is certainly important, since every consumer wants a product to fulfil its purpose well, but it should not be viewed in isolation, since consumers are emotional as well as logical beings. A product which is regarded by scientists as being at technical parity with its competition, may nevertheless be regarded by consumers as superior for non-technical reasons.

Most people prefer brown eggs to white ones although they taste the same. That is why they buy brown eggs even though, in a free supply situation, they cost rather more than white eggs. Our urban society nostalgically associates the brown colour with country wholesomeness and is therefore prepared to pay more for brown eggs.

Consumers are also influenced by the derivation of a product. Faced by two products which are technically identical, they are likely to prefer the one containing the most natural materials or appearing the most home-made.

In the USA, Heinz white vinegar is easily the brand leader in spite of being priced 30-40% higher than its competitors on a unit weight basis, and even though in a blind test situation consumers cannot differentiate it from its competition. The basis for Heinz's leading market share is its long establishment and the natural derivation of its raw materials. Heinz is the only brand that can describe its vinegar as 'natural' on the label, being made from natural grain—mainly corn, barley and rye—whereas the majority of other producers derive their vinegar from industrial alcohol, synthesized from petroleum.

The other side of this coin is that formulations which clearly have technical superiority in the laboratory may be seen as parity products by the consumer.

Crest toothpaste undoubtedly has technical superiority in reducing tooth decay among children and arresting it among adults, through its stannous fluoride ingredient. This was proved by a long series of clinical tests at Columbia University, spread over a number of years and accepted by the American Dental Association. Unfortunately, efficiency in reducing cavities is extremely difficult to demonstrate to consumers, even over a very long period. And people have become so sceptical about exaggerated advertising claims that when a genuine one comes along, they are inclined to disbelieve it.

Crest was only a moderately successful brand in the USA, until the American Dental Association endorsed it, and it failed to make any impact in the UK, together with other fluoride toothpastes, which in total account for less than 7% of the UK toothpaste market.

Finally technical superiority may be achieved at the expense of some non-technical emotional benefit. This can add up to inferior consumer acceptance.

Technically Campbell's condensed soup offers much better *value* than Heinz ready-to-serve soup. It tastes good and is a lot less expensive—a plateful of Campbell's costs 25% less than a plateful of Heinz. Yet Campbell's share lags far behind Heinz.

Consumers have reservations about its product form, which involves adding milk or water. They are not convinced that it has the wholesomeness, richness and natural qualities of the ready-to-serve form.

3. SUPERIOR PRODUCT BENEFITS CAN USUALLY BE DEVELOPED

'Our trouble is that we're in a commodity market*—all that matters is price.'
'No, we don't aim for product superiority because we have tied distribution.'

In some markets—like many industrial goods, cars and consumer durables—it is easy to see how, with skilful marketing and R & D, superior products can be developed. For example, many products made by Hoover have distinctive features—its new automatic machine is very compact in size, its gas fire is the only one with an illuminated display shelf, and its fan heater is angled to cut down noise. But in many markets for fast-moving consumer goods and services, superior product benefits are hard to come by. One can either accept the difficulties as insoluble, and the quotations with which this section opened take that line, or one can follow a basic belief that product superiority can nearly always be developed. There is more hope in the latter approach, and it often pays off.

The major petrol companies in the UK (and elsewhere) have made little attempt to build superior consumer benefits into their petrol or oil products. They have tended to regard them as commodities, and with tied distribution, different brands of petrol rarely compete head-on.

While they have attracted little outside competition in petrol, except from low price producers, the major companies have failed to dominate the motor oil market. They were unable to prevent Duckham† gaining a 25% market share, despite its lack of any tied distribution outlets. Duckham innovated multi-grade oil, developed a distinctive product colour and aimed at the motoring enthusiast.

Nor have they been able to shake Castrol, the brand leader

*'Commodity market' is marketing slang for a market close to nature, where it is hard to build in product differences. Typical commodity markets in this sense are tinned fruit, flour, tea and sugar.
† Duckham was an independent company until 1969, when it was acquired by British Petroleum.

in oil, with a share of 30%. Castrol also aimed for superior consumer benefits, and its GTX is strongly branded, with a high performance image. Although Castrol is owned by Burmah Oil, it has no tied distribution outlets and, like Duckham, has built up distribution as a result of consumer demand and aggressive trade margin policy.

There are many other examples of successful efforts to develop superior benefits in commodity-like markets. In frozen peas, Birds Eye has in the past achieved superiority through the size, sweetness and tenderness of its product. In the American canned French beans market, Green Giant's beans are sliced diagonally, thereby justifying the claim that they are 'angle-sliced for freshness'. In the grocery store business, Sainsbury has built a reputation for the superiority of its meat. Fairy Snow had a significantly superior product compared with Persil in the mid-1960s due to its higher content of real soap (although in any *named* packet research comparison, Persil always won hands down, because its strong emotional image blurred Fairy Snow's actual *performance* superiority).

A good example of near-commodity market whose participants have successfully sought to develop superior products is instant mashed potato.

The instant mashed potato market was pioneered by the Mars subsidiary, Dornay Foods, through its brand Yeoman. But growth was slow and the market was worth less than £1 million at retail prices as recently as 1966.

This was the year of Cadbury's entry with Smash, a de-hydrated mashed potato powder like Yeoman, but of better quality. Smash's product superiority and fine marketing enabled it rapidly to overtake Yeoman, and turned it into Cadbury's most profitable brand (ahead of Dairy Milk chocolate). In November 1970 Dornay Foods bounced back with Wonder-mash, which consisted of dehydrated pieces of mashed potato, claimed to taste better than powders and offering greater convenience in use. By early 1971 Wondermash had a 14% share and the instant mash market had expanded to around £10 million at retail prices.*

Perhaps the ultimate achievement is to build a product difference into water.

The bottled water category in the USA is worth £33 million

* Adapted from Gwen Nuttall, 'Will Smash get Mashed?' (*Sunday Times*, 21 February 1971).

annually and growing at 15–20% per year. It was given a boost
by a Federal Government study in August 1970, which showed
that 2·9 million out of a total of the 18 million people in the
sample were drinking water which was either dangerously
contaminated or inferior in colour, taste or odour.

The premium brands of bottled waters like Vichy and Perrier
are priced at 20–30p per quart [21–32p per litre]. Distilled tap
water retails at 8p per quart [8½p per litre]. Among the major
companies which have made acquisitions or carried out tests
in this market are Nestlé, Coca-Cola and Canada Dry. In
Los Angeles, which is very often the pace-setter in new
trends, 1 person in 6 drinks bottled water, compared with 1 in
200 in the remainder of America.★

Outlined in Table 9.2 is an inventory of consumer benefits,
which can be used as a check-list when searching for ways to differentiate or improve products. Although it is oriented primarily
towards fast-moving consumer markets, it is by no means exhaustive even for this category. Many of the benefits listed merely
summarize a cluster of possible improvement areas. For instance
'protective finish' covers non-stick, non-scratch, non-staining,
heat or dirt repellent, and flavour sealing.

TABLE 9.2   INVENTORY OF PRODUCT IMPROVEMENT
BENEFITS†

Category	Examples	Benefits
Convenience	Vesta meals: speed/ ease of preparation Polaroid cameras: speed of result Shift oven cleaner: speed/ease of use	Speed/ease of use, preparation, serving, disposal or dispensing from packet
Physical dimensions	Chunky dogmeat: shape of meat Mercedes 111: product styling Spillers Bonio: product shape	Thickness, size, shape, styling of product/pack [continued overleaf

★ Adapted from an article in *Business Week*.
† I am indebted for this basic approach to Mr J. E. Smilow, President of
International Playtex Corporation.

TABLE 9.2—cont.

Category	Examples	Benefits
Objective physical characteristics	Homepride flour: fineness/lightness Ariel washing powder: stain removal Playtex Living Bra: elasticity Fairy Liquid: mildness	Durability, shock-resistance, consistency, protective finish, stain removal, cleaning, water proof, colour, strength, absorbency, viscosity, safety, perforation, mildness, elasticity, smooth/lumpy, portion control, easier storage, transparent/opaque, insulation, longevity
Subjective physical characteristics	Wall's Cornish ices: enriched Tuc or Ritz crackers: unique texture Hartley's New Jam: taste Kodak Super 8 movie camera: more reliable results	Softness, taste, texture, freshness, crispness, comfort in use, smell, hotness, sweetness, purity, enriched, lightness, fashion, aesthetic appeal, more reliable results, versatility, personal hygiene
Health benefits	Sanka coffee (US): caffeine free Polyunsaturated fats: low in cholesterol Special K cereal: high in protein Mick dogfood: with calcium	Germicidal, calorie reducing, low in cholesterol, low in tar/nicotine, vitamins, insect repellant, protein, antiseptic, caffeine free, elimination of negative after-effects
Process types	Keg bitter: pasteurized Vesta meals: freeze-dried Maltesers/Aero: aeration Nescafé coffee: agglomerated	Sterilized, pasteurized, freeze-dried, air-dried, frozen, agglomerated, carbonated, homogenized, aerated
Product combinations	Harvey's Duo-Can (canned meat & rice) Quaker Sugar Puffs (cereal and sugar) Dual (cleans and polishes floors)	Various

4. BELIEVE THAT SMALL DIFFERENCES CAN MATTER

Apparently minor differences in product performance, which may even be spurned by a company's management as unimportant, can be significant to the consumer, especially in product categories with high purchase frequency. The expertise of the consumer is often underrated, especially by consumer protection bodies, who are too prone to regard her (or him) as naïve and easily deceived. On the contrary, the housewife can develop an expertise rivalling that of the industrial buyer in evaluating frequently purchased products.

But small differences only matter if they are in areas of importance to the consumer* and well exploited in advertising. Spillers Homepride flour illustrates this point well.

> During the 1950s Spillers rationalized all but its strongest local brands under the name of Spillers Flour but this move did no more than stabilize its market share. Until the early 1960s Spillers flour had parity consumer acceptance to McDougall, the then brand leader.
>
> In February 1963, Spillers flour was relaunched under the new name Homepride with a marginally superior product, which was preferred to McDougall by 55 : 45 on blind test, a preference which was statistically non-significant. The basis for the slight preference in favour of Spillers was its better texture. The relaunch advertising for Homepride stressed the traditional benefit of the baking end result, with only secondary emphasis on fineness of texture. At this time, Homepride had a 7% share of market, compared with 30% for McDougall.
>
> A new product management team arrived in spring 1963. After analysing a major consumer usage and attitude study on the flour market, it concluded that Spillers' advertising was based on the wrong strategy. This research showed that consumers did not regard flour as an important influence on the final baking end result (usually scones or cakes). Factors like oven temperature, age of eggs, the balance of liquid and dry ingredients and the use of butter versus shortening were the ones that mattered most. The new team concluded from this that

---

* This may sound like a contradiction in terms, but it isn't. For instance, in the washing powder market, a small improvement in whiteness performance may be important to the consumer because whiteness is the main benefit sought from the product.

advertising which positioned flour as having a major effect on the end result was not credible to the consumer, and therefore ineffective. Another conclusion drawn from this research was that fineness of texture and absence of lumpiness carried most weight with consumers in determining their choice of brand. This tallied with technical tests, which showed that a finer flour improved the rising, texture, and taste of baked products, though only slightly.

The spring 1963 relaunch had produced unimpressive results for Homepride, and by the end of the summer the brand's share had only lifted marginally despite a major increase in advertising level, which confirmed the diagnosis the new team had already made. Consequently the advertising was changed to a 'texture' strategy in the autumn and brand share began to lift dramatically. But Spillers was still not satisfied with the quality of the advertising execution, and changed its agency. The new one, Geers Gross, developed the 'flour graders' campaign at the end of 1964, and this has been runnning ever since. The main claim was 'Graded grains make finer flour', and the small cartoon characters in bowler hats who were a central feature of the commercial became widely known.

Spillers gained brand leadership of this declining market in 1970. Its share had increased from 7% to 30% in six years. It had exploited a small product difference very effectively.

5. LOOK FOR PROFIT IMPROVEMENTS

One should, of course, be continually seeking profit improvements in every part of the marketing mix, but there is often a reluctance to reduce the cost of the product due to a concern that quality will be affected. This reluctance is understandable, because examples of brands which have been downgraded, through lack of adherence to high quality standards, are not uncommon. But it is not valid, because there may be opportunities to reduce the cost of a product without affecting consumer acceptance.

The reformulation of Andrews Liver Salts in the mid 1960s illustrates the combination of bold thinking, but cautious and persistent testing, that is necessary to carry out such a move successfully.

Andrews Liver Salts was first sold by Scott & Turner* in New-

* Scott & Turner merged with the Chas H. Phillips Chemical Co. in 1960 to form the Phillips Scott & Turner Co., a wholly-owned subsidiary of Sterling Drug International.

castle upon Tyne in 1894. It grew steadily throughout the 1920s and 1930s but slowed down in the 1940s and by the mid-1950s had begun to decline in volume terms. However, it remained the brand leader of the 'stomach remedies' market, followed by Alka-Seltzer.

The Andrews formula, consisting of a mixture of sugar, tartaric acid, bicarbonate of soda and Epsom salts, had remained basically unaltered since the 1890s. Phillips Scott & Turner did not think it could be significantly improved, since it was very efficient both as a laxative and as an indigestion remedy. So it concentrated on seeking lower cost formulations which would achieve an equally good result. This approach helped stave off price increases, an important factor for Andrews since low price had been a key element in its past success.

The attempt to substitute citric acid for tartaric acid is one example of this approach. By the early 1960s tartaric acid was becoming increasingly expensive and in short supply. From a technical viewpoint, citric seemed to be a good substitute and a reformulated version of Andrews using citric rather than tartaric acid was tried out in one part of the country. When some letters came in from consumers, complaining that Andrews was 'not what it used to be', the company decided to carry out a sensitive consumer research comparison between the two alternative formulations. This research showed a clear rejection of citric acid by the Andrews user, and it was decided not to use it. However, further testing with a 50 : 50 combination of tartaric and citric acid proved acceptable, and this new formulation was adopted, giving a worthwhile saving in cost.*

SUMMARY

Product development is the most important activity in which marketing men are involved, because it has the greatest long-term impact on corporate profit. Five principles of offensive product development are summarized below.

(1) *Give priority to priority setting.* A decision should be made as to how to allocate R & D priority between genuinely innovative work and maintenance activity. Priorities should then be set for individual projects.

(2) *Products are pathways to consumer benefits.* Technical product

* Adapted from *British Cases in Marketing*, edited by J. S. Bingham (Business Books, 1969). The Andrews case was written by John Usher.

performance should not be viewed in isolation, since consumers have emotional as well as logical needs.

(3) *Superior product benefits can usually be developed.* This principle applies to any market, however close it is to nature.

(4) *Believe that small differences can matter.* They can be powerful profit-builders, if they are in performance areas that matter to the consumer.

(5) *Look for profit improvements.* Even if the product cannot be improved, its cost can often be reduced without impairing performance.

10:   *Market Research*

Market research enables a company to keep in touch with what consumers think about its products and those of its competitors, and to monitor their actions in the market place. It provides reasonably objective information on which to base decisions and forms a lifeline between the consumer and the firm. The key questions which market research usually answers quite well are:

(1) How do consumers evaluate our products against those of competitors?
(2) What are they looking for in this market and how far are we providing this effectively?
(3) How are consumer tastes changing?
(4) What are consumers buying in the market place, from whom, and why?
(5) How do consumers react to these new ideas we have thought up?

The techniques used are, of course, very widespread. A major one is the *product blind test*, in which two competing brands are evaluated by consumers in blank packets so that their reaction to the product itself, shorn of packaging, advertising and all the other attributes of the image, can be assessed. Then there is the *usage and attitude study*, which questions consumers about their habits and reactions to particular products in the market. And equally important are the two main ways of checking consumer purchases in the market place—the *consumer panel*, in which the purchases of a few thousand women are recorded, usually by keeping a detailed purchase diary, and the *retail panel*, in which actual sales out of shops are measured by auditors who regularly compare purchase invoices with stocks. Most consumer goods companies subscribe to at least one service for measuring sales out of shops, and usually receive continuous information on a four-weeekly or eight-weekly basis. In addition to telling you what your own share of the market is and how it is changing, retail and consumer panels also provide other useful data like levels of trade distribution, actual prices, proportion of promoted product moved out, brand loyalty levels and brand switching trends. From these figures, you can not only keep a beady eye on what is happening in the market, but will also be able to deduce why it is happening.

The underlying principle of market research is that a well selected sample of a few hundred people (or retail stores) will fairly accurately reflect the views and behaviour of a whole market. The level of precision will depend on the size of the sample, the sample selection method and the quality of the interviewing. This basic principle was brought into serious question both by the press and the public at large, following the unsuccessful efforts of many market research firms to forecast the 1970 UK General Election result correctly. Their lack of accuracy underlines the importance of size and selection of samples, but does not challenge the usefulness of market research as a business tool. Apart from the 1948 American Presidential Election and the most recent UK one, the efforts of pollsters on both sides of the Atlantic have been of a high standard. And whereas poll forecasts are expected to be within $\pm 1\%$ of actual, research with a $\pm 3\%$ accuracy is usually adequate for most business decisions.

As with any other specialist activity, the marketing man must understand the basic principles of research, appreciate its value and limitations, and know enough to be capable of cross-examining the research experts on the suitability of any particular technique they propose. With that preamble, let us take a look at 6 principles of offensive market research:

1. RESEARCH PRODUCES DATA, NOT DECISIONS

Research is a device for improving the quality of the information on which decisions are based. It is not a substitute for decisions, although it can make decisions easier and more certain. Market research is sometimes wrongly regarded by executives as a kind of 'answer machine' into which they can drop any questions or problems which bother them, in the hope that it will make judgement unnecessary. Applied in this way, research is bound to be misused and stretched beyond its capabilities.

A few years ago, a UK food company, which is now trading quite successfully, got itself into a terrible fix. It was producing a good turnover but making a net loss. After having done no product blind testing between 1960 and 1966, it had the shock of its life when its largest brand lost by a 30 : 70 margin on blind test against a major competitor. What is more, its inferior product was premium priced.

The product was rapidly improved, and some research undertaken to try to provide guidance to the sorely worried management team. The big question, of course, was whether to reduce the price and, if so, by how much. Three research studies were carried out, and these purported to show the following results:

(*a*) There was little consciousness among retailers of the brand's unfavourable price.

(*b*) Consumers had little awareness of the differences in prices between the various brands in the market. This deduction was based on direct questioning of consumers about their knowledge of prices, through interviews conducted in the home.

(*c*) An experimental study also apparently suggested that price was unimportant. Two packets of the brand were exposed to the consumer, each marked with different prices (there was a 10% difference between the two prices). Consumers were asked which one they were most likely to buy, and showed no preference between the two differently priced packets.*

Opinion within the company was divided as to what action should be taken, and it was undoubtedly a critical decision. One camp was opposed to cutting the price. They argued that a price cut would only be viable if volume increased substantially, and instanced the three research studies as clear evidence that it would not. In addition, they felt that the brand's higher prices had in the past helped it establish a feeling of premium quality among its own users.

The other camp strongly favoured a price cut. They agreed that a large increase in volume was necessary to justify a price reduction, but felt confident that this would happen. The argu-

---

* This strange result was probably due to consumer confusion about the question. Consumers no doubt thought the interviewer wanted to know if they saw any difference between the two products, and therefore ignored the obvious price difference. It was another bad piece of research.

ment they put forward was based on general principles—
the product was frequently purchased and in a high turnover
food category, and it could therefore be assumed that consumers
would be sensitive about price; in addition, a marketing policy
based on premium pricing a Number Two brand, whose
product acceptance was at best on a par with the brand leader,
was untenable; and thirdly, the premium pricing would not
enhance the image of a fast-moving food brand (unlike a
cosmetic or fashion product.)

They also dismissed the three research studies as useless and
misleading, saying that research on pricing is never effective
because it deals with a speculative future situation, and that
making predictions for researchers and making actual purchase
decisions were two entirely different things. Furthermore,
the inability of consumers to recall actual prices in the home
did not prevent them from observing them in the store.

Fortunately, the second camp won out, and the prices were
reduced. As expected, volume rose sharply, and the company
moved back into a profitable position. The moral is that the decision
could have been made without doing any research, just by following
general business principles and using common sense, as the successful opinion group in the company did.

Research can also be wrongly exploited as a delaying tactic
for postponing hard but obvious decisions. The weak manager
uses research in the same way as the politician uses Royal Commis-
sions.

2. LOOK FOR THE ACTION

Every market raises questions which it would be interesting to
research. But unless the research is likely to lead to action, it is
not worth doing, because business is run for profit, not for the
interest of employees. Each piece of research should be related to
a specific decision, to which the results of the research will contribute.
The Procter & Gamble practice of insisting that every research
request has an 'expected use of results' paragraph is a sound one.
Ironically, the case below, showing how not to do it, concerns a
P & G product, although P & G neither authorized nor paid for the
research.

In 1961–2 P & G tested out Mr Clean, a straw coloured household cleaning liquid, competitive with Handy Andy and Flash. The test was in the Tyne–Tees TV area and Mr Clean soon outstripped Handy Andy, gaining a 25–30% share of the household cleaning market. It was not expanded nationally, however, because it took most of its business from Flash, another P & G brand.

The Mr Clean brand was American in origin and still flourishes there. (In fact, the leading Democratic challenger for the Presidential Election, Senator Muskie, is known as 'Mr Clean' because of his achievements in enacting anti-pollution legislation.) The 'real' Mr Clean, a bald-headed, virile-looking cartoon character of distinctly Mongolian appearance, was the focus of the whole brand. He personified its cleaning efficiency, dominated the advertising and was featured on the package.

The advertising agency, with commendable enterprise but unclear objectives, decided to do some broad-ranging research on consumer attitudes to Mr Clean. People were invited to look upon him as a real person and to let their imaginations roam. Had he fought in the Korean War? What rank had he held? Who did he most look like? How many children did he have? The answers were fascinating. Most consumers thought he had been an NCO but not an officer. Quite a few guessed that he had ten or more children, a tribute to his virility. Many believed he looked like Mr Kruschev, and an inspired 1% said 'he looks like the head of your firm'.

The research was imaginatively conceived, and very interesting to the agency and to lower level company personnel like myself. But it did not contribute to any action, and it is difficult to see how it ever could have done.

3. THE BEST INFORMATION MAY COST NOTHING

Potentially first class internal company data about sales, consumer complaints or selling efficiency may never see the light of day just because they have not been analysed. Every organization keeps records of monthly sales on a national basis. There are numerous ways in which these data can be usefully broken down: by sales district or unit, by TV area, by major outlet type, size of customer or individual products and by sizes and varieties. And regular analysis of these raw data often pinpoints new problems and opportunities, as the example below shows.

Following two quite stable years, sales of a US brand began to fall away, and during the period of January–June they were 16% below the corresponding period in 1966.

The company in question had excellent internal data break-downs. Sales were analysed by territory, and it was dis-covered that five territories (out of 150 in the whole country) accounted for three-quarters of the brand's national deficit. The five salesmen in question had excessively loaded the trade on a bonus the previous December, and consequently had to accept a large amount of returned product during January–June 1967. Outside these five territories, the brand was only 3% behind the previous year and, in relation to its very limited marketing spending support, was reasonably healthy.

There are other fruitful sources of internal data. A careful tabulation of letters of consumer complaint and appreciation can provide a gauge of quality control effectiveness. Analysis of sales-men's reports yields stop press information on average daily call rates, sales per call, distribution gains and losses, and display levels. A great deal of potentially actionable financial data is often left unprocessed or is circulated to the wrong people.

In addition, there is usually a considerable amount of valuable published data about all markets. It varies from government statistics and reports to general interest newspaper articles and again to trade journals. The variety is such that one can often initially screen the potential of a possible new market without spending more than £100.

Most firms could probably make better use of internal and low-priced external data, but one hopes that the horror story below is untypical.

> This major American company had no sales breakdown of its products by variety, geographical area or type of account. There were no data on the minimum breakeven volume for new lines, nor any information on profitability by type of product. Facts were entirely lacking on who bought the product, attitudes to the company and its brands, and reasons for purchase. Nor did the company know its market share, even on a national basis.
> Almost unbelievably, they are still in business!

4. SEE THE PEOPLE BEHIND THE NUMBERS

The impact of a legal case, especially one involving a jury, can only be dimly communicated in the Law Reports. Many of the incidents will have been omitted, the atmosphere of the court is absent, the appearance and manner of the participants is not described, and there is no reference to the demeanour of the accused or the witnesses.

Equally, a research report can only be fully appreciated by businessmen with up-to-date and first-hand knowledge of their company's customers. Marketing men are sometimes justifiably accused of being 'chair-borne' and more in tune with their own Chelsea or Park Avenue set than with typical consumers. It is important to get out 'where the rubber meets the road', to use an American phrase, and to talk frequently to consumers and the trade if only to gain a background 'feel' in interpreting formal research. Marks & Spencer, with its northern origins, keeps very closely in touch with its grass roots. As Lord Sieff put it: 'Most of our stores are in places like Wigan, and middle aged men in Wigan do not wear yellow shirts.'*

Professionally conducted research and informal customer contact should be run in harness, since each has limited value in isolation.

5. GOOD RESEARCH REQUIRES IMAGINATION

The objective of much research is to uncover consumer attitudes and feelings. Although the means of measuring these may be highly mechanical, the thinking behind the technique and the questioning must be imaginative.

Consumers rarely analyse their real reasons for buying even major commitments like cars and houses, never mind instant coffee and tinned fruit. For example, if you ask a housewife a direct question about why she buys a particular brand, you are likely to get this kind of playback, which tells you nothing:

Reason for using last brand	%
Always used	20
Mother/relative used/recommended	15
Saw advertising	10
Recommended by friend/neighbour	14
Bought on special price offer	12
No particular reason	21
No answer or don't know	8
	100

* Goronwy Rees, *St Michael: a History of Marks & Spencer.*

Finding out what the consumer really thinks involves more than throwing a broadly directed question at her. In order to bring out real as opposed to surface motivations, the interviewer has to stimulate the consumer's interest, and this requires a creative approach. Some examples of imaginative techniques were given on page 55. This need for imagination in research is often overlooked by marketing people who reserve all their creativity for advertising, promotions and packaging.

6. BLIND TEST . . . WITH YOUR EYES OPEN

I have a complex about blind testing, probably because I have seen so many invalid examples of it in the past four years. A blind test result is very important. It tells you whether or not your brand has that much prized asset of product superiority. And if the answer is positive, you are likely to make important investment decisions on the basis of it. For a new brand, a blind test win represents 'permission to move into the market place'.* For an existing brand, a blind test result may determine the amount of marketing support received, since companies are rightly prepared to back superior products more heavily than parity ones.

When I add that blind testing is simple and inexpensive, any logical bystander knowing nothing about marketing will be astonished to hear that many large consumer goods companies do either very little blind testing or none at all, and that some of those which do employ blind testing use invalid techniques. Here is an example of the latter.

An American food company conducted an invalid blind test, which purported to give its new product a 70 : 30 win over its competitors. It was invalid because the base of consumers was only 100, the test was conducted in a hall rather than in the housewife's home, and the method of use specified bore no relation to normal consumer habits. Based on this blind test 'win', the company decided to deliver samples of its 'superior' product to some millions of homes at a cost of £200 000. The sampling operation proved a total failure because, having tried the sample, only a very small proportion of consumers subsequently purchased the product in a store.

The poor response of this brand to sampling, its inability

* This apt phrase comes from George Scott, Manager of R & D at Procter & Gamble.

to transform new triers into regular users, and the results of technical assessments all indicated that the product was at best on parity with competition. A properly run blind test would have shown this, and enabled the company to save the money it wasted on sampling.

While this is probably an exceptional example, invalid blind testing is by no means restricted to a few unfortunate cases, and the main errors are made as follows:*

(*a*) Consumers are given special usage instructions, instead of being allowed to use the product according to their normal habits. For example, telling a mother to taste a babyfood would be invalid, because many mothers never do this but give the product to their babies straight away.

(*b*) Consumers are prompted and their attention directed to particular performance areas. This type of direct questioning is less valid than the consumer's unprompted response to products.

(*c*) Products of uneven age are compared. Sometimes the company product is taken fresh from the factory, while samples of the competitive brand are bought in the market place. This naturally favours the company product.

Because of the importance of good blind testing to offensive marketing, the basic principles governing valid techniques have been listed in Appendix E.

SUMMARY

Market research provides reasonably objective information on which to base decisions and forms a lifeline between the consumer and the firm. It is not a substitute for decisions, although it can make them easier and more certain. Any piece of research should be related to an expected use of results. It is unbusinesslike to conduct research merely for the sake of interest.

Some of the most useful information available to a company—about sales, consumer complaints or selling effectiveness—costs very little to process but often lies neglected in department files.

Research is about the opinions and reactions of people and the

* And beware of the 'majority fallacy'—see Chapter 17, on market segmentation.

numbers in research reports will have most meaning for readers who are themselves closely in touch with events in the market place, on a first hand basis. Consumers rarely give much thought to their reasons for buying products, and any form of research requires imagination if it is to penetrate beyond their surface motivations.

Blind testing is important because the results may dictate major marketing investment decisions. Unfortunately, a considerable amount of invalid blind testing seems to be conducted, but this can be avoided if a number of simple principles are followed.

11: *Pricing*

A. BASIC PRINCIPLES

Together with product performance, pricing is the main determinant of a brand's value to the consumer. In making a purchase decision, three questions are likely to flit through his or her mind, albeit often unconsciously:

(1) What do I think of the product compared with the alternatives?
(2) How is it priced compared with the alternatives?
(3) How much do I get for my money?

Pricing is a very comparative affair. If consumers reckon your product is better than competitive ones, they will pay more for it, but otherwise they will not. Advertising and promotions play their part in influencing the consumer too, and a really good package can take a brand a long way, but for most brands the rating of its product and price is the most important factor.

With the rise of private label brands,* price is becoming an increasingly important influence on purchase decisions. Should the housewife buy the heavily advertised brand made by a major manufacturer, or should she go for the cheaper brand with the retailer's own brand label? When she cannot tell much difference between the quality of the two brands, and will perhaps save 20% by buying the private label brand, this becomes a relevant question. Tesco and Fine Fare each have about 400 private label lines and these account for 12–15% of their total turnover. Sainsbury's private brands clock up over 30% of its turnover. There is some evidence that purchasers of these brands are younger and better off than average, and perhaps in the 1970s and 1980s, as consumers become more discriminating and better educated, price will gain further in importance.

* Brands with the retailer's label on, e.g. Tesco Instant Coffee—produced for the retailer by a manufacturer.

Pricing is one of the most difficult marketing decision areas, because there are so many variables involved. The reaction of three groups has to be considered before setting or changing a price— consumers, the trade and competitors. There is no more un- comfortable situation than making a price increase in the expectation that your competitor will follow, and then finding that he does not. Or alternatively, all brands in a market may raise their prices only to discover that everyone has lost profit, because adverse consumer reaction has caused the value of the whole market to drop. So the response of those groups and their interaction are hard to read. And pricing decisions often have to be taken quickly without test- ing, but usually have a major effect on profit . . . one way or the the other. This all places a high premium on good management.

The most favoured approaches to pricing are cost-plus and demand-pricing.

Cost-plus involves taking your costs and adding on a fixed percentage for profits. It is used most by retailers and heavy industry, less often by packaged goods manufacturers. The advantages it carries are simplicity and, quite probably, less price competition between companies. But the drawbacks of the method are over- whelming for manufacturers in highly competitive markets, since it does not take into account consumer or competitive reaction. A company putting up its prices just because its costs have risen may be leading with its chin if its competitors do not follow. This happened to Spillers in the petfood market in the mid 1960s. Even though it was only Number Two in the market, it raised its prices when costs of raw materials shot up. Petfoods responded by holding its prices and advertising its advantage, thereby gaining a major share increase.

The other trouble with cost-plus is that it takes no account of the demand curve for the brand or the category. A rise in price due to cost pressure could reduce profit if sales revenue fell heavily. And in a number of markets today—cakes and crisps, for instance— a 5% rise in price by all brands would probably result in a volume fall of over 5%, thereby reducing profit for all.

Demand-pricing is the better method, because it takes market response into account. The only justification for a price increase is that it will increase profit, and unless a company is badly strapped for cash or is deliberately milking a brand, profit should be looked at from a longer term viewpoint.

With this method of pricing, one wants to know what would happen to the sales revenue trend if the price were increased by

10%—whether it would remain stable or fall so heavily that a price increase would reduce profit. If a price increase could be expected to deflate profit, it should obviously not be pursued. And if rising costs are a big problem, the solution should be found through means that seem more likely to increase profit, like perhaps cutting costs, or reducing the marketing budget. In essence, demand-pricing ignores cost. If an increase in price looked likely to raise long-term profit, it would be adopted, even though costs remained stable or even declined. Value rather than cost is what determines pricing.

No one faces pricing decisions with 100% confidence, but the pursuit of five principles of offensive pricing outlined below should increase the likelihood of effective decision making in this area.

1. KNOW YOUR PRICE DYNAMICS

Although pricing decisions often have to be taken quickly, the quality of even very fast decision making can be vastly improved by having a long and hard look at the price dynamics of a market beforehand. One should never be in the position of not really knowing whether price matters in one's market, like the people involved in the food case history on page 159.

Before embarking on the details of this examination, let us underline the important distinction between markets and brands. A total market may be insensitive to price changes while consumers may be very price-conscious between individual brands, or the reverse. The cigarette market is in the former position.

The total market for cigarettes is very price inelastic. Unit consumption of the market has been growing at 2–3% per annum over the past few years, despite increases in duty and manufacturer prices.

However, the price elasticity of *individual cigarette brands* is very high. Price is an important determinant of brand choice, together with image and coupon schemes. As prices have increased in recent years, consumers have traded down to smaller and less expensive cigarettes, and although there has been growth in the number of cigarettes bought, total tonnage of tobacco consumption has declined.

So any analysis of price dynamics should query not only the effect of price changes on the volume of a brand but also how the total market responds to price changes.

The application of general common sense principles is a good start. *Frequency of purchase* has a major influence on the sensitivity of individual brands to price changes. Brands in markets where frequency of purchase is high—like babyfoods, cigarettes, petrol, bread and tea—tend to be very price sensitive. *Degree of necessity* affects markets rather than brands within them. If a product category is very necessary to its users, changes in the prices of all brands are unlikely to affect its size—we have already seen this principle operating in the cigarette market and it also applies to petrol. But discretionary markets—like crisps, ice cream, cake or even consumer durables and cars—are adversely affected by general price increases. *Unit price* is another factor—high priced items like holidays, cars, furniture and consumer durables tend to be subject to long deliberation and considerable price-consciousness, although status and styling may also affect the outcome. *Degree of comparability* also influences the price sensitivity of brands—consumers are less price-conscious about cereals than about most other grocery products, because cereals are so different from each other. *Degree of fashion or status* affects pricing, but very often in reverse—some fashion or cosmetic brands use high price as a way of establishing quality. Table 11.1 illustrates the operation of these general principles on a number of rather different markets.

TABLE 11.1 FACTORS INFLUENCING IMPORTANCE OF PRICE, BY MARKET				
	MASS MARKET			
	Babyfoods	*Toys*	*Bread*	*Cars*
Purchase frequency	V. high	Low	High	Low
Necessity	High	Medium	High	Medium
Unit cost	Low	Medium	Low	High
Comparability	High	Medium	High	Medium
Fashion	Low	Medium	Low	High
Importance of pricing:				
on markets	Medium	Medium	Medium	High
on brands	High	Medium	High	Medium

You can draw some general conclusions about the likely price sensitivity of your brand and market in about five minutes flat, by applying these broad principles. Add to this some close analysis of the effect of previous price changes in your own market, and you may be able to draw a rough graph showing the effect of in-

creases or decreases in your brand's price on its profitability. This
background knowledge helps take the ulcers out of pricing decisions.

2. CONSIDER THE ALTERNATIVES

Pricing is often regarded as a somewhat mechanical aspect of
marketing, but in fact it provides plenty of opportunity for creativity, and this can pay off handsomely. For a start, price is only one
part of the marketing mix, and the profitability of a change in price
should be compared with all the other viable alternatives. Suppose,
for example, that a 10% increase in price was being considered,
and say that it was expected to bring in £300 000 extra sales revenue
and £100 000 additional net profit. Before recommending such
an increase, it would make sense to consider whether various other
possible combinations would raise profit by more than £100 000,
like these:

(a) Increase the price by 5% and run an extra major promotion.
(b) Hold the price and reduce the advertising by £150 000.
(c) Raise the price 15% and adopt a major product improve-
    ment.

Even when it has been agreed to follow the price increase route,
the alternative ways of implementing it may be numerous. Among
the possibilities might be:

(a) Hold the price but reduce the product weight by, say, 20%.
(b) Maintain the weight and raise the price by 10%.
(c) Raise the price by 5%, reduce the product weight by,
    say, 10%.
(d) Improve the package design and marginally improve the
    product (without adding much to its cost) concurrently
    with a price rise of 11%.
(e) In certain industrial markets, other options can be exam-
    ined, like altering the ratio between down payments and
    rental charges, or changing the conditions of free main-
    tenance or technical assistance.

3. BEWARE OF PROFIT CANNIBALIZATION

The development of private label brands has already been referred
to, and another major trend in packaged goods marketing in the
past twenty years has been the growth of larger sized units of purchase. We haven't quite reached the point of a drive-away truck of
washing powder, but the multi-packs and economy sizes are taking
over in many grocery categories.

These trends are a challenge to the manufacturer. Can he gain business by introducing lower priced versions of his own brands or by manufacturing for private label supply? The answer is undoubtedly a resounding 'Yes', but when the question is rephrased to 'Can he increase profit?' the answer is much less audible. A similar problem/opportunity situation faces the manufacturer in relation to larger sizes. He has to give the consumer a lower price in relation to weight on bigger sizes, but can this be done without reducing profit?

This is what profit cannibalization is all about—it happens when a company allows its lower profit brands or sizes to take business from its higher profit ones, thereby reducing its profitability in the market as a whole. As with all the more difficult marketing questions, there are no magic formulae for exploiting these opportunities in one's favour, but a few general guidelines can help, as indicated below.

Private Label

The subject of private label is a vexed one, and keeps many manufacturers awake at night as they see the shares of their brand leaders being eaten away by low priced competition. A great deal of emotion is expended on the issue, and private label brands are sometimes accused of being parasitic, in that they merely feed on the innovation of others—namely, the manufacturers. Let me therefore make it quite clear that I am very much in favour of private label brands as an economic phenomenon. They usually give consumers good value for money and by introducing strong price competition they prevent manufacturer brands with a dominant share of market from becoming fat and complacent.

A quick profile of private label is in order here. A private label brand can usually price itself some 10–25% below the brand leader, because it has no selling, advertising or promotion costs, and may make further savings through lower cost formulations and packaging. Its product quality will probably not be far behind that of the brand leader, and it may even be on a par. The brand leader will usually retain its leadership position, even though it may lose share if private label is particularly strong, because it got into the market first, has a better image and may have a superior product. Private label brands do best in unsegmented* markets where products are not strongly differentiated—like the frozen food, instant coffee,

* Sugar and tea have very few segments, while babyfoods and soup have many. See Chapter 17 for detailed discussion of market segmentation.

baked beans, sugar, dishwashing liquid and fruit squash markets. By contrast, they do quite poorly in markets where status is important, like cigarettes or beauty aids, and in those which are heavily segmented—like cereals, babyfoods, confectionery, soup, shampoos and washing powders.

The first thing manufacturers want to know about private label competition is how to stop it. The options they usually consider are reducing the price of their leading brands to narrow the gap versus private label, or beefing up marketing spending. The answer usually reached is to hold price and to strengthen advertising and promotion. The hope is that advertising, in particular, will be successful in stressing the higher quality of the manufacturer's brand, so that consumers will continue to think it is worth paying extra for. In my experience this approach usually fails, because it takes advertising of remarkable skill to persuade consumers that an essentially parity performance product is worth 20% extra. Heavy advertising of average quality may arrest the development of private label, but will rarely drive it back.

If private label is very well established, the only way to take business from it is to develop unique new products, to differentiate existing ones, or to dream up a really outstanding advertising campaign (one that is just 'good' or 'very good' is not strong enough for this task). Where private label is already thriving, the introduction of a low priced brand by a manufacturer, to complement his premium price brand leader, is unlikely to succeed because the trade will probably refuse to stock it.

It is a lot easier to prevent the private label beanstalk from growing at all than to try to cut it down in its prime (few succeed in this gigantic feat). A manufacturer who pours a number of products on to the same market, each with a distinctive benefit, goes some way towards preventing private label growth because there is no single mass appeal brand for the private label operator to copy. If this is combined with the early introduction of a low priced brand by the manufacturer himself, the oportunity for private label will be slim indeed. The various petfoods companies of Mars apply this approach with great efficiency.

Petfoods Ltd is the brand leader in the UK canned petfood market, with a market share of around 60%. Its main brands are Chum, Pal, Lassie, Bounce, Chappie, Whiskas, Kit-E-Kat and Katkins. Effem GmbH is the brand leader in Germany, with over 90% of the canned petfood category. Pal, Chappie, Loyal,

Whiskas and Kit-E-Kat are its main brands. Both Petfoods and Effem are wholly-owned subsidiaries of the Mars organization, one of the largest privately owned companies in the world.

Their strategy is to segment each petfoods market by type of appeal with a multi-brand approach. The German dogfood market is a good example of this. Pal is premium priced, all meat, and its advertising majors on appetite appeal. Chappie is medium priced, offers complete nutrition, and stresses a health benefit. Loyal, by contrast, is low priced. In the UK, Petfoods has the market segmented in a more complicated way, but its floor price brands are Chappie (meat and cereal dogfood), Bounce (all meat dogfood) and Katkins (catfood), all of which are priced at the level private label would choose. There is little private label in either the UK or the German petfood markets.

But not every company could operate this system effectively. Petfoods and Effem can because they take a total marketing approach to business and, like Marks & Spencer, are very efficiently run organizations with low overheads.

To return to the title of this section—'Beware of Profit Cannibalization'—after this lengthy build-up, some readers may now be thinking 'Is it wise to introduce your own low priced competition to your higher priced brands? Surely there is a danger that you will switch consumers from your high profit to your low profit products?' This danger certainly exists, and some trading down of consumers will usually take place. But if there is a genuine market opportunity for a lower priced brand, someone will take advantage of it—if you don't, private label products or perhaps even other manufacturers will. And surely it is better to switch business from your own high profit brands to other ones on which you are making a profit, than to lose business to competition.

While the introduction of a low priced brand by a manufacturer will probably result in some switch in business from higher priced ones, it will, if successful, also expand the market or take volume from competition, thereby substantially increasing total company profit in the market. The typical profile of a good low priced entry is that its price and quality are comparable with private label, there is no advertising or promotion support,* and percentage

* You want it to be there on the shelf as a deterrent or alternative to private label. But don't advertise or promote it, because in that way you would really encourage consumers to trade down from your own higher priced brands. Cutting out advertising and promotion is also a means of keeping your price down.

profit* is the same as for other higher priced company brands. In summary, it is better to risk some element of profit cannibalization, and at least to share in the profits of the lower priced segment of the market, than to bury your head in the sand and ignore it.

The second matter which concerns manufacturers is whether they should produce for private label sale. This is no problem for a company with a low share of market and plenty of spare capacity—if the price is right, private label production is a good way to increase profits. But it is a more difficult question for a company which is already brand leader and is looking for a way to fill in spare capacity. On the one hand, by encouraging private label, it may cannibalize the sales of its own branded product. Against that, private label production offers a profit in its own right, and the fact of your turning it down won't stop other people taking up the opportunity. Never an easy question to resolve, and no magic formulae to help. The only sensible attitude is to be empirical rather than doctrinaire about private label and to examine it like any other profit opportunity. The decision will have short-term and long-term implications and these should both be examined. There will be a plus and minus on the balance sheet—the plus being the profit attributable to private label production, and the minus reflecting possible loss of business for the company's branded products. These should be compared as a basis for the decision and the plus element for private label ought to be considerable to make it worthwhile undertaking, because it is uncertain business and contributes nothing to the company's long-term consumer franchise.

Watching the Profit Mix

Profit cannibalization also raises important marketing issues, even where private label is not a problem, for companies with a number of competing brands in different price segments. A balance must be achieved between two extremes, which are most easily expressed in a negative form. You have to avoid unnecessarily trading down consumers to lower priced brands. And you have to be sufficiently aggressive in the lower end of the market to prevent competitors from taking it over.

The American motor car manufacturers faced this difficult dilemma throughout the 1960s and have only recently decided to compete strongly in the low priced sub-compact sector

---

* This, of course, results in lower *sterling* profit per pack sold for the low priced brand, compared with the higher priced ones.

dominated by Volkswagen and the Japanese. Their reluctance, which we have previously observed, was understandable because, by introducing their own sub-compacts, like the Ford Pinto and the General Motors Vega, they may appeal to users of their own higher priced cars as much as to the VW user. Consumers who would otherwise have bought a $3000 Chevrolet may instead go for a $2000 Vega. The question which is as yet unanswered is whether GM and Ford will take enough business from the imports and extra market growth to compensate for the loss of profit through trading down. According to *Business Week,*★ Detroit has to sell 5 small cars to generate the same profit as they would get from 3 big cars.

One company which seems to have handled a complex profit mix situation very well is Imperial Tobacco.

Imperial Tobacco is the market leader in the UK cigarette category, with a 66% share, through its Wills and Player companies. It markets an assortment of brands at different price levels, and although the quality and quantity of tobacco vary with the price paid, the absolute profit per pack sold is lower on the cheaper brands. Imperials' two leading brands are Wills Embassy, and Player's No. 6, both with shares of around 20%. Embassy is quite an expensive brand, costing 26p for 20, while Player's No. 6 is only 20p and dominates the low priced end of the market.

In the past twelve months Imperial has increased its market share from 65% to 68% and its 1969 profits (which include world wide sales) increased to £34·9 million. One of the reasons why Imperial appears to have achieved such good balance between competitiveness and profit mix is that its two subsidiary companies in the UK are completely separate organizations and compete quite strongly against each other.

Runaway Larger Sizes

In the mid-1960s, Fairy Snow giant size was returning a much lower % profit than its large and medium sizes, and yet the marketing strategy of the brand, in traditional style, gave special emphasis to developing sales of the giant size. In other words, the brand was placing most effort against its least profitable size as measured by profit per ton sold.

★ 11 April 1970.

The trouble here was that Fairy Snow was giving the consumer much too good a deal on the Giant size—enabling her to gain an economy of about 10% by buying giant as opposed to large size. The corresponding economy on Persil was under 2%, but consumers did not appear to recognize Fairy Snow's generosity, because the share of its sales accounted for by giant size was similar to that of the wise but tight-fisted Persil.

To Procter & Gamble's credit, they at least had good profit figures by size, and were fully aware of the problem. Many other companies are doing the same thing in blissful ignorance of the profit implications. The savings for the manufacturer in larger sizes are frequently rather lean and sometimes illusory. What is more, generous economies for the consumer on larger sizes are sometimes based on the expectations of market expansion and extra business gained from competition. All too often, these expectations are over-optimistic and not fulfilled.

The golden rule for the offensive marketer is to lead the introduction of larger sizes and to determine their price structure. This should only pass on to the consumer the actual economies that the company itself gains by producing the larger size—the main economy is likely to be in packaging. If this means only a 1–2% saving, so be it.

4. IF YOU MAKE A MISTAKE ON PRICING, ADMIT IT AND REMEDY IT FAST

Anyone can make a mistake on pricing, and the important thing is to face up to it and put it right—fast. There is usually no practical reason why this cannot be done. But it is difficult to put into effect, because neither people nor companies like to admit they have made mistakes. The irony is that mistakes don't matter too much if they're spotted and remedied quickly. This of course, applies to every area of the business—as one executive with wide experience in acquisitions said: 'The key is to recognise a mistake early and then move quickly to cut losses.'[*]

5. USE MARKET-TESTING OFFENSIVELY

If analysis of past sales data, following previous price changes, does not provide a clear picture of a brand's price dynamics, this can be developed through small-scale testing in the market place,

---

[*] Stephen L. Bogardo, Assistant to the President of Esquire, in *The Business of Acquisitions and Mergers*, edited by G. Scott Hutchison.

in a small group of stores such as that provided by the Contimart Tyne-Tees Marketing Laboratory. Testing of price alternatives is quite frequently carried out by American companies but is much rarer in the UK. Although it does not take into account competitive reaction, it is a good way to measure consumer reaction to pricing changes and can provide valuable knowledge on which to base an offensive pricing policy.

B. CASE HISTORY ON OFFENSIVE PRICING— FAIRY LIQUID

By 1963, four years after launch, Fairy Liquid was clear brand leader with a 35% sterling share of the dishwashing market. It had just overtaken the combined share of all three Unilever brands—Sqezy, Lux Liquid and Quix. Fairy Liquid's success was due to its product superiority,* the mildness reputation of the Fairy name, and strong advertising on a mildness platform with a 'cleaning' reassurance. The brand was highly profitable and premium priced.

However, in 1963 it was not without problems, especially in pricing. There was a growing challenge from low priced and very diluted regional and private label brands. Unilever had acquired Sqezy, the second brand in the market, from Domestos in late 1961, and it was now being marketed more aggressively. It was rumoured that Unilever would attempt a Square Deal approach with Quix by reducing its price or increasing its weight. And the launch of Fairy Liquid giant size at 3s 6d ($17\frac{1}{2}$p) in 1962 had not done as well as expected.

The conclusion drawn by Fairy Liquid management was that the brand would have to improve its value in order to maintain long-term growth, and that the risk of a reduction in short-term profitability was worth taking to achieve this. It was therefore decided to reduce the brand's price per ounce to the consumer by about 14% without changing product quality. In order to squeeze the most out of this move, it was also determined to improve the size impression of the packaging and to rationalize the size structure, which no longer reflected the needs of the market. Before relaunch, Fairy Liquid had three sizes, broadly as follows:

* On launch in 1959, Fairy Liquid used a new base material—a mixture of two sulphate actives. It was a clear blind test winner over all competition, with big wins for mildness and lather.

Size	Price	% of brand turnover★
Medium	1s 6d (7½p)	18%
Large	2s 6d (12½p)	67%
Giant	3s 6d (17½p)	15%

The medium size was becoming increasingly irrelevant—a tiny bottle for 1s 6d. It was being shown up by Sqezy's large size, which cost only 2s (10p), held almost twice as much liquid, and was often promoted at 1s 9d (9p). Consequently, a decision was made to increase the weight of Fairy Liquid medium significantly by about 37%★ and to put the price up to 1s 9d. The objective was to gain a similar size impression to Sqezy, and although this was never quite achieved, Fairy Liquid medium began to look a much more competitive value.

The price of the large size, which had been selling very well, was held stable but its weight was increased by about 14%. On the giant size, weight was left unchanged but the price was reduced by 6d (2½p) to 3s (15p) because its somewhat disappointing launch in the previous year was largely attributed to the fact that 3s 6d was too high an absolute price for a washing up liquid.

To improve size impression, the Fairy Liquid bottle was made taller and slightly thinner on all sizes. The resulting changes in price/weight are shown below:

Size	Price Change	Weight Change★	Improvement in Consumer Value
Medium	+ 3d to 1s 9d	+ 37%	+ 15%
Large	No change	+ 14%	+ 14%
Giant	− 6d to 3s	No change	+ 14%

The better value Fairy Liquid was introduced in 1964, and this move improved long-term profit, giving the brand new momentum and keeping the cheap liquids at bay. Due to this and other skilful marketing moves before and after, Fairy Liquid's market share in 1970 was in the upper 30s. By contrast,

★ Since this case has been quoted from memory, some of these figures may not be exact, but they are very close.

no premium priced dishwashing liquid in Canada, the USA or Germany has a share above 15%.

SUMMARY

Together with product performance, pricing is the main determinant of a brand's value to the consumer. It is one of the most difficult marketing decision areas because so many variables are involved. The reactions of consumers, the trade and competitors all have to be considered in setting or changing a price. The two main pricing methods are cost-plus and demand-pricing. The latter is preferable in most circumstances because it takes into account demand and value.

A first step in sound pricing policy is to ascertain the price dynamics of your brands or markets. The major factors affecting price elasticity are frequency of purchase, degree of necessity, unit price, comparability and fashion or status. Pricing decisions offer plenty of opportunity for creativity, and the full range of alternative actions should be carefully weighed.

Profit cannibalization through private label supply, or the introduction of lower priced company brands and new larger sizes, should be guarded against. But it is usually preferable to risk some degree of profit cannibalization and at least to share in the profits of the lower priced segment of the market.

Mistakes can be made on pricing. They are least harmful when recognized early and remedied fast. Market testing of alternative prices provides very useful data for future decisions, but is a curiously neglected art in the UK.

12: *Sales Promotion and*
_____Packaging

A. BASIC PRINCIPLES OF SALES PROMOTION

Description and Role

Sales promotion consists of immediate or delayed incentives to purchase, expressed in cash or in kind. It has only a temporary and short-term duration. Continuous incentives to purchase, like the Embassy cigarette gift catalogue, are according to this definition intrinsic parts of the product offered to consumers, and therefore not promotions as such. A promotion has only three targets and two modes. The targets are the trade, the consumer and company employees (normally salesmen or factory staff). The modes are the immediate incentive and the delayed incentive to purchase.

Incentives are *immediate* when they can be obtained concurrently with purchase, and straight price cuts are the simplest example. Incentives are *delayed* when the purchaser has to take additional action (like mailing in an application leaflet) or to wait the determination of chance (as in a personality promotion like the White Tide Man), subsequent to completing the purchase.

The role of promotion is to encourage purchase by temporarily improving the value of a brand. It is part of the overall marketing mix, and ties in with advertising, product performance and pricing. In general, the purpose of advertising is to improve attitudes towards a brand, while the objective of promotions is to translate favourable attitudes into actual purchase. Advertising cannot close a sale because its impact is too far from the point of purchase, but promotion can and does.

No Promotion is an Island unto Itself

Sales promotion is often mistakenly viewed in isolation from the other elements in the marketing plan, and is sometimes utilized as a desperation measure to prop up sagging products. Companies may also attempt to use sales promotion as a solution to problems of a more radical nature—like inferior product performance—without recognizing that such a task is beyond its capabilitites. In such situations, it only fulfils the function of heart massage, and may render a disservice by temporarily obscuring the serious state of the patient.

The limited yet important role of sales promotion is not widely recognized. The objective of a promotion is to achieve a specific number of new or additional purchases during its currency. If it accomplishes this objective, it has fully completed its task. Whether or not the brand continues to grow and prosper *after* the promotion is over says little about the quality of the promotion—it is purely a function of the brand's product performance, pricing and advertising. A promotion merely gets a brand an 'interview' with the consumer. The brand's long-term future with the consumer will depend on how he or she assesses its performance against other product candidates previously interviewed. Comments by marketing men like 'The promotion was not successful because it only achieved a temporary bump in business' are uncomfortably frequent and demonstrate a clear misunderstanding of the role of sales promotion.

It follows that promotion will always be most productive on brands with superior product performance:

From the time that Omo (Unilever) was introduced in 1955, Daz (Procter & Gamble) has never possessed any unique point of difference. Both Daz and Omo were blue powders, and they consistently broke even on blind test. Their prices were similar and neither was able to build up any perceived superiority through advertising (unlike Persil). Daz's share of the total laundry and dishwashing market through the 1950s to the late 1960s* was normally around 12%, and Omo's around 9%. Daz's slight edge was probably due to its being first on the market.

In the absence of any distinctive advantage, both Daz and Omo relied greatly on heavy consumer promotion. But predictably, promotions never gained more than a temporary bump in business for either brand. Daz got up as high as 18% when it first gave away free plastic roses in 1961, but had soon dropped back again to its normal 12%. Neither Daz nor Omo had any performance basis for retaining new users attracted by a promotion.

* Both Daz and Omo predictably lost share to Ariel and Radiant, introduced in 1969.

By contrast, Fairy Snow (P & G) had a superior performance to its competitive soap powder (Persil) in the mid-1960s. At this time, Fairy Snow would successfully hold some of the new users gained on promotion, after the promotion had finished, because they were impressed by its superior product performance.

The long-term share charts of these two categories of brand would look something like Figure 3.

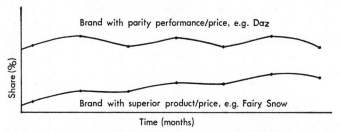

Figure 3 Effect of promotion on brand share

The Wide Repertoire of Promotions

There is a great variety of types of consumer promotion. The main ones are described on the following pages and are intended to serve as check-lists for practising marketing men. Most of these consumer promotions can also be adapted as incentives to the retail trade.

Some types of promotion techniques—like price cuts, free gifts, coupons and samples—have been in use for over a hundred years, and still work efficiently when applied to the right situation. Others come and go, and it is advisable to avoid using a promotion technique which was very strong a couple of years ago but is now declining in effectiveness. Personality promotions (e.g. the White Tide Man) used to be strong in the early 1960s but are much weaker today. Some of the more transient promotion types have life cycles, just like products.

Suiting the Technique to the Occasion

Faced with such a bewildering range of possible promotions to use, the uninitiated will naturally wonder how to choose the right one for each situation. This indeed is one of the key skills in promotion development. There are four stages in developing a promotion, as follows:

(1) First work out the objectives and strategy for the promotion.

[*Text continues on page 193*

TABLE 12.1 SUMMARY OF TYPES OF IMMEDIATE CONSUMER PROMOTION INCENTIVE

Promotion type	Brief description	Advantages	Disadvantages
(1) Reduced price packs (sometimes called *price off label* packs).	Price reduction marked on package by manufacturer, e.g. *1p off* Chum dogfood. Value of typical price reduction varies between 10% and 20% of retail price.	(a) Universal appeal of money. (b) Trade prefers price reductions. (c) Reliable results can be expected. (d) Can be mounted quickly without prior testing. (e) As effective for small as for large brand because no economies of scale.	(a) Undistinctive and easily matched by competition. (b) Price off amounts can escalate into mini price war. (c) Unless amount of reduction exceptional, most likely to be bought by regular users of brand and bargain-hunters who switch brands frequently.
(2) Free merchandise packs (sometimes called *on pack* premiums).	Free premium item attached to brand package, e.g. free sponge with Fairy Liquid.	(a) Usually more effective in getting trial among non-users than equivalent value price pack. (b) If a set-building item, can attract new users and hold them for a number of purchases. (c) Usually possible to give consumer an item worth twice what company paid for it, due to purchase of millions. (d) Distinctive and unique, hard to copy.	(a) Appeal hard to predict and requires prior testing. (b) Premium supply and quality control often time-consuming. (c) Limited number of high appeal items within affordable price range which can be banded to pack. (d) Extra packaging costs for banding and special outer cases often high.
(3) *Near pack* premiums. Can be either free to consumer or, less often,	Same as (2) above except that free premium is available near, but not attached to, package due to bulky size, e.g. free Pan books with Nescafé.	Same advantages as (2) above; in addition, more bulky premiums can be run as near packs, so wider choice available.	(a) Same disadvantages as (2) above. (b) Unpopular with trade. (c) Totally ineffective unless display achieved. (d) Risk of pilferage of premiums by

		Advantages	Disadvantages
	intrinsic value, e.g. Maxwell House packed inside glass percolator.	(b) Consumer can be sold large quantity of product. (c) Unique and hard for competition to copy. (d) Strong visual impact even if not specially displayed.	related, and must protect product quality like any other packaging. (b) Major manufacturing complexities and long lead times. (c) High risk and requires prior testing.
(5) Bonus packs (sometimes called *free product* packs).	Consumer is given extra product at no additional cost, e.g. ½ lb (227 g) of Omo free. Often a large size is offered at same price as size below.	(a) Alternative to price pack. Offers incentive in form of extra product rather than lower price. (b) Has most of advantages of price pack. (c) Forces consumer to use up more product. (d) Can accustom consumer to using larger size, i.e. consumer can be traded up.	(a) Must offer quite large amount of extra product to make impact. Even more likely to be bought by regular users than price off pack. (b) Expensive and time-consuming to produce unless bonus pack is standard package size. (Economics versus a price pack depend on internal company accounting system.)
(6) Home sampling (distribution by hand or mail to individual homes).	Free sample of a brand (usually a new one) is delivered to the home. The manufacturer hopes that, having used the sample, the consumer will then purchase the product at a store.	(a) Strongest possible promotion for new or improved brand with superior performance to competition and a mass market appeal. (b) Helps force trade distribution of product. (c) Best technique for gaining trial among non-users. Virtually assures widespread trial usage of product.	(a) The most expensive available promotion. (b) Of little value to brand with minority or special interest market. (c) Hopeless for a brand without superior product performance. (d) Often requires development and production of special sample size. (e) Because of high fixed cost of distribution, usually only affordable by large brands.

[Continues overleaf

TABLE 12.1—CONTINUED

Promotion type	Brief description	Advantages	Disadvantages
(7) Cross rough sampling.	Free sample of one brand is banded to another brand which is retailed at normal price. The two brands may come from the same company (e.g. free Silvikrin with Macleans toothpaste) or different companies (e.g. free Tate & Lyle lump sugar with Nescafé).	(a) Very inexpensive way of sampling a product. (b) Has promotional benefit for brand carrying sample. (c) Carrying brand may penetrate specific minority group aimed for, e.g. young mothers via baby-food brands.	(a) Less controlled way of sampling than home distribution method. Effectiveness depends on how far target consumer of each brand fits. Carrying brand must have low frequency of purchase, otherwise consumers will each get a number of free samples. (b) Some wastage. A proportion of consumers will not even use sample, or will give it to a friend. (c) Trade may press for the margin they would have made if sample had been sold rather than given away free.
(8) Home couponing.	A valuable coupon, redeemable against a specified brand, is distributed to homes, e.g. 3p coupon. Value of coupons varies widely, from minimum of around 10% of retail value to a maximum of 100%. Redemption levels on mass appeal brands 20–40%.	(a) After home sampling, the best way to achieve trial for new or improved product. (b) Usually less expensive than sampling, but still an expensive promotion. (c) Requires no special packaging or factory handling.	(a) Misredemption, i.e. consumers redeeming coupon against a brand other than that for which it was specified. This can run as high as 33% of all coupons redeemed. (b) Unpredictable cost, hard to estimate accurately ahead. (c) Wastage. Up to 80% of con-

		(e) Inefficient for high share brands. (f) Hard to achieve effective display of a coupon promotion. (a) Much less expensive than home delivered coupon, but usually less economic on a 'cost per new user' basis because redemption is so low. (b) Little regional flexibility for including or excluding specific geographical areas.
(9) Magazine or newspaper couponing.	Same as in (8) above, but coupon has to be cut from magazine or newspaper. Redemption levels tend to be less than 1% of all coupons printed.	(a) Same advantages as in (8) above but at much lower level. (b) Publication may be tailored to target audience, e.g. *Honey* or *19* for teenage girls.

TABLE 12.2   SUMMARY OF TYPES OF DELAYED CONSUMER INCENTIVES

Promotion type	Brief description	Advantages	Disadvantages
(1) Personality promotion.	A number of 'personalities' tour an area and call on housewives in their homes. Those called upon who can answer a simple question, and have the appropriate brand on hand, win a prize, typically worth £5–10. *Examples:* White Tide Man, Miss Camay, Omo Rainbow Man. On the best run promotions, about 1 in 1000 homes will be called on. Promotion usually lasts 4–8 weeks.	(a) Most appropriate for large brands because of high fixed costs in administration and TV advertising support. (b) Generates trade excitement and high display levels. (c) Can significantly increase consumer sales. (d) Does not require special promotion packaging and is effective against existing trade stock.	(a) Prohibitively expensive except for major brands. (b) This promotion type over-used in the 1960s. Housewives who were never called on (the majority) are sceptical. (c) Law restricts degree of noise (e.g. bell chiming) that can be made to attract attention in urban areas. (d) Complex to organize, and function usually delegated to outside firm. (e) Only small proportion of total promotion reaches consumer, as prizes. (f) Lacks immediacy.
(2) Free premium.	Consumer mailing in specified number of packet tops or labels (known as *proofs of purchase*) will be sent free premium by manufacturer. *Example:* free *Book of Football* to all those mailing in 20 packet tops from Park Drive cigarettes. Free premium offer usually made on limited quantity of special promotion pack. Redemption typi-	(a) Manufacturer can pass on to consumer major savings in mass purchase of premium. (b) Can be useful loading promotion for holding regular users loyal to brand. (c) Manufacturer benefits from 'slip-page': consumers collecting packet tops with view to mailing in and	(a) Appeals primarily to existing users. Ineffective in attracting new ones. (b) Low trade appeal and poor display co-operation. (c) Lacks immediacy. (d) Requires careful prior testing of effectiveness and redemption levels. Hard to judge likely cost.

		Advantages	Considerations
	3 special pack tops required by each applicant, therefore 3m opportunities to redeem. Actual redemption 1m, or 33% of opportunities.		(f) Only effective against proportion of users who start collecting for premium: at best 1 in 4.
(3) Buy one and get one free.	Consumer sending in 1 packet top or label from a brand will receive coupon entitling him/her to free 2nd packet. A variant of this is *buy 2 packets and get 1 free*. Redemption usually high: 15–40% of special promotion packs put out, if offer featured on packet.	(a) Sound loading promotion for holding regular users. (b) Can be mounted more quickly than free mail-in promotion. (c) Less risk of failure than free mail-in, no problems of premium supply. (d) Most effective for brand with low market share.	(a) Undistinctive, easily copied. Lacks immediacy. (b) Even less effective than (2) above in attracting new users. (c) On equal cost basis, less effective than reduced price pack. (d) Low level of trade interest and display. (e) Prior testing to check redemption is prudent.
(4) Refund offer.	Consumer sending in specified number of packet tops will be mailed a fixed amount of money in return. Simple form of offer is *20p for 5 labels*. Refund may, however, be escalated, e.g. 10p for 3 labels, 20p for 5, 30p for 6. Redemption varies, depending on proportion of all households using brand, value of offer and number of labels required from consumer.	(a) An alternative to (2) and (3) above for sustaining loyalty from existing users. (b) Cash has universal appeal. (c) Allows great flexibility in design. Offer can be escalated, and made high or low in value. (d) Can be mounted very quickly. Featuring on packet not essential.	(a) More distinctive than (3), less so than (2). Easily copied. (b) Limited trade appeal but certainly higher than for (2) or (3). (c) Prior testing wise to check redemption. (d) Appeals primarily to existing users: insufficient immediacy to attract many new ones. (e) Usually only applicable to brand with high purchase frequency since at least 3 or 4 labels have to be requested to make minimum refund value economic to company.

[Continues overleaf

TABLE 12.2—CONTINUED

Promotion type	Brief description	Advantages	Disadvantages
(5) Game promotion.	Two main types. (a) *Card and stamp games:* Involve skill but have appearance of chance. Answers look easy but are in fact difficult. Consumers usually given cards on which stamps from packets have to be arranged skilfully. *Example:* Gallaher Cadets 'Treasure Isle'. Correct picture of treasure scene had to be built up on card with stamps from cigarette packets. (b) *Matching half games:* Consumer gets half notes, e.g. half of £1, £5 and £10 to simulated note. Consumers who get matching half notes can claim face value in cash. *Example:* Shell 'Make Money'. This type of promotion is difficult to run on packaged goods brand because product purchase requirement not legal.	(a) Can be very effective in building extra consumer sales if well designed, e.g. Petfoods 'Big Name Bingo', Robinson's 'Fruit Machine'. (b) Apparent ease of winning creates high consumer involvement. (c) Consumer interest can be sustained over period of 6–8 weeks. (d) Most effective on brands with high purchase frequency, e.g. crisps, tea or petfoods. (e) Distinctive promotion, which can be tied in with brand advertising theme. (f) More effective in attracting new new users than (2) (3) or (4).	(a) Complex to design or execute and requires assistance of outside promotion house. (b) Requires home distribution of cards to be effective in case of card and stamp games. (c) Unless carefully designed, can be difficult for consumer to understand. (d) Special promotion pack production can cause problems. (e) Lacks immediacy.
(6) Charity promotion.	For every label or packet top sent in, sponsoring company will contribute specified amount to named charity. *Example:* Birds Eye 'Launch a Lifeboat'. 3 sizes of fish fingers carried tokens of value 2p, 3p and 5p. Birds Eye donated money equivalent of all tokens mailed in to Royal National Lifeboat Institution towards cost of	(a) If really well done, can have significant effect on consumer sales. (b) Group collection by schools, scouts and womens organizations often a major factor. (c) Can generate significant trade support and display. (d) Charity may place organization	(a) Can be difficult to find charity with necessary broad appeal. (b) Manufacturer risks accusation that he is exploiting charity for commercial ends, unless promotion tactfully handled. (c) Only suitable for large brand because major charities not in-

| | | | consuming. |
			(e) Lacks immediacy.
(7) Self-liquidating promotion.	Consumer mails in 1 or more labels plus some money and receives premium in return. Consumer has advantage of getting item in this way at below normal cost, since manufacturer passes on advantage of bulk buying and takes no profit. Typical cost to consumer is 50–70% of equivalent retail price. Most self-liquidators cost consumers from 75p to £1.50. Redemption of special packet tops usually below 0.5%, or under 20 000 applications for premium. *Example: Bobby Moore's Book of the 1970 World Cup* for 19p and 1 Shredded Wheat packet top.	(a) Very occasionally has measurable effect on consumer sales. (b) Will achieve some display if item attractive to trade. (c) Creates impression of activity on package. (d) Low cost.	(a) Usually has no effect on consumer or trade sales. (b) Usually has nil level of interest for trade. (c) A very over-used promotion technique. (d) Absorbs management and sales force time to no object. (e) Very few housewives send in for self-liquidators. (f) Danger of being left with surplus stocks of premium, or of losing consumer goodwill due to delays in mailing out, if demand unexpectedly high.
(8) Skill competition.	Consumer has to fulfil simple test of skill (typically arranging 6 phrases about the product in order of importance) and mail in 1 or more labels, thereby entering a competition with prizes. *Example:* Mini Minors to be won with Heinz soups. Typical entry level under 50 000 but can very infrequently run into millions—Vaux Beer Contest (4m entries), Danish Bacon House Contest (2m entries).	(a) Very occasionally has measurable effect on consumer sales. (b) Does not involve premium supply problems and can be set up very quickly. (c) Usually attracts more entries than typical self-liquidator. (d) Low cost.	(a) Low level of consumer interest. Usually has no effect on sales. (b) Costs more than self-liquidator, though still an inexpensive promotion. (c) Even less display potential than self-liquidator. Nil interest to trade. (d) Absorbs management and sales force time to no object.

[*Continues overleaf*

TABLE 12.2—CONTINUED

Promotion type	Brief description	Advantages	Disadvantages
(9) Sweepstake contest.	Similar to (8) above but no skill needed. It is illegal for manufacturer to require proof of purchase from consumer, in running sweepstake. This promotion technique over-used in USA but rarely employed in UK.	(a) Typically attracts more entries than equal value skill competition. (b) Less common than skill competition. (c) Otherwise, same as for skill competition.	(a) Proof of purchase cannot be requested. (b) Otherwise, same as for skill competition.
(10) Cross rough couponing.	Brand A carries a coupon, either on label or inside pack, redeemable against Brand B. The 2 brands may be from the same or different companies. *Example:* 3p coupon for Robertson's jam on every packet of McDougall's flour.	(a) Very inexpensive method of coupon distribution. (b) Provides selling point for carrying brand at no cost. (c) Can increase consumer sales of carrying brand if a broad appeal, high value coupon is included (but this is unlikely). (d) Can enable the couponed brand to reach a specific target group (e.g. slimmers, if carrying brand is a low calorie one).	(a) Little control over who gets coupons. The same consumer may gain 3 or 4 coupons from buying carrying brand frequently. (b) Coupon redemption tends to be low and very slow in building up. (c) Usually has no measurable effect on consumer sales of either carrying or couponed brand. (d) No trade appeal or display potential.
(11) Coupon on next purchase.	A brand carries a coupon redeemable against consumer's next purchase of same brand. *Example:* Maxwell House 3p coupon on next purchase. Consumer tears coupon off the label and gets its face value deducted from subsequent purchase of same brand. Normally used as alternative to reduced price pack.	(a) Can offer higher face value than equivalent cost on reduced price pack: a 5p coupon redeeming at 30% will only cost company 0·75p per pack because 2 packs were moved at a cost of 1·5p. (b) Can increase frequency of purchase among existing users. (c) A suitable holding promotion to	(a) Normally less effective in driving up consumer sales than reduced price pack because no immediacy, and appeal is almost exclusively to existing users. (b) Less trade appeal or display potential than reduced price pack.

(2) Then run through a list of all the promotion techniques, and draw up a short list of those which fit the strategy and the budget.

(3) Next think up creative ideas, stemming from the half-dozen or so techniques short-listed.

(4) Finally pick out the best idea and develop it in detail.

The first two stages are the ones which require some elaboration, since the other two are self-explanatory and simple to describe, though of course essential to the quality of the final promotion.

The objectives of a promotion cover what it is supposed to achieve, and usually requires a given percentage increase in sales to the trade and the consumer, perhaps accompanied by additional trade distribution.

The strategy specifies which groups the promotion is aimed at, and what it is designed to make them do. If the target is the trade, which particular parts of it are to be given priority, and how far are sales, as opposed to extra distribution, price cutting or display, the main aim? If the consumer is the main target, is the promotion to be directed at non-users, occasional users or regular users? And is it designed to make them buy once, or a number of times during the promotion? All these elements have to be weighed in the strategy, and priorities allocated to each one.

In building a strategy for a promotion, one of the most important issues, which bears very much on the particular technique eventually chosen, is whether to aim for consumer *trial* or *loading*. Trial involves gaining a single purchase from a wide range of consumers, many of them non-users, whereas loading seeks a number of purchases from a smaller group of consumers, most of them probably regular users. Trial is obviously the more positive of the two strategies, and is followed by most brands with growth ambitions. The theory behind it is that if you have a superior product, and consumers can be persuaded to try it, they will be so impressed by the experience that some will continue using the brand even after the promotion is over (as in the case of Fairy Snow in the case history above). Loading is most frequently followed either by brands that are badly on the slide, or by perfectly healthy brands faced with a powerful competitive new product introduction. In each case the object is to hold on to the brand's regular users and to prevent them from slipping away quietly to competitors.

Most promotions can be categorized as either trial-getters or loaders. The difference is obviously not starkly black or white, because every promotion performs both functions to some extent.

But promotions with an immediate purchase appeal—like sampling, couponing or free gifts attached to the packet—are most likely to achieve trial. And those with a delayed effect—like skill competitions, and money or gifts that have to be mailed in for—usually appeal to regular users, and have a loading effect.

The two lists of promotion techniques in Tables 12.1 and 12.2 are divided into the two categories of immediate and delayed incentives. They also list the advantages and disadvantages of each promotion type. Anyone armed with a strategy, and applying it to the appropriate list should therefore be able quickly to pick out the few promotion techniques that match it, before setting the creative juices flowing.

Should Promotions Tie in with a Brand's Advertising?

If you are talking to a really good promotion consultant who knows his job inside out, and you want to get him frothing at the mouth, there is one sure-fire way to do it. Tell him that you want a promotion which 'ties in with our advertising'.

He will probably start by saying that this will severely restrict the search for an outstanding promotion, which is hard enough to come by even with an entirely open brief. Next will come a short homily on the different roles of advertising and promotion—the the one being designed to influence long-term attitudes, the other to achieve an immediate rise in consumer sales. And he will no doubt end by throwing in your face all kinds of highly successful promotions which had nothing to do with the advertising or usage of the brands that ran them—like Omo plastic daffodils, Daz table mats, Shell 'Make Money', Nescafé free books, the Golden Wonder Olympics promotion, and so on.

And he would of course be right. A promotion with broad consumer appeal will succeed whether or not it ties in with the advertising. And close relevance to a brand's advertising theme will not save a low appeal promotion from disaster. A close tie-in with an advertising campaign may add 'a little something' to an already strong promotion—like the Homepride flour grader or the Maxwell House coffee percolator—but it will certainly not make the difference between success and failure.

B. OFFENSIVE PROMOTION ATTITUDES
1. Set Clear Strategies

A common mistake is either to start thinking about detailed promotion ideas without the benefit of a strategy, or to develop a strategy which sets no clear priorities and is merely an inventory of all the things a brand would like to achieve. A clear strategy provides the discipline necessary to develop a strong promotion.

2. *Give Promotions the same Priority as Advertising*

Most packaged goods companies spend as much money on trade and consumer promotion as they do on advertising, and yet promotions are a strangely underrated and neglected marketing tool. Advertising is developed by outside agencies with specialized skills, and every new campaign involves numerous meetings with company personnel, as well as some participation from top management, and yet promotions are usually developed by marketing people with no specialized knowledge of them, in the time they have left over from other tasks. Top management is not particularly interested in promotions, even though expenditure on them may be as high as 10% of the company's sales. Many writers on marketing subjects also seem to share this disdain for promotion. If book indexes are to be believed, Theodore Levitt does not mention sales promotion once in either *The Marketing Mode* or *Innovation in Marketing*, nor does it appear in Esmond Pearce's *Marketing and Higher Management*. Philip Kotler's *Marketing Management*, a fine work, only devotes 3 of its 607 pages to the intricacies of sales promotion.

Why the deliberate neglect of such an important marketing tool? Well, many marketing men especially the more senior ones, share the 'middle class' attitudes that promotions are rather grubby and lacking in social or economic value. And there are other reasons, but they are not important. What is important is that the relatively low status accorded to promotions in many companies gives the offensive marketer a chance to gain an edge by giving promotions the priority they deserve. At present, the amount of genuinely innovative thinking applied to promotions is minute compared with that lavished on advertising and R & D . . . which leads to the next point.

3. *Aim to Innovate New Promotion Techniques*

New promotion techniques are not often developed, and even when they are, there is of course a risk that they will lack appeal. But companies inventing or exploiting successful new techniques gain the large rewards due to innovators.

Shell pioneered the matching half promotion with 'Make Money':

Make Money was a very successful promotion and paid for itself many times over. It enabled Shell to increase its sales by

50% over a ten-week period. When the promotion was over, sales remained above the pre-promotion level for some months because some motorists who had changed to a Shell station during the promotion stayed with it afterwards.

Make Money was very simple. Every time a motorist bought Shell petrol, he received a half-note with a 10*s* (50p), £1, £10 or £100 denomination. If he was able to match the two halves of a similar face value, he won the amount printed on the note. The cost was controlled by making available only a limited number of winning halves. The reason for the promotion's success was its simplicity, immediacy and apparent ease of winning.

In the summer of 1970 Brooke Bond innovated a promotion technique with the 'Half-Million Giveaway', and gained a large increase in business as a result.

In May–July 1970 a leaflet was distributed door to door offering half a million prizes, ranging from Ford Capri cars and colour TVs to art prints. Consumers were invited to collect and mail in as many stamps as possible from special packs of PG Tips and Brooke Bond Dividend tea. Prizes were awarded according to the number of stamps mailed in—i.e. the three people mailing in most stamps won a car, the next ten a colour TV set, and so on until the half million prizes were awarded. The vast majority (495 000) of the prizes were art prints, which had a retail value of 25p but cost Brooke Bond very little because they bought in such large quantities.

The promotion was highly successful. Over eight million stamps were mailed in, and Brooke Bond's share hit an all-time high point.

The Half-Million Giveaway was very different from the conventional skill competition, where you typically have to arrange half a dozen rather boring statements in order of importance and send in packet tops. Its novelty lay in the fact that *all* you had to do was send in packet tops and the people sending in most, rather than those with the brightest intellect or greatest luck, won the prizes. In addition, the number of prizes offered was exceptional. The promotion worked well because entrants felt they had a good chance to win, and the competition was novel and easy to enter. Another of its strengths, from Brooke Bond's viewpoint, was that it encouraged people to buy large numbers of packets rather than the two or three which most promotions require.

4. Creativity can Build Dramatic Results from Humdrum Techniques

An original exploitation of an ordinary promotion technique can produce remarkable gains. A skill competition usually rates as a lightweight promotion, and has no impact on consumer sales, but the Brooke Bond PG Tips 'Happy Reunion' in 1969 proved an exception to this.

> The Happy Reunion competition offered 20 prizes of flights for two people to anywhere in the world, for a reunion holiday with relatives or friends. Entry forms were printed on the inside of packets. Consumers had to rank reasons for a reunion on the entry form and there was a tie-breaker.
>
> The competition pulled 1·3 million entries, and increased brand share of PG tips to 20%. The major reason for the promotion's success was the 'reunion' theme, which had great emotional appeal.

A self-liquidating offer is also a lightweight promotion, and very rarely affects brand share, but the Spillers Homepride flour premium achieved exceptional results.

> A kitchen flour shaker, shaped like the Homepride cartoon flour grader, was offered to consumers for 3s 4d (17p) and two proofs of purchase. 500 000 entries were received, and Homepride brand share increased by 15% over a two-month period. The success of this promotion was due to the appeal of the premium and to its uniqueness, since a flour shaker of this kind could only be obtained by purchasing Homepride flour.

The technique of the charity promotion has been widely known for years, and was used as long ago as the 1930s. Few manufacturers have exploited it, however, due to the difficulty of finding a charity of wide appeal and concern at the possibly explosive implications of mixing commerce and charity. Golden Wonder was successful in overcoming these potential problems with its Olympics charity promotion.

> During May-August 1968 Golden Wonder offered to donate 2d (1p) for every five empty crisp packets, and 2d (1p) for every

empty peanut packet mailed in, to the British Athletic Board Olympics Fund. Nine million empty packet tops were returned, and Golden Wonder's brand share increased from 48% to 52% in grocers during the promotion.

5. *Don't Waste Time on Ineffective Lightweight Promotions*

For every promotion like the Brooke Bond Happy Reunion, and the Spillers Homepride flour grader, there are thousands of skill competitions and self-liquidating premium* promotions which sink into grateful obscurity without making the slightest ripple on a brand's business.

Out of the hundreds of promotions of this type which I have come across, only five had any noticeable effect on brand share, even though a number of the unsuccessful self-liquidating offers brought in over 200 000 applications. Most marketing men would acknowledge that, with the occasional exception, skill competitions and self-liquidators are weak promotions and yet they continue to be widely run. The justifications for persisting with them are unconvincing, the most common being 'they give the sales force a talking point', 'They will gain us some display' or 'They provide a change of pace'.

The essence of offensive marketing is to concentrate as much time as possible on development projects which, if successfully concluded, will have a measurable effect on the business. In this context, time spent on working up self-liquidators or skill competitions of the normal mediocre standard is wasted time.

6. *Insist on Results from Trade Promotions*

There was a time not so long ago when retailers were passive middlemen who gratefully received goods from manufacturers at whatever terms they were offered and resold them to the public. The manufacturer was very much in control and the trade played second fiddle because the supply of goods was restricted.

The number of industries in which any semblance of this type of relationship now remains must be minute. In the grocery trade, in particular, the large retailing companies have gained the initiative from the manufacturers and over the 1960s have succeeded in raising the proportion of the sales pound accounted for by trade expenditure. This item covers spending by manufacturers on trade

---

* A self-liquidating premium is one which the manufacturer sells to the consumer at no profit. An example is a carving knife worth 75p for only 49p plus two packet tops.

margins, overriding discounts and special promotion expenditure. The sufferers in this transfer of funds have been advertising, consumer promotion and manufacturer profit. By contrast, profits of the more efficient retailers have boomed in the 1960s and even the less competent ones, with their paths to profit smoothed by the aggressive approach of retail industry leaders, have done much better than expected.

The dilemma confronting the grocery manufacturer, and any other company facing a well organized and aggressive retail trade, is simple. In order to sell his goods, he has to persuade the retailer not only to stock them, but to give them a fair share of shelf space. To carry out his marketing programme, he will also aim to get the retailer to display and price cut his brands periodically.

Faced by these requirements, the retailer is in a strong bargaining position. Sitting across the table from a major manufacturer, he knows that the amount of shelf space, display and price cutting which he allocates to a large brand in his stores will strongly affect its sales. And if he reduces the priority given to a major brand he may lose little or no turnover, because consumers will just buy more of the competitive brands. Although the retailer does not want to risk throwing out a major brand completely, most large manufacturers also have cherished minor brands, which the retailer could easily delist without feeling any pinch. Furthermore, in most markets there are at least two substantial manufacturers, and the retailers can play the one off against the other. With this substantial bargaining power behind them, and the skill to exploit it, it is not surprising that retailers (and wholesale groups) succeed in squeezing extra volume discounts and larger promotion allowances out of manufacturers. There is nothing vicious or unethical about this, since any organization is entitled to drive the hardest bargain it can.

This leaves the manufacturer in a vulnerable position. To begin with, he is giving the larger groups in the trade extra discounts and not getting much back in return. Then, when he pays the trade sums of money to run their own short-term promotions on his brands, he is allowing the trade to spend the money in the way that is best for them rather than himself. And the way this money is normally utilized by the trade—in price cuts—may give the manufacturer's brands a short-term volume boost but will in the long term blur their distinctiveness by focusing so strongly on price. This in turn tends to make markets more commodity-like in nature, where price is the major determinant and the distinctiveness of individual brands receives less stress. And this, of course, provides the ideal climate for the growth of low price private label brands! It all sounds like one of those lengthy discussions about the state of the British economy, with the customary unpleasant conclusion.

Before examining how the offensive marketer can remain offensive in this situation, let us just nail a couple of points about the trade which are often misunderstood or overlooked. First of all, the interests of the manufacturer and the retailer are very different, and the cant which is sometimes talked avout their having common objectives is misconceived. The manufacturer's aim is to increase the sales and profits of particular brands, while the retailer is concerned to raise the total turnover of his store, and he doesn't particularly care which brands he sells in doing so. The manufacturer is also interested in furthering the image of his brand, while the retailer thinks about the image of his store. Secondly, manufacturers sometimes forget that retailers also have competitors— Tesco is always very interested in what Fine Fare, Pricerite and ASDA are doing, for instance—and that they need the promotion allowances which manufacturers can provide.

With that short background, let us see what offensive marketing action can be taken by the manufacturer. Here are a few common-sense suggestions.

(*a*) A good starting point is to evaluate carefully just how profitable your trade spending is, in terms of extra product moved through to the consumer. If you spend £50 000 on a trade promotion, how many additional *consumer* sales does this generate? Some companies make the mistake of relating trade spending to extra volume sold into the trade—but if this just adds to the trade stocks of your product, it is not worth much.

(*b*) Compare the profitability of trade spending with that of alternative expenditures like advertising or consumer promotion, and try to divide your spending between the three on the basis of profitability. Take a medium to long-term view, if your annual budget targets allow this, because trade spending always looks attractive in the short term, whereas the claims of advertising become more convincing as your perspective lengthens.

(*c*) If you have one or more high volume brand leaders, you are in a strong bargaining position and should take advantage of it. For a start, you should insist on paying a lower *percentage* than your competitors on both overriding discounts and on short-term promotions. After all, 5% on £10 million is much more than 10% on £2 million. You can drive a hard bargain with retailers—they want to display and price cut your brand because they know that this may attract new consumers to their stores.

(*d*) Set conditions on the money you give the trade. Insist that it is spent in the way that suits you best, and don't just hand it to the trade on a plate. For example, a brand leader may ask the trade to widen the distribution of some of its less popular sizes or varieties as a condition of granting a short-term trade allowance. Or your brand may respond better to display than to price cutting, in which case you would demand display.

(*e*) Check on the trade's performance of the agreements they undertake at head office. There is often a gap between the undertakings made by the HQ of a large retailer and the actual implementation at store level. If there is a complete failure in local implementation, the manufacturer should bring this to the notice of HQ with a well documented case, and ask for a re-run of the promotion.

(*f*) Remember that the trade prefers to promote the highest volume brands, and it follows that trade promotion money is more likely to be passed on to the consumer on larger brands. On smaller ones, the trade may well pocket the money, and apart from the contribution it may make to retaining distribution, trade expenditure is usually much less effective on this type of brand. On smaller brands it is often better to reduce the retail price permanently or to run reduced price offers flashed on the pack, than to spend heavily against the trade.

(*g*) Ignore threats and if your competitors wish to throw away their money, don't feel any obligation to follow them.

The degree to which you can actually achieve your objectives with the trade will naturally depend on the size of your business. The small manufacturer will have less bargaining power than the large one. And it is, of course, much easier to talk about principles than to apply them in action. But the trade has a ready eye for a 'softie' whom it can take for a ride, and it also quickly recognizes the hard bargainer who knows exactly what he wants for his money. In the long term, the latter inevitably achieves the best results.

7. Make the Effort to Test

Major★ promotions involving untried ideas are worth testing for the same reason as new products—it is hard to assess them except in the market place, and it is cheaper to have a failure in a TV area

---

★ The word 'major' is related to expense. It would not, for example, be worthwhile pre-testing a promotion that would only cost £10 000 nationally.

than in the whole country. Another big advantage of promotion testing is that is enables you to try out completely new concepts, which you would not dare to run nationally merely on the basis of judgement.

The case for pre-testing new promotion ideas is weaker than that for pre-testing new products, because of the smaller amounts of money at risk. But it is still a good case, because the cost of a national promotion may exceed £100 000. And what company would ever dream of spending £100 000 on the purchase of capital equipment with no prior pilot testing and no clear ideas as to whether it will function or not? Yet few companies pre-test, and few run innovative new promotions. Most just rake over the mediocre old favourites like the reduced price pack or the trade allowance.

One of the exceptions is the indefatigable Procter & Gamble, which carefully market tests all new promotion ideas, including untried free giveaway premiums.* And it is no coincidence that this particular company has been the greatest innovator of new promotion techniques in both the UK and the USA—in the UK it was first in its market† with personality promotions (the White Tide Man), in-pack chance games (Daz Cross 4), free on-pack give-aways (Daz roses), on-pack self-liquidators (Fairy Snow Pyrex cup for 7p) and bonus packs (Daz). All of these promotions would have been much too risky to run nationally on judgement, and most came to fruition through careful market testing. The story of the Daz Cross 4 game illustrates the widsom of testing new ideas.

Daz Cross 4 was a chance game on the pack, run in the Anglia TV area in 1960. I cannot remember the exact details, but the principle was that of matching numbers. Numbers were printed on the inside of the packet (under the perforated opening device), and had to be matched with numbers on the outside. People with matching numbers then had to fulfil a simple test of skill, to satisfy legal requirements,‡ and the prizes ranged from re-frigerators to sets of knives. The exact prize won would depend on the identity of the winning numbers.

The cost of the promotion was to be controlled by limiting the quantity of winning numbers. As I recall it, there were 72 losing combinations and about a dozen winning ones, and the

* Like a free Christmas spray or a free toy car on the packet.
† Many of these promotions were 'firsts' in the UK in any market.
‡ The law has now changed, and this particular promotion would no longer be legal.

plan was to have a winning number in every few hundred packs. However, an error was made by an outside supplier in checking the proofs of the numbers. As a result, one of the losing combinations, printed on large quantities of packs, became a winning combination entitling winners to the top prize of a refrigerator. But this was only discovered after the promotion hit the market place.

Housewives and retailers in Anglia soon sniffed something special about this promotion. Shoppers ordered whole cases of Daz, and some retailers decided not to resell the Daz Cross 4 pack, but instead opened all the packets in their stockroom in the hope of winning a prize. One small retailer won eight refrigerators, and engaged P & G in correspondence for some months subsequently, claiming that he was entitled to a ninth.

At the first sign of trouble, P & G acted with characteristic speed. All shipments of the Daz Cross 4 pack were stopped. Local salesmen and half the marketing department trudged around the Anglia TV area, buying back all the Cross 4 packs they could. Despite this, at the end of the day the promotion test had cost about £50 000, compared with the original budget of about £5000. One shudders to think what the cost would have been if P & G had not been such firm believers in pre-testing.

It is easy but mistaken to laugh at such examples as this, because there is always a risk for anyone pioneering new territory, and in 1960, knowledge of the correct control procedures for games of chance was at a rudimentary stage. But the innovator usually wins out in the long term. The promotion testing equation can be spelt out simply, as follows:

promotion testing = promotion innovation + reduction of risk

PACKAGING

Packaging will be covered briefly, not due to any feeling that it lacks importance, but because functional packaging is governed by the same principles as product R & D and package graphics follow many of the same rules as advertising.

The purpose of packaging has changed greatly in the past twenty years. Its original function was to protect the package contents and it discharged this function in a utilitarian way. With the advent of self-service shopping, packaging became an important selling vehicle in its own right. In addition to its more basic purpose, it was used to create impact for the brand on the shelf and to make the product appear attractive to the consumer. The package was also an appropriate and inexpensive device for carrying promotional messages.

Now some progressive companies are taking packaging a further stage and making it into an inseparable part of a product's performance. This trend is likely to continue, since it is becoming increasingly difficult in certain markets to develop products which are superior in their own right. And new combinations of packages and their contents can turn up novel product ideas, which would not have been apparent if the product had been viewed in isolation.

General Foods in the USA has been particularly successful in developing new brands, where the package adds importantly to product performance. In these instances, the function of the package goes well beyond conventional norms. Two of the most interesting examples are Good Seasons salad dressings and Shake & Bake seasoned breadcrumbs for coating meat and fish prior to baking (instead of frying, which is messy).

The bulk of the salad dressing market in the USA is of the wet/pourable type, packed in glass bottles. Kraft is the brand leader, and the best selling varieties are French and Italian. Good Seasons introduced dry salad dressings in small sachets and the consumer had to add her own oil and vinegar. To facilitate this, Good Seasons also permanently offered a glass 'mixing decanter' which could be obtained free when two sachets were purchased. This decanter contributed greatly to the brand's success. It had no protective function at all, since the dry sachet was self-sufficient, but gave consumers a stimulus to try the product and a means for preparing it in the home once they had become regular users.

Shake & Bake was also an entirely new kind of product. It consisted of a conventional cardboard box (about the same dimensions as a large packet of Flash cleaning powder). Inside this box was a plastic bag, and a packet of seasoned breadcrumbs. To use the product, the consumer would place the crumbs and pieces of meat or fish into the bag, shake them together until the meat or fish was evenly coated with crumbs, and then just bake in the oven. Again, the packaging for Shake & Bake played an important role in product preparation, by providing extra convenience, an even spread of breadcrumbs on the meat and less cleaning up afterwards.

Packaging is one of the lowest cost and highest leverage areas of marketing activity, Changes in design are relatively inexpensive but can bring quite large business gains, especially on small brands which do not normally catch the attention of either the consumer or the trade. Functional improvements in packaging cost more, but can provide large payoffs and boost whole product categories. The aerosol spray can, for example, built the hairspray market and has been the major influence behind the dramatic growth of the deodorant market in the past five years.

Packaging, unlike advertising, can close a sale since it operates at the point of purchase. In the case of lesser known brands, it may even trigger off the whole cycle of interest, attention, desire and action by itself. Most often, however, it will work hand in hand with the other elements of the marketing mix—especially advertising. A package should protect the product, appeal to the consumer and the trade and, ideally, enhance product performance. Table 12.3 shows a check-list of points to note in package design and development.

TABLE 12.3 CHECK-LIST FOR PACKAGING DEVELOPING	
Heading	*Check points*
Protects against	moisture, air, heat, cold, separation of product, tearing, explosion, leakage, staleness, breakage, crushing, dirt, corroding, scuffing
Consumer convenience	ease of opening, disposal, storage, dispensing and handling, safety in use, reusable, reclosable, clear instructions for use, light to handle, stands easily
Trade appeal	ease of stacking, shelving, displaying and identification of both individual products and outer cases; economic utilization of space and good protection
Consumer sales appeal	good size impression, attractive shape and design, easily identifiable, distinctiveness from competition, appearance ties in with product purpose

SUMMARY

Sales promotion consists of immediate or delayed incentives to purchase, expressed in cash or in kind. Its role is to achieve a specified number of new or additional purchases over a limited period.

Whether or not the promotion achieves a long-term increase in business depends on the performance and value of a brand compared with its competitors.

There is a very wide repertoire of promotion types to choose from, and to ensure that the most appropriate types are selected, objectives and strategies should be developed for each promotion. A promotion with broad consumer appeal will succeed whether or not it ties in with a brand's advertising.

Certain attitudes, related to the offensive marketing approach as summarized by 'P–O–I–S–E', improve promotion effectiveness and these are listed below:

> Clear strategies should be agreed as a basis for creative idea development.
>
> Promotions are an underrated marketing tool and should be given at least the same priority as advertising.
>
> New promotion techniques, or a creative adaptation of an existing promotion type, can bring large rewards.
>
> Most lightweight promotions are a waste of time, which could be better applied on projects of higher priority.
>
> Many manufacturers are spending large amounts of money ineffectively against the trade, and could significantly improve the efficiency of their trade effort by following certain principles uncompromisingly.
>
> Promotion testing increases the level of innovation and reduces risk.

13: *Advertising**

'*There is probably no other part of the business to which we allocate resources that provide so little justification for their use.*'†

A. BASIC PRINCIPLES

How Advertising Works

Advertising makes people aware of the existence and advantages of goods and services. It is a form of personal salesmanship‡ designed to make consumers see a brand in a more favourable light. For a familiar brand, consumers will have formed a number of different impressions, probably both favourable and unfavourable, based on previous usage, recollections of past advertising, attitude to packaging and price, opinions of friends and so on. Advertising will add to this set of impressions, attempting to reinforce favourable attitudes and to loosen or eliminate unfavourable ones. The devices used are information, reason and emotion. Advertising therefore interacts with all the other elements that make up the image of a brand, which is why its effect is so difficult to isolate.

The most important relationship is that between the advertising and the product—advertising may build up a wonderful picture of a brand for consumers which can be shattered when they actually try the product. It follows that advertising is unlikely to succeed in selling an inferior product more than once. And since it is applied most heavily against fast-moving consumer goods, the purchaser's right not to buy a second time is a powerful sanction against both misleading advertising and inferior products.

* Readers will notice that this chapter concentrates on TV advertising. This is due to limitations of space. However, the principles of developing and assessing TV advertising can also be applied to other forms of advertising.

† Malcolm A. McNiven (editor), 'How much to spend for advertising?' (*AMA*, 1969). Mr McNiven is Vice-President of Coca-Cola.

‡ But advertising differs from personal selling in a variety of ways. Most significantly, it cannot close a sale and trigger off a purchase on its own.

The Varying Effectiveness of Advertising

Advertising is usually most effective on new brands, because people take time to form definite opinions about them and are not deterred from buying by previous poor experience. What is more, new product advertising is likely to attract above average interest, since novelty holds great fascination. Once a brand has been on the market for some time, it becomes harder for advertising to make an impact. Most consumers will already have a firm opinion about the brand. Here, the advertising has to change attitudes rather than create fresh ones.

Advertising expenditure is usually more efficient than promotion spending for large brands, and the reverse is generally true for small ones. A '1p off' price offer costs the same amount (per packet sold) for any brand whatever its size. But a £500 000 advertising campaign will have a lower cost per packet for a large brand than a small one because the lump sum can be spread across a much higher sales volume.

TABLE 13.1   ADVERTISING SPENDING BY MAJOR US
COMPANIES IN AMERICA, 1969*

Name of company	Category of business	Advertising spending £m	% of sales
Procter & Gamble	Soaps and cleansers	115	9·2
Colgate-Palmolive		50	22·9
General Motors	Automobiles	71	0·7
Ford Motors		47	0·8
General Foods	Food	63	8·5
Kraft		26	2·4
Bristol-Myers	Drugs and Cosmetics	48	12·5
American Home Products		40	9·8
R. J. Reynolds	Tobacco	35	3·8
American Brands		31	2·8
United Airlines	Airlines	12	2·0
Eastern Airlines		10	2·7
Standard Oil of New Jersey	Oil	12	0·2
Shell		11	0·6

Advertising Percentages

Advertising is a much more important cost ingredient in some markets than in others, and since this is a practical book I don't intend to theorize as to why this is so. Based on figures from the USA, the largest market in the world, pharmaceutical companies have the highest ratio of advertising spending to sales, followed by household cleaning firms and food and tobacco groups. Car manufacturers, oil companies and airlines all spend quite large *absolute* amounts on advertising, but these represent only a very small proportion of sales. Table 13.1 summarizes advertising spending, both in absolute levels and as a percentage of sales, for the two leading American companies in each of these categories, in 1969. It includes spending by these companies in the USA only. Advertising as a proportion of sales varies from a low of 0·2% (Standard Oil of New Jersey) to a high of 22·9% (Colgate-Palmolive). General Motors was the second largest advertiser in the USA, but its sales volume was so great that advertising only accounted for 0·7% of turnover.

Logic and Emotion

There are two basic types of advertising. The first relies on rational argument to convince consumers of a brand's superiority and is sometimes called the 'hard sell'. Very specific benefits are claimed for one brand against others in the same market. This kind of advertising is most often used on products whose performance can be logically measured and compared with competitive brands. It is most common in advertising for washing powders (whiteness results), aspirin products (speed of action), food (amount or quality of ingredients) or retail stores (low prices).

The second type of advertising aims to convey more emotional benefits, such as status, safety, personal fulfilment or sex appeal, and is often referred to as the 'soft sell' approach. Product categories using emotional appeals extensively are cigarettes, cosmetics, cars and beer. Most airline advertising is also directed at the senses rather than the mind and is based on a concealed safety theme.

Safety is a matter of prime concern to all passengers, and fears about it are one of the main reasons why so many people have

---

* Figures from *Advertising Age*, 1970. American figures have been used because comparable ones for the UK are not readily available.

never flown (even in the USA, less than 40% of the population
has ever been airborne). But airlines are not prepared to advertise safety on a competitive basis, because a good safety record
could be wiped out overnight through just one major disaster.
Consequently, the safety theme is muted in alluring and
emotive executions, but it shows through in the claims of most
well known campaigns for airlines:

> 'Pan American—the world's most experienced airline';
> 'BOAC takes good care of you';
> 'Fly the friendly skies of United';
> 'Eastern makes it easier to fly'.

Most advertising falls mainly within one category or another
but some brands mix rational and emotive appeals almost equally.

One of the most consistently well advertised UK brands over
the past twenty years is Persil. In the washing powder market,
where most advertising is wooden and dull, Persil's campaigns
have been distinctive and effective.

Back in 1945, the three brand leaders in the washing powder
market were Rinso (Lever), Oxydol (Procter & Gamble) and
Persil (Lever), all of them soap powders as opposed to synthetic
detergents. Rinso and Oxydol never really survived the introduction of detergents in the 1950s, Rinso being withdrawn
some years ago, and Oxydol now having less than 3% of the
total market. Persil remained brand leader until 1969, when
enzyme products were introduced, and it is still the second largest
brand after Ariel. One gains some understanding of the hurdles
which Persil has surmounted from the fact that soap powders
have been virtually eliminated by detergents in the USA,
Canada and Germany. The outstanding quality of Persil's
advertising support must be a major reason for its continued
survival against very long odds, because there is certainly
nothing special about the product itself.

Persil advertising has always been based on a whiteness claim
—'Persil washes whiter'—which ran continually from the
1930s. However, the whiteness benefit was related to the wider
frame of the family, and the Persil user portrayed as the good
mother (though not cloying), who always did her best for the
family. One aspect of this was the use of Persil. The advertising
appeal was a combination of product benefit and emotional

satisfaction. The treatment was credible because the choice of Persil was shown to be merely one aspect of the housewife's life, rather than, as in much washing powder advertising, a question of universal significance and interest. Since the launch of enzyme powders, Persil has sensibly added a softness benefit to its advertising, but maintained the whiteness claim and the quiet but emotive family approach.

If publicity about the health hazards of enzymes continues to build up, Persil may well regain brand leadership—the advertising campaign of the Swedish Co-op washing powder—'Unpolluted by enzymes'—is a symptom of what could become a more widespread onslaught on enzyme brands.

Finding Out Which Half is Wasted

The comment 'I know that half of my advertising budget is wasted, but I'm not sure which half' was made many years ago and has now passed into advertising folklore.* It raises a disturbingly relevant issue, to which no satisfactory solution has yet been found. Setting advertising budgets and assessing the effectiveness of advertising campaigns remains an approximate art, and although techniques are available for making the whole business more scientific, they are acknowledged to have serious weaknesses. The evaluation of advertising still relies heavily on the personal judgement of experienced executives.

Every company would give a lot to know the effect of advertising on its sales, but this can rarely be done with any precision, except in the case of mail-order sales. The trouble is that advertising is only one of many variables which also affect sales. Indeed, an advertising campaign is itself influenced by four sub-variables—the content of the message, the amount of money placed behind it, the choice of media and the amount of competitive activity.

Tradition and guesswork play an important part in the setting of advertising budgets, and any sharp accountant in search of corporate cost savings could have a field day in challenging the basis of advertising appropriations in most companies. In 1968 the National Industrial Conference Board conducted a survey among 267 senior American marketing executives on how they spent their budgets. The overwhelming majority used either arbitrary or highly subjective methods, and the main ones were as follows:

* Most frequently attributed to the first Lord Leverhulme.

(1) the task approach;
(2) the historical approach;
(3) the percentage of turnover (or case-rate) approach;
(4) the share of market approach;
(5) the 'match competition' approach.

Because none of these methods are ideal, they are not elaborated upon here, but for those who are interested, Appendix F contains an examination of each one. Of all the possible approaches, the percentage of turnover one looks to be the best, provided allowance is made for the well argued exception. The snag is, however, that advertising budgets cannot be effectively established by using mechanical guidelines and formulae on their own. These must be supplemented by the results of market-testing of alternative advertising weights, and this point is taken up again later on, since it is one of the principles of offensive advertising.

Techniques for assessing the strength of individual advertising campaigns are much more advanced than those for establishing the budgets, but they are still far from perfect. A long-standing technique is the *recall and playback* method. This involves interviewers calling on homes owning TV, usually 24 hours after the TV commercial has been screened. Their purpose is to check whether the audience recalled the commercial and, if so, the detailed points remembered. The assumption behind this technique is that advertising can only affect purchase in so far as it is remembered by potential purchasers. It has many opponents and numerous weaknesses. For example, a consumer may recall a TV commercial perfectly but find the message totally unconvincing; or may remember things he or she doesn't like in the commercial. In addition, a commercial whose story is easily verbalized may be recalled better than a more persuasive one relying on mood and emotion.

Then there is the *consumer attitude study*, in which detailed attitudes to various competing brands are compared, often at different points in time. This is useful in highlighting the aspects of products to which consumers atttach most importance and in getting a rating of each brand against these yardsticks. It is also invaluable as a guide to developing advertising strategy. But it has the disadvantage that attitudes are slow to change and are affected by many marketing influences apart from advertising.

Thirdly, there are various techniques for measuring the *persuasiveness and interest level* of advertising. Among the methods used are electronic rating scales, by which each viewer of commercials in a hall rotates a hand-held dial, indicating his or her level of interest throughout the advertising. In this way, variations in degree of interest throughout a commercial can be monitored. Other methods involve recording changes in the blood pressure, discussing the advertising in depth with individuals or groups, or simulating a purchase situation.

Many of these techniques for evaluating persuasiveness or interest levels have been greatly refined over the years, but still fail to reproduce the consumer's real viewing situation, which very often involves a family group at the end of a hard day, with many distractions. Table 13.2 summarizes the purpose of the main techniques for testing the quality of TV advertising. Most of them are appplied before or shortly after the advertising is first shown in the market place.

TABLE 13.2 FACTORS WHICH EACH RESEARCH TECHNIQUE
AIMS TO MEASURE

	Strength of strategy	Strength of advertising execution
Recall and playback	No	Yes
Attitude studies	Yes	Sometimes
Persuasion/interest studies	Yes	Yes

B. PRINCIPLES OF OFFENSIVE ADVERTISING

Advertising is a product which manufacturers buy from an outside agency. But the quality obtained can vary from the very good to the very bad, and it is much more difficult for a manufacturer to obtain the best possible results from an advertising agency than from any supplier of raw materials or capital equipment. Everyone knows that good advertising costs no more than bad, and that one company spending £250 000 well may achieve greater impact than another using £1 million poorly.

It is hard to develop outstanding advertising because this requires *relevant* creativity on the part of the agency, and an open-minded response from the manufacturer. A new idea is fragile and easily crushed by traditional thinking or highly elaborate approval procedures. The manufacturer taking an offensive marketing approach to advertising will work closely with the agency in developing strategy, and beyond that will build up a relationship in which creativity can flourish. The principles of offensive advertising follow the objectives listed below.

1. Set Crystal Clear Advertising Strategies

Strategies are more essential in advertising than in any other part of the business. The need for 'relevant' creativity has already been stressed. Advertising is unlikely to be effective, however creative, unless its message stresses a benefit which is important to the consumer.

An advertising strategy forces the client and the agency to work out the overall impression they wish a campaign to convey. This will involve them in establishing priorities between the various communication aims—an important exercise, because a major cause of poor advertising is the attempt to establish too many points in too short a time. The strategy should be highly competitive, and aim to establish an impression of superiority on at least one important score. Once developed, it will provide a valuable brief to the agency's creative staff, and facilitate the approval of the advertising subsequently turned out.

2. Create a Climate Where Creativity can Flourish

Few would deny the desirability of this objective, but there is a diversity of sometimes conflicting opinion as to how it can best be achieved, and this section will therefore inevitably be rather subjective. I feel pretty confident that the approach used by many large companies—formal agency presentations, tiers of approval levels and a failure positively to encourage radically new ideas—does not produce an atmosphere from which outstanding advertising can emerge.

Perhaps a good starting point for the manufacturer is to tell the advertising agency that he values its freedom from the traditional thinking in which he is enmeshed, and hopes the agency will exploit this objectivity to develop radically new ideas. He might add that, while he appreciates innovation involves risk, he is prepared to accept this subject to appropriate testing.

No company ever tells an agency openly that it is not enthused at the prospect of breaking new ground and quite satisfied to ring the changes on humdrum and conventional approaches. But, through response to new ideas, it can spell out this impression loud and clear by implication. And no agency, however determined, will continue to generate radically new thinking for a client who clearly finds it rather frightening. Many companies like the thought of new ideas in the abstract, but will not accept the iconoclastic approach that can make them a reality—and the caption to a *New*

Yorker cartoon of the chairman addressing his Board sums this up well: 'What we need, gentlemen, is a completely brand new idea that has been thoroughly tested.'*

But the manufacturer has to go further than giving the agency a charter to think freely. He has a part to play too in bringing his knowledge of the consumer to bear on the communications task, and in approving the advertising. This part can either add or detract from the final quality, depending on the system he adopts. In large companies a number of people are involved in the advertising process—usually too many. They typically fall into two groups—junior and middle management, who work closely with the agency in developing the advertising, and top management which gives final approval. The problem is how to ensure that the brilliant new advertising idea will run through this formidable gauntlet successfully.

As ever, there is no magic formula to apply. But certain guidelines can be followed, which help to nurture and protect innovative thinking. Firstly, it is advisable to clear the advertising strategy with senior management before embarking on creative executions, because nothing is more frustrating for the copywriter who has sweated over a new campaign for weeks than to have it turned down on strategic grounds. Secondly, it is usually best for the client to have frequent informal meetings with the agency, in which the advertising can be developed on a partnership basis, rather than to have occasional full-dress presentations, since these tend to lead to confrontation and entrenched positions. Finally, the fewer people involved in the advertising process at the client end, the better, which is why I don't believe in having company advertising managers or executives in addition to marketing personnel.

3. Assess Advertising Systematically

Every advertising agency has its own stock of horror stories, about the client who wanted the print ad to be green because it was his wife's favourite colour, or the Board of directors which informed the agency of its desire for a cartoon or jingle campaign this year please. Naturally, the client has the ultimate responsibility for profit, and he is entitled to comment upon any advertising proposal or to reject it out of hand. But advertising is a very subjective business, and an agency has a right to expect a client to assess it in a disciplined way.

If a professional code of conduct were drawn up for offensive

* Quoted in the chapter on 'Iconoclasm' in *Plotting Marketing Strategy*, edited by Lee Adler.

marketers when evaluating television advertising proposals, it might run something like this.

Article (i) Client has an obligation to ensure that he fully understands what the agency is trying to achieve with the advertising. If he does not follow the action of the commercial or is confused by the technical instructions, he should say so. Client should ascertain whether the commercial is envisaged as a 'once only' effort or as part of a continuing campaign. He should also be clear as to the type of voice-over proposed, the nature of the music and the kind of characters envisaged—if possible, a tape of the sound track and a casting specification for the actors should be provided before the storyboard is approved for production.

Article (ii) When the agency has completed its presentation, which will preferably be simple and informal, the client should read through the pictures on the storyboard, ignoring the words. The message of the commercial ought to be understandable on the basis of the pictures alone, because TV is a visual medium. Client should then read the words in conjunction with the pictures. He is not advised to go through the storyboard more than twice at this stage, since he should be putting himself in the shoes of the viewer seeing the commercial for the first time. After the second reading, client should close his eyes and recollect the action of the commercial. The basic impression he gains from the commercial should be consistent with the agreed advertising strategy.

Article (iii) Client should satisfy himself that the commercial will be interesting to the viewer and command close attention. In doing this, client will do well to recall how his own attitudes vary from those of the consumer, so that he can allow for the difference. The viewer has a low degree of interest in most everyday products, regards television as entertainment rather than as a selling vehicle, and is more likely to live in Birmingham than in Belgravia. Client should look for advertising which combines his objective of selling a product with the consumer's interest in being entertained.

Article (iv) Client must feel confident that the commercial will get across the points intended. Bad communication is due to failure by one party to understand how the other party looks at things. In a commercial something which is intended to be incidental could dominate, and cause the viewer to miss the main selling point. For instance, unsuitable casting can completely distract a housewife —a presenter she doesn't like, a mother and daughter where the mother looks too young and glamourous, a child behaving rudely.

Each one of these things, though only conceived as a background by the maker of the commercial, can send the housewife's mind running off on a completely irrelevant train of thought.

Article (v) Client should consider whether the advertising is likely to be understood by the average viewer. Commercials which contain too many selling ideas, numerous changes in location or complex execution are unlikely to be comprehended and should be simplified. Client must expect neither special knowledge nor deductive ability from the viewer, and any message which jumps a stage in the selling argument will not be absorbed. Finally, client should check that the words and pictures knit up. If the two are pulling in different directions, the effect will be like two people talking at cross-purposes and neither will be understood.

4. Test Out Alternative Spending Levels

The most effective means of establishing the optimum level of advertising, but by far the least frequently used, is market-testing of alternative spending levels. For example, advertising weights equivalent to £0·5 million, £1·0 million and £1·5 million could be tested in different TV areas and the sales results compared six months later. Even though it is never easy to find areas which are typical of the national situation, and varying competitive activity is a factor outside your control, the results of higher and lower spending tests are nearly always useful. They are most effective when the levels of spending chosen for comparison vary widely.

Since the setting of advertising budgets is a problem of acknowledged difficulty, it is surprising that more companies do not run continuous tests of different spending levels. It is hoped that programmes of this kind will become more widespread in the 1970s, as general and financial management insists on better justification of advertising expenditures.

SUMMARY

Advertising makes people aware of the existence and advantages of goods and services. It relies for its effectiveness on information, logic and emotion.

Advertising is hard to evaluate, because it is only one of many variables affecting sales. The main approaches used to set advertising budgets are task, historical, percentage of turnover, share of market, and 'match competition'. The percentage of turnover appears to be the best of a poor bunch, but market-testing of alternative weights of spending is much more effective than any mechanical technique.

A manufacturer taking the offensive approach will set crystal clear advertising strategies, create a climate where creativity can flourish, and develop a system for assessing advertising systematically.

A. BASIC PRINCIPLES

A channel of distribution is the means by which products are moved from the *manufacturer* to the ultimate *consumer*. It is best envisaged as a railway line connecting these two extreme points. The product may run straight down the line without interruption, as in the case of brushes sold door-to-door, or it may have to pass through a network of junctions, commonly known as middlemen. Distribution channels are customers of the manufacturer just as surely as the ultimate consumer. Any company applying the offensive marketing approach to distribution channels must therefore study their needs closely, and aim to meet them as far as is profitable.

Types of Distribution Channel

Distribution channels vary greatly in complexity and efficiency. The channel for electricity is simple and almost ideal—the manufacturer has mass distribution and the consumer has instant availability, literally at the turn of a switch. By contrast, the channel for man-made fibres is extremely complex—the chain runs through spinners, dyers, weavers or knitters, garment manufacturers, retailers, and finally reaches the consumer. Figure 4 (overleaf) shows the most common types of distribution channel.

Most products reach the consumer by more than one type of distribution outlet:

(1) Airline tickets can be bought direct from city ticket offices, from the travel department of large companies, through travel agents or at the airport.

(2) One can purchase crisps from pubs, ice cream kiosks, petrol stations, vending machines, grocers, confectioners, newsagents and tobacconists, and also through a variety of wholesalers.

(3) Women's underwear is available from department stores,

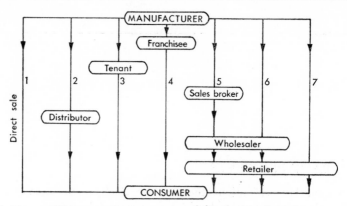

Figure 4   Common types of distribution channel

mail-order firms, specialist clothing shops or Marks & Spencer, and in the home.

For the majority of markets, one type of distribution outlet is predominant, even though others of less significance may exist. The main types of channel are direct selling, distributors, franchises, sales brokers, lessees, wholesalers and retailers.

In *direct selling* the product is sold by the manufacturer straight to the consumer. Brushes, life assurance, encyclopaedias and certain toiletries are sold in this way. It is most suitable for products of high value which benefit by demonstration.

Distributors usually act as the manufacturer's agent in selling his product, often on an exclusive basis. Most of the cars and petrol in the UK are sold through distributors. They normally own their premises, and provide capital and labour. The manufacturer is responsible for the product and its advertising or promotion. He may also help with personnel training, technical advice or financial loans.

Franchising is the way for the ambitious young man to make £10 000 a year at the drop of a hat, if you believe some of the ads. Under the franchising system, a company will provide a product plus know-how to an entrepreneur with capital. Franchising is common in soft drinks, launderettes and snack food operations (e.g. Wimpy). Coca-Cola is the most famous franchiser of all, and anyone holding its franchise would regard £10000 a year as a small sum. It provides specially prepared syrup to the bottlers, and is responsible for advertising, promotion and merchandising. The bottlers dilute and carbonate the syrup, and then distribute it throughout their franchised area. The advantage of franchising for a company is that widespread distribution can be achieved quickly and at low cost.

Sales brokers are independent sales companies who sell the products of a number of non-competing manufacturers and get a commission on sales in return. Their customers are either companies too small to have their own sales force, or larger ones who use brokers temporarily to meet a short-term situation like a distribution drive or the launch of a new brand. Sales brokers are common in the USA, but not so widely used in the UK.

The lessee is a feature of the licensed drink trade. Unlike the distributor, the lessee only rents his premises from the brewer. The lessee usually has little freedom of manoeuvre in the product he can purchase and can only sell those authorized by the brewer.

Wholesalers and Retailers are too well known to require any elaboration.

The Changing Face of Distribution

Distribution channels resemble the hour hand of a watch. They are always moving, but each individual movement is so small as to be invisible in isolation. The cumulative movement over a number of years can, however, be massive.

> For example, there have been major changes in distribution patterns in the 1960s. The proportion of non-food sales accounted for by mail-order has risen from 2·5% in 1961 to 7·1% in 1969.* Chemists and other specialist shops have lost out to grocers in many categories. Cash-and-carry methods now dominate much wholesale distribution. The location of stores is turning away from high streets to housing estates, following the movement of population. And self-service shops increased their share of grocery turnover from 15% to 64% in the ten years from 1959.
>
> Other changes will take place in the 1970s. Discount stores, 'one stop shopping' near out-of-town arterial roads, self-service petrol stations and further growth in supermarkets are all likely to develop dramatically. Because of the seeming permanence of distribution channels at any single point in time, it is easy for manufacturers to respond too slowly to their evolution.

Key Factors in Channel Selection

In selecting distribution channels for new products, or reviewing channel arrangements for existing ones, six key factors need to be

* From Department of Trade and Industry figures.

considered—exposure to target consumers, product performance requirements, control, flexibility, manufacturer profit and distributor needs. Each one is assessed below.

(1) *Exposure to target consumers*   From the viewpoint of the manufacturer, the primary purpose of any distribution channel is to make his products available to his target consumers. A good product may fail because it is in the wrong channel and not exposed to the people most likely to buy it.

(2) *Product performance requirements*   The distribution channel should deliver the product to its consumer in the form the manufacturer requires and, at minimum, maintain quality and freshness of stock. This is of particular importance to producers of frozen foods, newspapers, bread, meat and fruit. In addition, the manufacturer may wish the channel to maintain minimum retail prices or to provide certain skills which are a necessary part of the product sale (e.g. advising on choice of cosmetic, servicing cars.)

(3) *Control*   A manufacturer's control over his channels depends upon his degree of ownership, the number of channel steps and the consumer appeal of his products. Large and powerful manufacturers like General Motors or Coca-Cola have a lot of influence over their independent distributors or franchisees, because their strong *consumer* appeal provides the channel with a large profit opportunity. At minimum, a manufacturer needs enough control over his channels to achieve his aims of exposure to the right consumers, maintenance of product quality and profitability. Those with worthwhile consumer franchises do not usually require any ownership.

(4) *Flexibility*   Channel decisions are almost inevitably long-term in effect, but even so it is desirable to retain maximum flexibility to alter channel emphasis.

(5) *Manufacturer Profit*   Offensive marketers will seek the type and mix of distribution channel that gives them maximum revenue at minimum cost in the long term.

(6) *Channel needs*   Owners of distribution channels are also in business to make a profit and will refuse to handle products which don't meet their financial needs.

Product and Channel Fit

It follows from the previous section that the existence of an effective distribution system depends on both the manufacturer and the channel deriving worthwhile benefits from it. The cigarette companies have a good fit with their distribution channels:

The major channel for cigarettes is through CTNs (confectioners, tobacconists and newsagents). What the cigarette companies want from their channels is the widest possible availability and display, and CTNs provide that.

From the viewpoint of CTNs, cigarettes are an attractive product, even though the low profit margins often cause grumbles. Volume and product turn are high, the category has broad appeal and draws 'traffic' to the store, there is little price competition, and no problem of storage, perishability or seasonality. In this case a reasonable balance has been struck between distributor and manufacturer and both derive major benefits.

By contrast, magazines have a relatively poor fit with the same distribution channels:

Magazines of all kinds are also distributed primarily through CTNs. The distribution requirements for magazines are similar to those for cigarettes—availability and display—but CTNs do not meet these objectives effectively. With a few notable exceptions like W. H. Smith, they do not display magazines attractively, and repeatedly run out of issues before their expiry date, because they are more interested in minimizing waste than in maximizing profit.*

From the angle of the CTNs magazines are not ideal. They are bulky in relation to their retail value, highly obsolescent, difficult to display effectively in a restricted space and unpredictable in demand. Of course magazines also have undeniable advantages. They attract customers to the shop, are not subject to price competition, and offer good margins even when allowance has been made for waste. But present channel arrangements leave a lot to be desired for both manufacturers and distributors.

B. PRINCIPLES OF OFFENSIVE CHANNEL MARKETING

1. Give Priority to Channel Marketing

Because distribution channels are outside the company framework, they are sometimes wrongly regarded by businessmen as fixed,

---

* Few magazines are offered to CTNs on a sale or return basis. The retailer usually has to absorb the cost of unsold copies. Waste is only 1% in UK, compared with up to 20% in parts of USA.

and are rarely given as much priority as the product, the packaging or the advertising which are entirely controlled by the manufacturer. As Peter Drucker points out: 'many businessmen—especially makers of industrial products—are as unaware they use distribution channels, let alone that they depend on them, as Molière's Monsieur Jourdain was of the fact that he spoke prose'.* Add to this the fact that the long term nature of channel decisions gives them a tendency towards the *status quo*, and it is not hard to understand why many companies folllow such non-offensive channel policies.

And yet, as we have seen, the structure and balance of distribution channels is constantly changing. At any moment in time, old channels are dying and new ones springing up. This dynamic situation, together with the lethargic attitude of most companies towards it, gives the offensive marketer a fine opportunity to innovate. New approaches to distribution are often easier to develop than superior products, and yet can lead to equally large breakthroughs in profit, as various examples quoted later on show.

2. Audit Existing Channels

The first step in an offensive programme is to audit existing channels. Perhaps one or more channels should be dropped because they have become obsolete or unprofitable. Hoover took a bold decision of this kind in the early 1960s:

> Hoover built up a very successful washing machine business in the 1950s, using the door-to-door sales approach. By the early 1960s, the company had 4500 sales servicemen. They would call on the housewife in her home, demonstrate a machine, sell it and then have it delivered via a local appliance dealer stocking Hoover products. The dealers were making a trade margin on every sale but in many cases doing very little to earn it, since most of the sales were being made by Hoover personnel.
>
> Hoover decided that this duplication had to be eliminated, since distribution costs had become too high, and now that washing machines were well established, there was less need for demonstration. Another practical problem was that Hoover was widening its range and there was a limit to the number of products the salesman could lug around for demonstration purposes. So Hoover executed the Net Dealer Plan. The number of sales servicemen was cut drastically from 4500 to 360, and the responsibility for selling was placed

* Peter F. Drucker, *Managing for Results*.

squarely on the shoulders of the dealers, who underwent intensive sales training programmes.*

Few companies ever make such radical changes in channel policy, but every organization can benefit by conducting a channel audit each year. This involves working out the relative profitability of each distribution channel, taking into account the allocation of sales force time, discount levels and delivery costs.

An audit of this kind can produce some real surprises—for example, one grocery company discovered that it was making a net loss in its trading with multiples after carefully allocating overheads and that all its profits were being earned in the independent and wholesale sectors of the trade. The problem was caused by giving excessive overriding discounts to multiples and by devoting an unreasonably high proportion of sales force time to them. To solve this, a new discount structure for multiples was worked out to tie in more closely to revenue performance, and costing the company less on a percentage basis. The sales force was also reorganized so as to give less attention to multiples.

Channel policy should always look ahead. A useful rule of thumb is to relate the proportion of sales force effort to be placed against a channel *this year* to the channel's estimated share of company profit the *following* year. In other words, if multiples were expected to account for 42% of your profit in 1972, you would allocate 42% of your sales effort to them in 1971. This is a useful starting point, although in practice it may be rightly modified by other factors, such as the sales task to be done in multiples.

3. Investigate Existing Channels not Used by your Markets

A suitable new channel for your market may be lying unexploited, waiting to give an innovator's advantage to the first company to discover it. As observed earlier, there is an inbuilt *status quo* in distribution channels and some channel arrangements are based more on tradition than on logic. Why, for instance, do national beer brands in America not franchise local brewers to use their names and so enable them to benefit from heavy advertising and skilful merchandising? Why are packaged tours not sold through

* Adapted from Doina Thomas, 'The Hard Times of Hoover' (*Management Today*, March 1970).

department stores and supermarkets rather than solely through travel agents? The travel agent has no access to the mass market and his original role was to provide specialized advice or to make complex booking arrangements. But a packaged tour has nearly all the service built in and is a product which, in January or February, can be sold almost as easily as baked beans.

In the 1950s and 1960s, a number of product categories previously restricted to specialist outlets moved into the grocery trade, and for the first time reaped the benefits of mass distribution. There is often, of course, a conflict between the old channel and the new, and the manufacturer has to balance the possible loss from the one against the likely gain from the other. When ICI decided to give more priority to the do-it-yourself market in the mid-1950s, it did so in a way that did not offend decorators.

> In the early 1950s Valspar was the brand leader, and ICI trailed well behind. The majority of paint was used by decorators, and bought by them from wholesalers. The retail side of the market was at that time quite undeveloped. ICI saw the potential of the do-it-yourself market and decided to give priority to achieving good retail distribution (via wholesalers) to complement its plan to build up strong consumer brand awareness of the name Dulux.
>
> To sweeten the pill for the decorators and maintain their goodwill, Dulux opened a campaign of 'Say Dulux to your decorator'. This helped reassure the decorators while ICI built up retail distribution in ironmongers and specialist paint shops, and spent heavily on advertising, by the standards of the paint market. By about 1957, Dulux became brand leader in the paint market, a position it has never since relinquished.

In order to get the most out of a new distribution channel, a manufacturer may have to develop a new product, tailored to fit the channel's needs. This was the case with *Family Circle* and *Living*, two magazines jointly owned by the Thomson Organization and the *New York Times*.

> Both *Family Circle* and *Living* are women's service magazines; one concentrates on recipes and cookery, the other on home design. They have in common a sensible down-to-earth approach, and are unique in being distributed through grocery stores, in contrast to the other women's magazines which are

sold via newsagents or on subscription. The grocery store is an ideal channel for these magazines. They achieve permanent display, have no competition within the store, and are exposed to the mass market. In addition, they can run joint promotions with grocery products (like Oxo and Brooke Bond tea), using linked displays.

Family Circle and *Living* also have a lot to offer the grocery store. They take up no floor or shelf space, because the special dispenser unit can be placed near the cash register. Their 49% margin is well above the average for grocery brands. And the recipes they contain are geared to supermarket products.

Unlike virtually every other major woman's magazine, both of these publications are showing impressive growth, even though they are priced at $6\frac{1}{2}$–$7\frac{1}{2}$p, compared with *Woman* and *Woman's Own* at 5p. Comparable circulation figures for 1969–70 were as follows:

	1969 ('000)	*1970 ('000)*	*% Change*
Family Circle	1160	1200	+3%
Living	420	500	+19%
*Woman**	2508	2051	−18%
*Woman's Own**	1967	1703	−13%

The reason for the success of *Family Circle* and *Living* was a combination of appealing product and unique but highly appropriate distribution channels. If they had been distributed through conventional newsagent channels, it is hard to believe that sales would have reached their current levels, since they would have faced the disadvantages of direct competition with other magazines, limited visibility and display, and lack of exposure to a mass public. Equally, if the magazines had not been tailored to the needs of the grocery trade, they would never have gained a worthwhile level of distribution.†

4. Create New Channels

Companies entering a new market from scratch may find that existing channels do not adequately meet their needs. If they are

---

* It is only fair to state that *Woman* and *Woman's Own* had a price rise from 10*d* to 1/- in November 1969, which deflated the 1970 circulation figures versus 1969.

† Adapted from Geoffrey Sheridan, 'How the magazine sisters found supermarket success' (*Campaign*, 5 February 1971).

particularly enterprising, they will pioneer entirely new channels of
their own making, like Avon Products, whose net profit has risen
from £7 million in 1961 to £32 million in 1969.

> Avon innovated direct selling techniques in the cosmetic
> market, and although it has had many followers, none has
> repeated its success. Avon products are in the middle price
> range for cosmetics and, though generally well packaged,
> they are at best of parity performance to the competitive
> brands stocked by retail stores. The products are sold direct
> to the housewife in her own home by Avon representatives,
> of whom there are 400 000 world-wide. They are part-time
> saleswomen, and most of Avon's volume is sold on promotion
> at large reductions below list price.
>
> The secret of Avon's success is that women feel more
> secure about purchasing cosmetics in their own home, where
> they have privacy and time. Cosmetics are very personal pur-
> chases, and women like to take their time in choosing between
> a range of alternatives (Avon has over 400 products). In
> addition, women sometimes feel intimidated by the knowledge
> and appearance of beauty counsellors at department stores.
> This is an especially potent factor in Germany, where middle-
> aged women were discouraged during their youth (when
> Hitler was in power) from wearing cosmetics and are conse-
> quently concerned at exposing their ignorance in public. Avon,
> which only started business in Germany in 1960, now has a
> higher sales revenue there than the top ten international
> cosmetic firms in combination.

Tupperware parties are another form of new distribution created
by the Rexall Drug Company in order to sell a new, high priced
product which benefited by personal demonstration.

5. Develop New Relationships with Distribution Channels

Some companies with a very enlightened approach to the consumer
apply quite different yardsticks to the trade. While they are concerned to discover consumer needs and fulfil them wherever
profitable, their attitude to the trade often approaches hostility.
A familiar line of reasoning is that the manufacturer can create
strong consumer demand by providing an appealing product and
heavy advertising, and that the trade has no choice but to stock it.
Very often the trade will co-operate because it will take a profit

opportunity even where it is offered by an unpopular manufacturer.

However, companies have more to gain from active trade support than mere passive co-operation. And the enlisting of trade enthusiasm for a manufacturer's products is not just a matter of offering high margins, any more than low price is the only way of building a consumer franchise. Companies recognising the trade as a customer, and searching for ways to fulfil its needs profitably, are likely to get the best out of their distribution channels. Even in the 1920s, General Motors was applying this approach:

In the American motor industry in the 1920s, the dealer or *vending machines!* distributor was usually given an exclusive franchise to sell General Motors cars in one area. He provided capital, a place of business, salesmen and mechanics. GM supplied the cars, and helped the dealer with advertising, promotion, training and technical advice. Over the years 1923–29, automobiles changed from a seller's to a buyer's market, and the position of distributors deteriorated. GM franchises were less in demand and the economic situation of many distributors was poor.

In the early twenties, manufacturers felt their task was over when they had sold and delivered a car to a dealer. His role tended to be minimized and many people in the industry felt that purchasers were already pre-sold by the advertising when they entered the dealer's showroom. As the twenties rolled on, three needs of distributors became apparent to GM, following a prolonged investigation. First of all, many dealers were being left with substantial stocks of the previous year's car when the new model was introduced. This meant losses for dealers, and a reluctance to buy either the old model in the latter part of the year, or the new model when it was first introduced. Secondly, few dealers had accounting systems at all, and those who did used rather primitive methods. This lack of financial control reduced the distributor's return on capital employed. And finally, some otherwise suitable entrepreneurs were being prevented from taking up GM distributorships through lack of capital.

At various points in the latter 1920s, GM acted to help distributors meet all these needs. It was the first motor car manufacturer to agree to share responsibility with dealers for the left-over inventory at the end of the old model year. In 1927 it set up the Motors Accounting Company, which developed a standard accounting system applicable to all dealers and supplied staff to install it. In 1929 GM established the Motors Holding Division, which provided temporary financing for dealers and concentrated mainly on developing new ones. Ford followed this move in 1950, Chrysler in 1954.

All this helped GM strengthen the efficiency and loyalty of its distribution channel. Thanks to the improved financial control, GM now gets monthly financial statements from over 80% of its dealers, accounting for at least 95% of sales, and this is invaluable for monitoring the performance of distributors. And from 1929 to 1962, Motors Holding Division invested in 1850 dealerships, of which 1395 paid back their loans and only 198 were discontinued because of sub-normal operations.*

In a rather more modest way, BEA has successfully attempted to meet the needs of travel agents.

Most airline sales are made through travel agents, whose role is to offer specialized advice and service to the consumer. Like GM distributors in the 1920s, travel agents today tend to have inadequate statistics about their business and are rarely large enough to run their own staff training schemes. In addition, they show little enterprise in seeking out new business, and generally expect it to come to them.

BEA sets out to meet these needs in a number of ways, though in my view they are still too modest in scale. It runs training courses for certain agency personnel, covering reservations methods, ticketing procedures, handling of complaints and so on. It has excellent sales statistics, and produces for each major agent a monthly breakdown of its BEA sales by destination. This is available to the BEA salesman a month after the event and not only gives him a powerful selling tool but also enables the travel agent to identify the routes on which he has gained or lost business compared with the previous year. To a greater degree than most airlines, BEA salesmen also make a point of feeding local sales leads to agents—they might hear that a particular company is holding a conference in Japan, or that another one is opening up an overseas subsidiary in France.

Much more could be done by manufacturers to meet the funda-mental needs of their distribution channels. An understanding

* Adapted from Alfred P. Sloan Jr, *My Years with General Motors* (Sidgwick & Jackson, 1965; Pan, 1969).

and imaginative approach to channels is much more profitable in the longer term than continued face-to-face confrontation with them over margins and discounts.

SUMMARY

A channel of distribution is the means by which products are moved from the manufacturer to the ultimate consumer. The main types of channel are direct selling, distributors, franchises, sales brokers, lessees, wholesalers and retailers.

Six factors should be considered in selecting or reviewing channels—exposure to target consumers, product performance requirements, control, flexibility, manufacturer profit and channel needs.

The principles of offensive channel marketing are summarized below.

Distribution channels should be given high priority, since new approaches are often easier to develop than superior products and yet can lead to equally large profit breakthroughs. They are often neglected because they are outside the company framework.

Existing channels should be audited, and adjustments in priority made in line with their changing importance. A useful rule of thumb is to relate the proportion of sales force effort to be placed against a channel this year to the channel's estimated share of company profit the following year.

Presently available channels not used by your markets should be investigated for potential, and if existing channels are not effective, a company may pioneer entirely new channels of its own making.

Companies regarding the trade as a customer, and searching for ways to fulfil its needs profitably, are likely to get the best out of their distribution channels.

V OFFENSIVE MARKETING
_____*FOR THE FUTURE*

All the techniques for offensive execution described in Part IV apply as much to new products as to existing ones. However, there are a number of separate issues and techniques which have special application to new products. Part V covers new product development and acquisition together, since they are both routes to the same destination—corporate growth—and should be seen as alternatives. Whenever a company decides to diversify into a new field, it should examine the economics of acquisition as compared with internal new product development.

There are four chapters in Part V. Chapter 15, 'New Products—the Difference between Success and Failure', draws conclusions from 100 new product launches in the 1960s and identifies the factors separating success from failure. Chapter 16, 'New Products—Offensive Techniques', outlines a number of techniques and attitudes whose acceptance will increase the effectiveness of a company's new product programme. Market segmentation is a device for improving the positioning of existing brands and for uncovering new product opportunities, and Chapter 17 outlines how it can be used effectively. Chapter 18 deals with the marketing approach to acquisitions, and establishes that the use of marketing as well as financial yardsticks is an essential part of offensive marketing.

Offensive marketing is intimately concerned with innovation and it has the greatest payoff when applied to the corporate development areas of new products and acquisitions.

15: New Products—the Difference between Success and Failure

'There is a mythical corporation known as Lip Service Inc. It does not manufacture pomades for chapped lips. Instead, it manufactures executives who say "We're determined to mount an aggressive acquisition program," and "Our company is dedicated to being in the forefront of key breakthroughs in the all important field of new products."

'Of course all the key men thrusting forward and breaking through at Lip Service are only expected to talk about these things, not to do them. New product development and marketing, especially, is the "motherhood" of management. You never read a president's letter to stockholders that says "New products could cost this company its shirt and we're going to steer clear of them". Just the opposite. New productry is a synonym for success and executives desperate to appear "modern" make it the order of their day.

'The doing, not the talking, is a traumatic experience for any company.'★

WHAT IS A NEW PRODUCT?

New products need to be distinguished from line extensions, since the two are often confused, especially by companies who wish to make their new product record sound much better than it really is. Under the definition used here, a new product is seen by the consumer as a separate entity, rather than as a development or modification of an existing brand. The key element is consumer perception, rather than degree of technical change. Line extensions are developments of existing brands. They are typically given little or no separate advertising support, and no attempt is made to create a separate image from the 'umbrella brand'.

The differences between these two classes are easier to describe than to define. Products with a new brand name, like Ariel, obviously qualify as new, under any definition. And new flavours, perfumes or sizes of existing brands are always line extensions— a new variety of Heinz soup or babyfood, a lemon version of Silvikrin shampoo, or a king-size of a detergent for instance. Brands

★ David J. Mahoney, President of Canada Dry, quoted in J. T. Gerlach and C. A. Wainwright, *The Successful Management of New Products* (Pitman, 1970).

launched under family names create the greatest difficulty in definition—for instance would a Lyons Viennese Whirl be regarded as an extension of the Lyons cake line or as a new brand? The only reliable guide is to guess how the consumer would see it.

These distinctions have practical importance, because while new brand introductions are properly regarded as development activity, line extensions are usually no more than a maintenance obligation. Successful new brands improve a company's overall market position and move it forward in the long term. Line extensions, however, are usually essential to hold a brand's standing, merely because they are housekeeping activities in which the rest of the market will also be indulging. Every brand is continually seeking flavour or size opportunities. Those with large lines like soups or babyfood should be adding a few new flavours every year and also withdrawing the poorest selling ones as a matter of routine.

Consequently, companies which fail to distinguish between new products and line extensions, and lump them together under 'new brand activity', tend to overrate their level of innovation. This means that they may be too easily satisfied and not set their sights high enough.

CLICHÉS ABOUT NEW PRODUCTS

Most subjects have their stock of clichés, and new products have an ample ration. But some of the clichés are nonetheless real, and so cannot be ignored.

Only the eccentric would deny that new products are important. It is commonplace now for companies to have 50% of their sales today in products which did not exist ten years ago—for certain companies the figure may be nearer 100%. The critical role of new products does not need to be stressed.

Another cliché is that the majority of new products fail. This is a fact whether you take your measure in the laboratory or in the market. Studies by the Nielsen Company in the UK and North America* show that about one in every two brands test-marketed fails, and some of those which go on to national expansion are also unsuccessful—for example, McVitie's and Cadbury's range of cakes, Gerber babyfood and Campbell's soups do not appear to have generated worth-while profit levels.

However, new brands actually appearing in the market only represent the tip of the iceberg of new product development,

* A. C. Nielsen Co., *How to Strengthen your New Product Plan.*

since the majority of new ideas are discontinued before they get there. A study by Booz, Allen and Hamilton conducted across 51 American companies in 1966* showed that it took 58 ideas to yield one successful new product. The idea mortality rate is built up as follows:

Number of ideas needed to produce one successful new product	
NUMBER OF IDEAS	58
Number left after screening	12
Number left after business analysis	7
Number left after product development	4
Number tested	3
NUMBER SUCCESSFUL	1

It would, however, be naïve to take these studies too literally. The number of ideas needed to produce one successful new brand will depend on their quality, on the distance of the new product field from the company's present base of operation and on the organization of the company's new product function.

These well documented analyses do, nevertheless, highlight the fact that new products do not come easily, and that a company undertaking the task with anything less than the highest degree of professionalism is unlikely to succeed.

TWO STUDIES ON NEW PRODUCT FAILURES

Just as each sales manager will reel off a different list of the qualities of the ideal salesman, so most marketing people have a favourite list of reasons for new product failures. Each one tends to be different. An analysis by Nielsen of 44 new product failures in the grocery field† pointed to the following main reasons for failure:

Reasons for failure	%
Product/package	53
Price/value	20
Trade acceptance	18
Advertising	9
TOTAL	100

This kind of analysis is of limited value because it looks at the various elements of the marketing mix in isolation. A product's

* Booz, Allen & Hamilton, *The Management of New Products*.
† A. C. Nielsen Co., *How to Strengthen your New Product Plan*.

performance cannot be evaluated except in relation to its price, and a parity product may be very successful if it is lower priced than its competitors.

The list drawn up by Theodore L. Angelus,* President of New Products Action Team, is much more to the point because it takes a broader view of the reasons for failure. It is based on an analysis of 75 new product failures in the food and drug trade, and although the findings refer to the American market, they have relevance to the UK:

Reasons for new brand failures	%
Vague or nil consumer difference	56
Poor product positioning	32
Bad timing	16
Product performance	12
Wrong market for company	8
TOTAL	124

Note: The total is higher than 100% because there were two or more main reasons for the failure of some brands.

As Angelus's list implies, the main reason for failure (56%) is that most unsuccessful new products do not have a significant point of difference. The next most important reason was poor product positioning (32%). In some cases, this was a direct reflection of insignificant product differences; in others, the positioning was mismatched because the advertising failed to stress the product's point of difference; and sometimes the positioning was plain confusing. The onus is on a new product to prove that it is better than existing products. If it fails to establish this superiority, consumers will see no reason to switch from the brands which served them well in the past.

HOW SUCCESSES DIFFER FROM FAILURES

The few pieces of authoritative data on why new products fail are rather general in scope, and in the hope of delving more deeply into this question, I have analysed 50 new product successes and 50 failures, introduced in the UK since 1960. They cover 38 product categories, mainly in the grocery trade. In order to ensure accuracy each case study was discussed with someone having first-hand

* Theodore L. Angelus, 'Why do most new products fail?' (*Advertising Age*, 24 March 1969). Angelus has had fifteen years of full-time experience on new products, and this excellent article is well worth reading.

knowledge of the brand—often the brand manager or assistant at the time, or the marketing manager. The analysis does not pretend to be comprehensive, but it is sufficiently representative to support the points made. The majority of the conclusions are consistent with the findings of Angelus in his American study of 75 new product failures.

Although every attempt has been made to use objective criteria, subjective judgements inevitably creep in. For example, even within the same company there may not be unanimous agreement as to whether a given new product is a success or a failure. I have defined as unsuccessful all test market brands which were not expanded and new national brands which have been withdrawn or appear not to have paid out after three years. Appendix G gives some details of the categories and brands covered.

There are exceptions to every rule about new products but, in general, successful new products tend to differ from failures on three scores:

Successful brands	Failures
Significant price or performance advantage	Marginal advantage, if any
Significant difference from existing brands	Marginally different or similar
First in with new idea	Follower

Let us look at these in more detail.

1. Significant Price or Performance Advantage

TABLE 15.1   DIFFERENCES IN VALUE BETWEEN SUCCESSFUL AND UNSUCCESSFUL NEW PRODUCTS (%)

Difference	50 successes	50 failures
Significantly better performance, higher price	44	8
Marginally better performance, higher price	6	12
Better performance, same price	24	0
Same performance, lower price	8	0
Same performance, same price	16	30
Same performance, higher price	2	30
Worse performance, same or higher price	0	20
TOTAL	100	100

Note: Level of performance was based as far as possible on blind product tests among target consumer groups where the benefit was a product one, and on judgement in other cases.

It will be seen from Table 15.1 that 74% of the successful products offered better performance than existing brands, though usually at higher prices. The corresponding figure for failed brands was 20%. Only a minority of successful brands (18%)* were of parity or inferior value, whereas 80% of failed brands were in this category.

As many as 20% of failed products had better performance at a higher price, which on the face of it is surprising. However, they failed either because their price was too high or because they did not communicate their advantage clearly to the consumers. Quite a few brands in this category failed because, although they offered a superior performance to their target segment of consumers, this segment proved too small to support a profitable business. An example of this is the segment for low sudsing washing powders.

> Owners of automatic washing machines require low sudsing products. General purpose powders like Ariel or Persil cause over-sudsing (on to the floor!) when the right amount of product to do a good cleaning job is used. However, a number of low sudsing brands, specially targeted at the automatic machine owner, have failed. Procter & Gamble's Cheer and Unilever's Skip were both unsuccessful. P & G's Bold, which is an outstandingly good low sudsing enzyme powder, is doing poorly on test in the Southern TV area at present. The only brand to have succeeded in this market is Persil Automatic.
>
> The problem is that there are not yet enough automatic washing machine owners in the UK to support a major brand. These are expensive to communicate with through TV advertising, and hard to locate with an introductory trial-getting promotion like sampling.

One very clear pointer from this analysis is that the successful products more often had advantages in areas that mattered to consumers, whereas the point of difference among the failures tended to be in a fringe area. For example, housewives are most interested in getting better whiteness or stain removal from their washing powders, and even a marginal technical improvement in this can be pretty important to them. But a new washing powder with much more acceptable perfume or lather levels than existing brands would be very unlikely to succeed, because housewives attach much less weight to these characteristics. The UK toilet

---

* These were mainly cigarettes and snack brands, for which packaging and product positioning are particularly influential.

soap market in the 1960s illustrates this conclusion, which Angelus found also applied to the USA.

A favourite source of self-flagellation for Procter & Gamble, Colgate and Unilever in the past decade has been the UK toilet soap market. It is quite evident, from even a superficial look at the pyramids of available research, that housewives deciding which brand will be used in the home want the mildest possible soap at a relatively low price. They take it for granted that all soaps will clean reasonably well.

All the long established UK soaps—Palmolive, Lux, Camay, Knights Castile and Imperial Leather—cater to this demand for mildness and complexion care. The only odd man out is Lifebuoy, which is famous for its BO campaign and seen by the consumer both as a masculine product and as a deodorant brand.

New product failures in the toilet soap market have been legion since the late 1950s. Instead of giving the consumer what she clearly wanted, the major soap companies have tried to feed her brands which make the very opposite impression— synthetic detergent bars often with a deodorant incorporated, at a hefty premium price. Technically, these synthetic bars had a lot to offer. They all eliminated the bath tub ring because they did not form scum, and some had effective deodorant properties. On mildness, they scored as well as soaps and sometimes slightly better. But as far as the housewife was concerned they had no appeal. She equated any cleaning or deodorant claim with harshness, and was just not interested in paying a price premium of up to 50% for a brand offering, in her terms, exactly what she didn't want. The synthetics were further handicapped by not being legally able to describe themselves as soap, a word which itself carries strong mildness connotations.

However, encouraged perhaps by the fact that a synthetic bar, Dial, is the brand leader in the USA, the three major 'cleaning' manufacturers have made repeated attempts, all unsuccessful, to introduce synthetic or deodorant bars in the UK. First, Unilever's Lyril appeared in 1959. It was introduced nationally, but had an unfortunate tendency to dissolve rapidly in water and was soon withdrawn. Unilever has since tested Caress and Apollo, neither of which succeeded. Other synthetic test market failures were Procter & Gamble's Dawn, Armour's Dial and Unilever's ubiquitous Dove, which has been bobbing in and out of test markets since 1958. Premium priced soap formulations which have failed are Unilever's Rexona and Colgate's Choice and Espri.

P & G eventually did the obvious in 1968 by introducing Fairy Toilet Soap, a parity performance soap bar priced 10% below Lux, Camay and Palmolive. Together with its price advantage, it had a strong mildness impression, due to the millions spent over the years by Fairy Household Soap and and Fairy Liquid on 'mildness' advertising. It offered extra mildness for less money and, not surprisingly, rapidly gained a major market share.

New product introductions in the biscuit market also conform to a similar pattern, and most of the successful brands have been built on texture differences.

The UK biscuit market, worth about £120 million at manufacturer selling prices, is very fragmented and the largest individual brand—McVitie's Chocolate Home Wheat—has a turnover of under £6 million. The main opportunity for new products lies in finding new textures which appeal to the consumer. Taste is also important, as with any food brand, but virtually every taste is already catered for by existing brands, so it is hard to find a new one with enough novelty and appeal to form the basis for a new brand.

The three major new brand successes in the biscuit category—Ritz, Tuc and Butter Crumble—have all had unique textures. In addition to its novel texture, Ritz also had a buttery taste, a round bite-size shape and superior packaging. Despite its high price, it rapidly won consumer acceptance, but it has fallen back heavily since Tuc's launch and now has a turnover of under £1·5 million. Crawford's Tuc, made under licence to Parein, a Belgium company, has a distinctive texture. It was introduced in 1967 and its present turnover exceeds £2 million. McVitie's Butter Crumble has an unusual crumbly texture, based on the traditional 'Abernethy' biscuit, which was little known outside Scotland. It was introduced in 1969, with a hexagonal cardboard pack and its turnover is now hovering around the £1 million mark.

Many of the new brands that failed in the biscuit market were built around differences that the consumer couldn't care less about. McVitie's Tropical Creams were very similar to the existing brand Digestive Creams, a cream sandwich biscuit. The only point of difference was that Tropical Creams offered a variety of cream flavours in each packet, whereas Digestive Creams only had a custard cream filling. Tropical Creams, introduced in around 1969, got good distribution but little consumer trial, and never looked like succeeding.

Crawford's Golden Glen shortcake was another failure, originally brought in to compete with Peek Frean's shortcake. It contained butter, unlike the Peek Frean's biscuit, and was premium priced. The brand was couponed and quite heavily advertised, but not widely tried; the butter taste was hardly detectable and the brand's advantage marginal.

A third failure was Premium crackers, introduced with heavy advertising by Nabisco in the early 1960s. Although it had a slightly different texture from cream crackers, its main point of distinction was the small size and large number of biscuits offered. But consumers did not consider this marginal advantage worth paying a heavy price premium for. Premium crackers' volume is now quite small, and I would be surprised if it has ever paid out.

2. Significant Difference from Existing Brands

The previous section viewed new products from the standpoint of product performance related to pricing. This one concentrates on the extent of differences between new brands and existing offerings. A new brand can perform better than existing ones even though it is not dramatically different in appearance or formulation, and a unique new product may fail.

The purpose of this study was to check whether there was any correlation between new product success and degree of innovation. All new products were divided into three categories—dramatically different, very different, and marginally different or similar. The judgement was inevitably subjective, but certain yardsticks were consistently used. Each new product was compared with the brand on the market nearest to it, and the criterion was how the consumer would view it.

The 'dramatically different' class was made up of those brands which had a radically new appearance or performance that would be immediately apparent to the consumer even before using the product. Among the brands in this class were Vesta, After Eight, Gillette Techmatic, Dual, Gold Blend and J-Cloths (successes), and Nestea, Spic and Wisk (failures).

The 'very different' group was composed of those brands whose differences were not fully apparent until they had been used.

Among the successes were Duckhams Multi-Grade, Ariel, Mick, and Johnson's Nappy Liners, and the failures numbered Cerola, Head & Shoulders, and others.

The third group comprised brands that were different in unimportant ways or straight 'Me Too's'. Fairy Toilet Soap, Ajax Liquid, and Embassy Regal were among the few successes in this group, and the list of failures was crowded.

Based on this analysis, it was found that 68% of the successful products were dramatically or significantly different, compared with 30% of the failures.

TABLE 15.2 RELATIVE DISTINCTIVENESS OF SUCCESSFUL AND UNSUCCESSFUL NEW PRODUCTS (%)

	50 successes	50 failures
Dramatically different	20	8
Very different	48	22
Marginally different	12	38
Similar	20	32
TOTAL	100	100

The 'dramatically different' or 'very different' new product *failures* are worth further examination, and seem to fall into three major categories. The first group consists of those which had major performance weaknesses, and Harvey's Duo-Can, Kellogg's Freeze Dried Fruit with Cereal, Wisk (a soap-impregnated disposable cloth for washing up) and Metrecal are examples. The second is made up of products whose benefits were insufficient to justify their premium price, and Gerber (glass jars for babyfood), Spic (pre-measured tablets of washing powder) and Downy (liquid fabric softener) are instances of this. The third group comprises new brands which unsuccessfully attempted to change established housewife usage habits—and numbered among them are Campbell's (condensed soup), Betty Crocker (cake-mix), Instant Breakfast (flavoured high protein powder to be mixed with milk) and Wisk again. It is possible to alter existing usage habits, as Shift, Cadbury's Smash, Dual and After Eight have proved, but this requires a product improvement of a high order allied to very skilful marketing.*

* *Note:* not all the product failures mentioned in this paragraph are included in the list of 50 on which the analysis was based, since I had insufficient information about the detailed product performance of some of them.

3. The Early Bird Catches the Worm

While examples can always be given of companies which have succeeded despite late entry to a market—like Avon in cosmetics, Volkswagen in the American car market and the Japanese in cameras and motor cycles—it is almost always better to be first.

There is inevitably a risk with a pioneer product that competitors will improve on the original technology and bring out a superior product. This risk is usually worth taking because the news value of an innovation is always at a peak in the early stages, and this enables the pioneer brand to obtain widespread consumer trial. The fact that the innovator gains initial possession of the consumer's usage means that the follower has to produce a better or less expensive product to make consumers switch. Certainly, in grocery markets, the dictum that 'First is best' is borne out by results in a selection of categories developed since the Second World War. In the eighteen markets in Table 15.3, the original pioneer has only been overtaken in six cases by a competitor *from another company* and in each case there was a specific reason. (See p. 246).

In almost every case, the overtaking brand (italicized) succeeded because it had a superior product or better market positioning.

Fairy Liquid overhauled Quix because its product delivered better mildness and cleaning, its packaging was superior, and it was the first dishwashing brand to be positioned single-mindedly on a mildness platform.

Kensitas lost out to Embassy because it had a poor quality image, due to the stress it gave to its coupon scheme. Embassy, by contrast, gave primary emphasis to product quality and only mentioned its coupon plan at a secondary level—a triumph of good positioning.

Wilkinson did not have the resources fully to exploit its success with the polymer-coated stainless blade, and Gillette was consequently able to recover.

Cadbury introduced with Smash a much better tasting product than Yeoman, and accomplished it with advertising of tremendous flair.

Golden Wonder was successful (in volume at least) at the expense of Smith's because its use of Rayophane bags gave improved product protection, resulting in a fresher product. It was also quick to exploit distribution channels which had been somewhat neglected by Smith's in the past—notably grocers and wholesalers.

Harmony edged Color Glo out of leadership in a market where product formulations underwent a major change in the mid-1960s.

Market	Pioneer (1st major brand)	Overtaker
	TABLE 15.3 18 UK GROCERY MARKETS—INNOVATORS VERSUS CHALLENGERS	
Dishwashing	Quix (Unilever)	*Fairy Liquid* (P & G)
Synthetic detergents	Tide (P & G)	Daz (P & G) then Ariel (P & G)
Dogfood	Chappie (Petfoods)	Chum (Petfoods)
Catfood	Kit-E-Kat (Petfoods)	Whiskas (Petfoods)
Hair sprays	Supersoft (Reckitt & Colman)	—
Coupon cigarettes	Kensitas (Gallaher)	*Embassy (Imperial Tobacco)*
Stainless razor blades	Wilkinson	*Gillette*
Mashed potato	Yeoman (Dornay)	*Smash (Cadbury)*
Crisps	Smiths (General Mills)	*Golden Wonder (Imperial Tobacco)*
Frozen foods	Birds Eye (Unilever)	—
Cakes	Lyons	—
Canned desserts	Ambrosia (Bovril)	—
Packet desserts	Instant Whip (General Foods)	Angel Delight (General Foods)
Household floor cleaners	Flash (P & G)	—
Spray oven cleaners	Shift (Phillips Scott & Turner)	—
Nuts	KP (United Biscuits)	—
Hair colourants	Color Glo (L'Oréal)	*Harmony (Gibbs)*
After shave lotions	Old Spice (Shulton)	—

THE AMERICAN NEW PRODUCT NEMESIS

While the list of 100 new products is too small a base from which to draw definitive conclusions, it is interesting to note that only 18% of the sucessful new brands were of American origin in formulation and positioning, compared with 30% of the failures.

Some American companies like IBM, Playtex, Kodak and Xerox (with Rank) have built up successful international businesses using standardized products world-wide. This has not, however, proved possible in the grocery market, and the most successful American companies have tended to use their American know-how as a base for tailoring a product to the UK market, rather than attempting a straight transplant.

This tenet can be illustrated in reverse by examining Procter & Gamble's new product record during the past fifteen years (Table 15.4). Overall this very effective company has achieved the fair* scoring rate of 5 successes out of 19 attempts, but if the straight American transplants were eliminated, the success ratio would have improved to 4 out of 8. Another point of note about P & G's new brand effort is that the company has consistently aimed for major volume and that all but one of its 5 successful new products have held leadership of their markets for sustained periods (the exception being Fairy Snow).

TABLE 15.4   ORIGIN OF P & G'S NEW PRODUCTS—1955–70

NEW PRODUCT FAILURES		NEW PRODUCT SUCCESSES	
Product	Comment	Product	Comment
Cheer US	Based on US Dash	Flash US	Based on US Spic & Span
Head & Shoulders US		Fairy Liquid UK	Completely different to US Ivory Liquid
Crest US		Ariel UK	
Gleem US		Fairy Snow UK	
Mr Clean US		Fairy Toilet Soap UK	
Golden Harvest UK	Parity product to Summer County		
Spic US	Based on US Salvo		
Downy US		*DOUBTFUL*	
Tempo US	Based on US Secret		
Bold UK	American only in name	Camay US	Achieved high share of toilet market but thought to have taken over 10 years to pay out
Gay Liquid UK			
Dreft Liquid UK			
Dawn Mixed	Heavily modified version of US Zest		

It is very easy for an American company to assume that a successful product in the USA will also do well in England, because of the

---

* 'Fair' in relation to the ambitious targets P & G had for most of its new brands. One would expect a much higher scoring rate from a company whose typical new products had lower volume objectives.

common language and related traditions of the two countries. The similarities may well be more important than the differences, but the latter have been sufficiently serious to trip up a long line of distinguished companies which attempted straight American transplants to the UK—Betty Crocker (General Mills), Campbell's, Gerber, Chesebrough-Ponds and Bristol-Myers being among the prime examples.

THE IMPORTANCE OF OBJECTIVE JUDGEMENT

A substantial number of new products among the 50 failures represented genuine attempts at innovation by the companies concerned, and offered a sufficient extra benefit at least to justify market testing. However, others brought nothing new to the market and, of the 50 failures analysed, 80% had a similar or worse performance to other products, at a similar or higher price. It is difficult to believe that this group of products was examined objectively by company management, and one is forced to the conclusion that judgements of their success were made with rose-tinted spectacles.

The case history below illustrates this, and shows how two major companies in the USA attempted to introduce new brands with no point of difference or superiority over the strongly entrenched brand leader. The law that the newcomer must have a meaningful advantage over established brands, in order to succeed, once more prevailed.

Crest, a blue-coloured toothpaste containing stannous fluoride and with wintergreen flavour, was the brand leader of the US toothpaste market, with a 34% share, in 1964. It was the only major fluoride brand, and the only toothpaste whose effectiveness in reducing cavities among children was endorsed by the American Dental Association. For some years its leadership had not been seriously challenged, but in 1965 two of its major competitors—Colgate and Bristol-Myers—introduced fluoride toothpastes.

Colgate's Cue was launched nationally in 1965. It was in test market for four years and only hit share target in one of these markets, but as soon as the ADA endorsement was received, Cue was expanded. As far as the consumer was concerned, the brand offered nothing more than Crest—it contained stannous fluoride, had ADA 'backing', wintergreen flavour, and an anti-cavity advertising campaign. Despite heavy spending of £2·8 million on advertising in the first year (14% of total market advertising expenditure), Cue only achieved a 3% share of market versus a 4·5% share objective. Share fell to 1·5% in 1966 and advertising was discontinued in 1967.

Bristol-Myers' Fact was launched nationally in December 1965. It was similar to Crest and Cue with no important point of difference—stannous fluoride ingredient, ADA endorsement, and wintergreen flavour. Advertising spending in the first year was just over £2 million but brand share was only 1·5% in 1966 and had declined to less than 1% in 1967.

Crest was able to shrug off these attacks with little extra marketing effort—in fact it continued to account for only 23% of total toothpaste advertising spending in 1965 and 1966, when the introductions of Cue and Fact were at their height. Cue and Fact failed because they offered nothing more than an imitation of Crest. Cue's only point of difference was its white colour (versus Crest's and Fact's blue). Both brands over-estimated the importance of their ADA endorsement, which did no more than bring their claims up to parity with Crest.

In fact, both Cue and Fact missed an important opportunity, since Crest's one weakness was its wintergreen flavour. All other leading US toothpaste brands use a peppermint/spearmint flavour, and this taste is preferred by the majority of consumers. Cue or Fact could have appealed to the large market segment which wanted both an effective anti-cavity toothpaste *and* a mint taste. It was left to Crest to do this itself a year or so later, thereby eliminating its major weakness, and also demonstrating the opportunity lost by its competitors.

This is by no means an isolated example, and one is left wondering why seasoned and intelligent companies so frequently plunge into new product projects which to the objective outsider appear notable only by their lack of promise. The clue lies in the word 'objective'. Marketing departments are under severe pressure to deliver successful new products and it is tempting to over-estimate the chances of the available candidates, because new ideas of the calibre of Shift, Gold Blend and J-Cloths are in short supply. In addition, the individual or group originating an idea has a natural tendency to press its claim. And once a new product project gets off the ground within a company, with its own brand manager and advertising agency, the basic momentum of events often obscures any reassessment of the merits of the idea. There is usually such a rush to meet deadlines and detailed approvals that no one has either the time or the inclination to ask fundamental questions.

This is also Kraushar's experience:* 'I find it surprising that large and sophisticated companies, well-staffed with marketing executives, can have failures which would often be apparent to the most junior marketing assistant—I am convinced that there is one general answer which goes some way to explain this strange phenomenon. The answer is largely *lack of objectivity*.'

What is the cure for this disease? A wider use of objective screening criteria for new projects would help, but would not provide the whole answer, because the best constructed yardsticks can be misapplied by over-enthusiastic interpreters. A system of regular check points for each new product project, so that its viability is monitored at various stages in its career, can also help. But the most significant advance of all would be an increased awareness on the part of general management, and those directly concerned with new product development, that lack of objectivity is a prime pitfall which should be allowed for at all times.

SUMMARY

A new product is seen by the consumer as a separate entity, and needs to be distinguished from a line extension, which is a development or modification of an existing brand. Companies which lump these two distinct activities together as new brand activity tend to overrate their level of innovation.

The failure rate of new products, both at the development and test market stage, is very high. The main reason for failure is the lack of any significant point of product superiority. Unsuccessful new products tend at best to have marginal performance advantages. In the few cases where they have clear advantages, these usually lie in areas of little interest to the consumer.

The early bird nearly always catches the worm, since the followers have to produce a better or less expensive product to make consumers switch.

There is some evidence to show that straight American new product transplants have a higher than average failure rate.

One of the most important, and elusive, ingredients in successful new product development is objective judgement.

* Peter M. Kraushar, *New Products and Diversification.*

16: *New Products—Offensive Techniques*

REMINDER

It is impossible to break down marketing into discrete compartments, because there is a continuous interflow between them. 'New products' is no exception to this, and inevitably a number of offensive techniques have already been described in previous chapters. In order to make this one complete, we will retrace this territory briefly.

Successful new product plans depend as much on effective organization and careful charting of corporate marketing strategy as they do on developing bright new ideas. As we have already seen, a good idea in an unimportant area, or one that is poorly positioned, is unlikely to succeed.

New product development is the ultimate test of marketing's effectiveness, and all the threads of offensive marketing must be brought together if the test is to be passed with flying colours. In particular, the organization for new product development must create a climate where innovation can flourish, and the concept of the diversification department was outlined in Chapter 4. The company should have clearly worked out strategies and objectives, designed to exploit its strengths (Chapter 5). And, we are assuming that it has already drawn up a short list of its target markets by using an offensive technique like the new market selection grid, described in detail in Appendix C.

On the basis that this all important groundwork has been carried out, the present chapter will concentrate on techniques for developing and screening new ideas. We are deliberately not covering the drawing up of the detailed pricing, advertising and promotion plan for new products, since these have received ample space earlier in the book. Three offensive techniques for generating and assessing new product ideas follow.

DEVELOP A NEW IDEAS SYSTEM

We observed earlier that a considerable number of new ideas is needed for each successful new product developed—perhaps as many as 50 rough starters. To take an unduly mechanistic view, over 200 reasonable new ideas may be needed to father 4 profit making new products. This is a large number and to help keep a flow of the right quality pouring in, the diversification department or new products group is well advised to set up a system for generating ideas. This ensures that the efforts of those responsible for new products are well directed, and that the whole company, rather than just a few specialists within it, can be mobilized to produce new ideas. And the contribution which outsiders can make as well is by no means negligible.

There are numerous ways to develop new product ideas, but it is difficult to forecast in advance which ones will produce the best results for a given company. The secret is to start by using them all, and then to drop the ones which are least fruitful. Some of the main sources of new ideas are listed below.

1. Internal Sources

Marketing and R & D people are usually the best internal sources for new ideas. Indeed, a National Industrial Conference Board survey of 150 American companies showed that 88% of new product ideas came from within organizations, and of these 60% originated from the marketing or R & D departments. Every employee should be regarded as a potential source of new ideas, but any company wishing to draw them out has to graduate beyond the hackneyed suggestion box, which is more often a repository for obscene suggestions than good ideas. The trick is to tell all employees which markets the company is interested in, to have the resulting ideas routed to one man, probably the new products manager, and to acknowledge all suggestions, giving clear reasons for rejection where ideas are deemed to be unusable.

Most important of all, people making suggestions which are developed should be given credit and reward. Clearly, they will be rewarded in terms of status and responsibility within the company, but whether or not to offer substantial financial incentives is a controversial question. A National Industrial Conference Board survey involving 86 US companies showed that about 60% gave special rewards to employee-inventors, whereas the others did not. Most of the rewards consisted of small sums of money, but as many as 11% of the companies surveyed offered royalties. Inland Steel is one company which rewards successful employee-inventors handsomely.

'Inland Steel gives awards as high as $5000 per inventor or $10 000 for each invention. For royalties, the scale is set according to an employee's duties. A research (R & D) man or someone directly concerned with inventions may get a 15% royalty, but someone from another department, where his duties are apart from inventions, may receive as much as one third of the profits.'*

On balance, it is probably worthwhile offering substantial rewards to employee-inventors of successful new products, and Gerlach and Wainwright† point out that the three countries with the greatest number of patent applications for new inventions —Switzerland, Sweden and West Germany—all have laws requiring royalties to be paid to employee inventors. However, any incentive system must be handled with extraordinary skill, to minimize piracy, undue secrecy and bad blood between employees.

2. External Sources

Advertising agencies, suppliers specializing in new consumer products (e.g. Monsanto) and banks should be acquainted with the company's new product requirements. Banks sometimes know of small organizations with a number of new ideas which they wish either to sell or to develop jointly, because they lack the capital to go it alone.

For security reasons, some companies may feel hesitant about making their new product interests too widely known. But it is difficult to see what action potential competitors could take, on the information that you have an interest in several markets. You may in fact never enter many of the categories listed on your new idea requests, and the very act of making your interest known could result in an approach from possible acquisition prospects.

---

* J. T. Gerlach and C. A. Wainwright, *Successful Management of New Products* (Pitman Publishing, 1970). Mr Gerlach is Director of Corporate Growth Development at General Mills.

† Ibid.

3. Overseas Sources

New ideas can be gained from overseas by subscribing to some of
the many information bulletins or by personal visits. At minimum,
it is worth while examining existing products in your present
or future fields of interest in the USA, leading European countries
and Japan. For a grocery manufacturer, this is just a simple matter
of catching a plane and wandering around supermarkets for a
couple of days in the foreign countries concerned. Cadbury's
Smash was based on an American formulation, Crawford's Tuc
biscuit is of Belgian origin, and enzyme washing products were
first marketed in Holland.

Licences for sales rights of foreign products in the UK are also
a worthwhile source of new products. Companies abroad may
prefer to license a UK company rather than set up their own organization. The Rank Organization's phenomenal growth in the 1960s
(profits up by 1207% in 1960–69) was largely attributable to its
interest in Rank-Xerox, which has the right to manufacture and
market all Xerox products outside the USA.

However, as indicated in the previous chapter, foreign countries
and America in particular should be regarded as a source of ideas
rather than of ready-made products, and strong overseas brands
should not be transplanted to the UK in their original form unless
it is clear from consumer testing that they require no modification.

4. Patents

Patent information is easily available at little or no cost. There
are many thousands of them, and the problem is to pinpoint those
of possible relevance. A good approach is to limit your search to
recently registered and expiring patents, in your areas of interest.
This will enable you to exploit ideas previously covered by patents
which have now expired, and to spark off fresh concepts arising
from new patents but not covered by them.

5. Previous New Ideas on File

Rejected old ideas can often be a source of new ones. The old
ideas may have been wrongly assessed, or circumstances may have
changed since they were last evaluated.

6. The Universities

Arrangements can vary from large-scale sponsored research
financed by a company, to the use of individual professors on a

consulting basis, to informal discussions with university staff or students. P & G's successful toothpaste Crest was the result of years of sponsored research on stannous fluoride at Columbia University, New York. The first electronic computer—the ENLAC—was designed by J. Mauchly and W. Eckert at the University of Pennsylvania, on money provided by the US Army.*

7. Other Methods

For every major product category, there will be other more specific sources of new product ideas. Let us take food as an example. Restaurant menus can be a good guide on changes in eating habits, and are a way of identifying popular dishes not yet covered by branded products. Leading printers of restaurant menus may cover as many as 500 different locations, and will usually supply copies of these for a small charge. New ideas for food products can also be found in the more popular recipe books, or in recipes included in magazines.

USE AND ANALYSE RESEARCH IMAGINATIVELY

The need to use market research creatively has already been covered in Chapter 9, and this is nowhere more true than in new product development. This section will give some examples of creative methods for turning up new product ideas, which can be used in addition to conventional direct or psychological techniques.

Dissatisfaction panels consist of small groups of consumers led by an experienced researcher. The panels cover one or more markets at each session, and are paid to grumble. The principle is that if the deficiencies of existing brands can be identified, exploitable new product opportunities may be revealed.

Brainstorming is most often carried out as an internal exercise, using qualified company R & D or marketing personnel. It can, however, be extended to mixed groups of company employees, consumers, retailers, with perhaps a couple of psychologists thrown in too. The richer the mixture, the better, provided there is a 'free' atmosphere, and quantity rather than quality of ideas is the objective. Brainstorming requires that the creation of ideas and their evaluation be handled as completely separate operations, because any attempt to assess ideas inhibits the flow of creativity.

Just as important as using imaginative techniques is the ability

* William Rodgers, *Think: a Biography of the Watsons and IBM* (Weidenfeld and Nicolson, 1970).

to interpret market research creativity. Quite often, the clues to a new product idea will be hidden in a number of different areas, and astute marketers will spot them and put them together. The development of the Ford Mustang is an example of this.

> The Ford Mustang was introduced in the USA in April 1964, and was one of the most original new cars of the 1960s. The Mustang was initially conceived in 1961 as a four-seater with the style and performance of a sports car, at a price between $2000 and $3000. The target would be the young married man who liked sporty cars and had to carry at least two passengers.
>
> Two important clues influenced the development of this concept. First, Ford had noted the peculiar sales behaviour of the General Motors Corvair. This was a four-seater compact car for the family, and when first introduced it looked like a flop. Then GM dressed it up with bucket seats and few sporty knick-knacks, and renamed it the Corvair Monza, at which its sales suddenly took off. Secondly sales statistics showed that the sales of sporty models was rising, and that teenagers were having a growing influence on the market.
>
> The concept for the Mustang was checked and re-checked through oceans of research, and the car proved very successful. One million Mustangs were sold in the two years following its launch, and 50% of these were 'conquest sales', made to people whose previous car had not been a Ford. Predictably, the main buyers were young marrieds—the average age of the Mustang purchaser was 31 years, and almost two-thirds were married.*

BUILD OBJECTIVE SCREENS

It is not much use generating hundreds of new ideas unless there is some system for assessing them, and separating those with promise from the non-runners. Most companies have good ideas bobbing around the place, but they often fail to spot the ones with the most potential. Conversely, as we have seen in the previous chapter, many poor ideas are progressed into the market place, when in fact they should have been screened out at a very early stage. Before proposing methods for screening ideas and projects, let us take a brief look at the four stages in the hatching of new

---

* Adapted from speech by Dr Seymour Marshak, Marketing Research Manager, Ford Division of Ford Motor Co.

products which precede national expansion. They are *raw ideas, business analysis, development* and *test marketing*.

The starting point is the generation of many unpolished ideas. Some of these can be quickly eliminated, but the more viable-looking ones will be subjected to preliminary business analysis, whose purpose is to check whether the idea holds together commercially. The business analysis need be no more than a page long and will estimate total market size, brand share, pricing, chance of R & D success, marketing spending and profit. It is usually a fairly rough-cut affair, but sufficient for the purpose of eliminating commercial lame ducks at an early stage. Using the business analysis, and applying the principles of the product development priority table (page 146), a decision will then be made whether to undertake laboratory development of the new idea. Once development is completed, a full test marketing plan will be drawn up, and the company will determine whether or not to move into test.

This describes the best practice of the most progressive companies, which is logical in a book concerned with offensive marketing. But even the most effective organizations do not find screening an easy process. Every successful new product requires a combination of objectivity in assessing its chances and enthusiasm in overcoming all the roadblocks and difficulties implicit in the development of any new idea. And there is always a danger that the enthusiasm necessary to bring an idea to fruition will cause a lack of objectivity in judging it. The ideal screening system would seem to have three elements—continuity, clear yardsticks and top management involvement.

Continuity in assessing new ideas is not a very general practice. A new concept is closely monitored in the beginning, probably before development begins, and unless any major snags occur, it rolls on merrily until it reaches the market. Once an idea achieves development status, the vested interests of the people involved directly with it create a bandwagon effect and it may never be fundamentally reassessed.

Continuous assessment of a new idea is essential, because as it moves through the four stages of product evolution, more becomes known about it. A project which looked very promising at the business analysis stage may be a lot less attractive by the time development of the product has been completed. New data on the market, raw material price increases, fresh legislation or the entry of additional competitors may reduce the appeal of the project to the point where it should be discontinued. The fact that a great deal of money may already have been spent on development is unfortunate but irrelevant—it is better to cut losses early than to incur larger ones in the future on a doomed project.

It makes sense to evaluate each project on at least four occasions and a schedule for this is outlined below:

Check point	Data	Assessor
(1) Raw ideas	Short verbal statements	New products manager
(2) Prior to R & D development	1 page business analysis	New products committee
(3) Prior to test market	Full recommendation	Managing director
(4) Prior to national expansion	Full recommendation	Board of directors

The second and third check points are the most critical ones. The value of a new products committee at the second stage lies in the added objectivity which a group of people, as opposed to one individual, can provide. However, its composition should be chosen with great care, because a stodgy committee may squash the more exciting new ideas. Equally, the person with ultimate line responsibility for new products, whether he be the marketing director or diversification director, should hold a powerful position on this committee. Obviously, in choosing members, personality and attitudes as well as job function need to be taken into account. However, a committee of four, consisting of senior people from R & D, finance and marketing and chaired by the marketing or diversification director, can work well. The chairman would have the casting vote, in recognition of his line responsibility for the new products function.

At the third check point, prior to test market entry, the managing director should question the strength of the basic marketing concept, and if he considers it fails to hold water, he should reject the test recommendation. As an objective outsider with a good knowledge of the company, he is well placed to examine the fundamentals. Unfortunately, top management does not always follow this tack, and is much more likely to focus on incidentals, such as the packaging design or the level of marketing spending, than to examine the basic merit of the project.

If the assessments of the new products committee or top management are to have any validity, clear pointers must be agreed to guide them. In fact, there is no need for a complex list of requirements, and only two simple criteria are necessary at each check point, but they must be pressed remorselessly:

(a) Does the concept offer significant improvements in product performance, pricing, or positioning, compared with existing brands?

(b) Is it likely to meet corporate requirements for minimum volume, payout period, and profit return on sales and capital employed?

Although in the difficult area of new products, there is no system which will guarantee success, any project which passes these tests at each check point is more likely to succeed.

SUMMARY

There are numerous ways to develop new product ideas. The best course is usually to try all methods first, then to persist with those that prove most fruitful. The main sources are company employees, external organizations like advertising agencies, raw material suppliers, new product shops and banks, similar fields of interest overseas, patents, previous new ideas on file and universities. The creative use of market research can also turn up useful hypotheses.

It is important to develop an objective screening system for new product ideas, since the enthusiasm necessary to bring an idea to fruition may cause a lack of impartiality in judging it. The ideal screening system has three elements—continuity of assessment, clear yardsticks, and top management involvement.

17: Segmentation—A Touchstone for Offensive Marketing

SEGMENTATION VERSUS MASS PRODUCTION

In 1947 Persil, Oxydol and Rinso held over two-thirds of the market for washing powders or liquids. They were used for washing clothes, dishes, floors, walls and even cars. Today this same market is segmented into a variety of sub-categories all satisfying specialized needs. Some of these are listed in Table 17.1. Including bleaches

TABLE 17.1	
Purpose	*Segments*
Cleaning clothes	Blue synthetic powders (Daz)
	White synthetic powders (Tide)
	Enzyme powders (Ariel)
	Soap powders (Persil)
	Low sudsing powders for automatics (Persil Automatic)
Cleaning dishes	Liquids stressing mildness (Fairy Liquid)
	Liquids stressing cleaning and convenience (Sqezy)
Cleaning hard surfaces	Low sudsing powders (Flash)
	Liquids (Ajax Liquid)
	Combined cleaner/polishes (Dual)
Softening clothes	Fabric softeners (Comfort)

and hard soaps as well as washing powders, the number of cleaning products on the market had risen from 92 in 1947 to 288 in 1969.*

The breakdown of large homogeneous markets into a variety of specialized sub-categories has been a feature of the post-war marketing of consumer products. Market segmentation is based on the fact that consumers have different needs, and that companies can achieve success by catering for the specialized requirements

* From a speech by Mr J. P. Napier, Managing Director of A. C. Nielsen Co., quoted in *The Grocer*.

of smaller groups. This can be illustrated by the law of averages. Let us suppose that you ask four people to list their preferred number, and they give you 3, 7, 1 and 9. If you had to plump for a single number representative of each of your 'guinea pigs' you would take 5, the average. In fact, it would satisfy no one completely and, although it is not far away from 3 and 7, it is a long distance from 1 and 9.

Bringing this closer to the market place, let us take a hypothetical example involving chocolate sponge cakes. One of the factors by which consumers judge chocolate sponge cakes is degree of 'chocolateyness', to concoct a horrible word. For the purpose of illustration, we will assume that the distribution of preference, following consumer tests between recipes containing different levels of chocolate was as shown in Figure 5. In this example, level

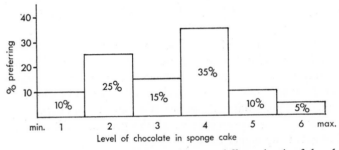

Figure 5 Distribution of preference between different levels of chocolate

4 is preferred by the greatest number, and would win a product blind test against any of the five other levels. The first manufacturer into the market would obviously be best advised to adopt level 4. Other companies taking a 'Me-Too' approach and developing a product with the highest majority appeal would also follow into level 4. Before long, there might be four manufacturers, all with similar products at level 4. If you were considering entry to this market as a fifth brand, you would have no chance at level 4, since it is already overcrowded. But a new product with level 2 of chocolate content would have a good prospect of success. It would be the ideal recipe for the 25% preferring level 2, and a big improvement on level 4 for the 10% who like level 1 best. A new brand at level 2 might well become market leader, since although it would appeal to only 35% or 40% of consumers it would have this segment to itself, while the remaining part of the market was being fought over by four competing but similar brands.

This illustration is, of course, over-simplified because consumers use other criteria apart from chocolate levels in deciding which brands of chocolate cake to buy. Texture, the type of filling, and price/value would also come into play. However, market segmentation is a two-edged weapon, and can easily turn into fragmentation (see page 273), where all the segments are so small that they hardly generate any profit. The aim should be to uncover segments which are still quite large, though smaller than the total market itself.

There is also a continual tug of war between the market opportunities provided by segmentation and the economies of mass production. In theory, it is possible to produce a different product for each consumer, and indeed, in the case of tailormade suits, this has been translated into practice. At the other extreme stands the Model 'T' Ford, which held over 50% of the American car market in the early 1920s, and was able to offer low cost motoring to the masses thanks to the economies made possible by mass production. The company aiming for a particular market segment will usually have lower volume than one that caters to the whole market, and this creates higher costs of production, inventory and marketing. But the lower volume segmented brand may also be successful in obtaining a premium price because of the absence of direct competition, and the higher revenue which this generates will often more than cover any higher costs.

STANDARD MODES OF SEGMENTATION

This section covers types of segmentation which are applicable to any market, irrespective of its particular characteristics. The next section will deal with segmentation modes which are only relevant to certain categories. However, it should be stressed that segmentation requires a creative approach, and that any market can usually be divided up in a number of different ways. There are no 'correct' answers, as in mathematics, and the secret of effective segmentation is to keep an open mind as to the possibilities.

Demographics are the most commonly used segmentation tool. Research studies of usage and attitudes are broken down by consumer's age, income, social class, sex, geographical location and even occupation. The fond hope is that somewhere in this whirlpool of statistics, a group of people will be found with different needs from the majority, but large enough to justify special marketing effort. Demographics are sometimes useful in pinpointing groups with special needs, and cereal manufacturers have applied this approach very effectively—more than half of Weetabix's volume comes from families with children under eight, while Welgar Shredded Wheat's business is primarily among adults, especially males.

However, many market segments are unrelated to demographics, since the fact that people are in the same age or income group is no guarantee that they will have similar attitudes to a market. For instance, an above average proportion of purchasers of the low priced private label brands are thought to be in the higher income groups, while the most expensive watches are bought by people with both the highest and the lowest incomes.★

Another segmentation mode, which was hailed as a possible breakthrough in the early 1960s, was segmentation by *personality variable*, but so far it has not fulfilled its promise. The theory is that if a substantial proportion of consumers in a particular market had a common personality characteristic, like aggression or desire to dominate, special advertising or even a different product could be tailored to appeal to this group. Two separate studies of the personality make-up of Ford and Chevrolet cars showed no significant differences, and the Advertising Research Foundation was not able to identify important personality differences among buyers of toilet tissues.† However, an investigation of the psychological make-up of aspirin users showed that compulsive persons, who were frustrated in their efforts to bring a high level of order to their lives, were more inclined to be heavy users of aspirins. One would also expect considerable personality variables to be present in comparing the owners of a Rover and a Jaguar respectively, with the latter being more aggressive and thrusting. As better methods for measuring personality differences are developed, this mode of segmentation should produce more usable results.

Value is one of the most frequently used methods of segmentation, and it is present in most markets. Value is the ratio between consumer satisfaction and retail price. Many categories have a small premium price/high quality segment, a large middle sector which is medium priced, and a low price segment probably dominated by private label. The cigarette market has a number of value segments.

The most important elements in new product success with

★ Daniel Yankelovich, 'New Criteria for Market Segmentation' (*Harvard Business Review*, March 1964).
† Information from Philip Kotler, *Marketing Management*.

cigarettes are pricing and positioning. There are differences in tobacco blends between the various brands, but these have much less influence on consumers than the imagined differences in image created by advertising and packaging. Pricing matters because most smokers purchase quite frequently, and cigarettes are a substantial item of their weekly expenditure.

At present there are five price segments for filter cigarettes, which account for about 80% of the market:

Segment	Price bracket (20 packet)	Leading brand
King size filter	28p & over	Benson & Hedges (Gallaher)
'B' filter	26p	Embassy (Imperial Tobacco)
Intermediate filter	22–24p	Embassy Regal (Imperial)
'A' filter	20p	Player's No. 6 (Imperial)
Sub-'A' filter	17–19½p	Player's No. 10 (Imperial)

With the exception of Benson & Hedges, all the segment leaders were introduced since 1961. The majority of new brands in the past five years have succeeded through entering a growing or unexploited price segment with a well packaged, advertised and promoted product. The development of the intermediate filter market in 1969 and 1970 is a good example of price or value segmentation.

Gallaher's Albany first created this segment in 1969. At that time, there was a gap of 6p between Embassy at 26p and Player's No. 6 at 20p, and the only brand in the middle was Guards (Carreras) at 25p. Albany was tested in Scotland at 22p without coupons, and subsequently went national. Over the next few months, three coupon brands were introduced at this same price point—Benson & Hedges Gold Bond, Carreras Cambridge (with Green Shield stamps) and Embassy Regal. This segment, which had not existed at the beginning of 1969, accounted for 10% of the cigarette market by the end of 1970.

Among other categories with many different value segments are petfoods and motor cars.

The other most commonly used segmentation mode is *level of usage*. In most markets it will be found that 25% of users account for more than 50% of volume consumed. Because the marketing cost of reaching a heavy user is the same as for a light user, companies often obtain the demographics of heavy users and beam the majority of their advertising against them.

To take an extreme example, Puerto Ricans are among the heaviest beer drinkers in the New York market and, as a result, some beer companies advertise in Spanish in local Puerto Rican newspapers, and place posters with Spanish copy in areas with a large Puerto Rican population. The Sheaffer beer company has even tailored its advertising message to appeal to the heavy user—the theme of its message being 'The beer to have when you're having more than one'. Another aspect of segmentation by level of usage is the proliferation of larger units of purchase—family sizes, economy packs and king sizes—which are also aimed at the heavy user.

A GLIMPSE AT THE SEGMENTATION REPERTOIRE

Market segmentation is a creative technique and no list of the possible modes can ever be exhaustive, because imaginative marketers are continually uncovering new ones. However, this section lists a number of types of segmentation, which will provide a good starting point for any marketer undertaking an analysis of possible modes.

1. Purpose of Use

Diverse groups of consumers derive different satisfactions from the same product. These variations can be exploited either by developing separate products, each of which ideally meets the need of a specific group, or by tailoring the marketing of a single product to appeal to all of them.

Vinegar in America is used for two entirely different purposes by distinct groups of consumers.

> In the USA bottled vinegar is sold in small sizes (pints and quarts) and large sizes (gallons). The small ones are used for making oil and vinegar salad dressings, and the prime consumer is urban and slightly upscale. There is not a great deal of seasonality in the sale of the smaller sizes, although volume is a little higher in the summer when salads are eaten most. Consumers of small sizes favour the premium priced brands with the backing of a famous name, rather than the wares of local bottlers or private label.
>
> The gallon market is completely different. Two-thirds of

gallon volume is consumed in June–September, the pickling season. This large size is used almost entirely by low income country people for pickling their home-grown cucumber. There is little interest in product quality among these consumers, because the vinegar itself will not be consumed, and is only used for turning the cucumber into pickle. Consequently, the larger size segment of the market is monopolized by low price private label and locally bottled products, and the premium priced nationally branded products hardly get a look in.

In a rather different kind of way, the airline market is segmented by purpose of usage and this also has an implication on pricing policy, especially on the transatlantic routes.

There are a number of segmenting factors in the transatlantic air travel market, but one of the most important is purpose of travel. Over 75% of transatlantic travellers are American citizens or residents and the main purposes of travel are:

(*a*) business;
(*b*) combination of business and pleasure;
(*c*) packaged vacation;
(*d*) individual vacation (i.e. not packaged tour);
(*e*) visiting friends and relatives;
(*f*) educational;
(*g*) home leave (military and government personnel).

Each of these groups of consumers has different needs and requires a separate marketing approach. Let us demonstrate this by looking at the four most important groups in more detail.

The businessman is interested in speed and convenience. Price is unimportant to him because his company will be paying his expenses. His choice of brand is most significantly influenced by the time of the flight, and he will pick the one that fits in best with his business arrangements. He is probably an experienced flyer, but his total demand is inelastic, because his need for air transportation is determined by the demands of his business, not by his personal preference. The implication of this for airlines is to charge businessmen top fares, to exclude them as far as possible from concessionary rates, but to give priority to reaching them through personal sales calls, direct mail or the business press, since they are the heaviest individual users of air travel.

The packaged vacationer will not choose his airline—he will pick a particular tour which includes air transportation. The buyer in this case, as far as the individual airline is concerned, is the packaged tour company, like American Express or Cooks. The sale is an industrial one to a specialized buyer, and pricing is of critical importance.

The individual vacationer is also price-conscious, and his demand is elastic. He can choose whether or not to go abroad on vacation and, if so, where to go. However, he is expensive for the airline to reach, and although television may be the best advertising medium, it is very wasteful, since most viewers have neither the money nor the inclination to travel across the Atlantic on vacation.

The majority of those visiting friends and relatives are first or second generation American immigrants who wish to revisit the 'old country', whether it be Ireland, Italy, Germany or England. They usually save up for the fare over a period of years and are very price-conscious. They are most likely to book a charter flight through an ethnic social or sports association in America. The distribution channel is therefore the ethnic social club and the ethnic travel agent. This type of traveller is also inclined to fly by the national airline of his home country.

All four of these groups, incidentally, are strongly influenced by nationality considerations. The vast majority of the passengers of any transatlantic airline consist of its own nationals.

2. Occasion of Use

In some markets the product needs of consumers vary according to the occasion when they are used. For instance, quite a few cigarette smokers use a lower priced brand like Players No. 6 during the week, and a prestige brand like Benson & Hedges or Dunhill on social occasions at the weekend. The switch to higher priced brands at the weekend is especially prevalent in Latin countries like Italy and Spain. There is a similar situation in the biscuit market, where consumers purchase the more expensive brands for entertaining, even though they may normally buy plain biscuits for family consumption.

The best example of segmentation by occasion of use is provided by Rowntree's After Eight mint chocolates, one of the most imaginative new product launches in recent years.

After Eight entered a declining market—the box chocolate category—but crystalized a number of existing needs in a single unique brand. Even prior to After Eight's introduction, there was an established habit of eating confectionery after dessert in the evening, but it was not very widespread.

After Eight positioned itself as being uniquely suitable for this occasion, which fitted in well with the upscale treatment of the brand. The product consisted of dark chocolate and cream mint packaged in individual envelopes inside a dark green box. It was unlike any other box of chocolates, the vast majority of which were assortments, and the advertising added to After Eight's social cachet. Only a minority of After Eight's volume comes from consumption after dinner. The eating occasion was used as much to add to the brand's exclusive image as for the extra consumption it would create.

3. Personal Characteristics of Consumers

People are too fat, too thin, have brown hair, grey, red, black or sometimes none at all. Some brunettes would like to be blonde. The variety of different skin types people have or think they have is too numerous to count. These real and imagined differences in personal characteristics create frequent opportunities for market segmentation. As Maurice Bale, President of Beecham Products points out: 'Once upon a time there was a single product called cold cream. Now cold cream, although it still exists, has also been "spun off" into foundation, cleansing, vanishing, nourishing, conditioning, hormone, astringent, lanolin, marrow and wrinkle cream.'* The shampoo market is segmented by products for dry, normal and greasy hair, the hair colouring category by various colours of hair and the analgesic market by all kinds of real or imagined ailments.

One clever piece of segmentation by personal characteristics was carried out by Mead Johnson in the USA with its brand Nutrament.

Mead Johnson was one of the pioneers of the market for slimming products in the USA. It introduced Metrecal, a 225 calorie milk based drink in a can, during the late 1950s and retained leadership of the slimming product category until the late 1960s, when it was overtaken by Carnation.

In the course of its research on people's attitude to their

* *Plotting Marketing Strategy*, edited by Lee Adler (Business Books, 1967).

weight, Mead Johnson discovered that as many as 10% of all Americans considered they were *underweight*. The largest proportion of this group were teenagers or students, and some had been consuming Metrecal in addition to a normal diet as a means of *gaining* weight.

Mead Johnson decided to exploit this market segment by introducing a new product. This was called Nutrament, and it was a milk based drink with a higher calorie count and more protein than Metrecal. Nutrament's marketing was targeted against the 15–25-year-old, and the advertising used a straight factual approach, since young Americans are unimpressed by commercial gimmicks like testimonial advertising by famous sportsmen. The basic promise of Nutrament was that it helped underweight people to gain 'strong' weight as opposed to flab, through its high protein content. It has proved to be a successful and profitable brand, with turnover of a few million pounds.

4. Characteristics of Related Products

If a new carpet is required for the living room, the size, shape and colour chosen will depend heavily on the dimensions and appearance of the room, because no normal person would buy a new house just to accommodate a particularly nice carpet. Many purchases of this kind are influenced by possession of a 'governing' product. People would not buy petrol if they owned electrically powered cars, they would be unlikely to order a car that was too large to fit into their garage, and so on. The characteristics of cars determine the kind of oil that is needed.

Duckham's now famous Q20/50 motor oil was initially put on the market in 1956* and at first did only moderately well. It was a heavy oil well suited to cars with fast-revving engines. Q20/50 took off soon after the Mini arrived in the early 1960s. The original Mini had a problem of high oil consumption, partly because the engine and the gear-box ran off the same oil. Duckham's Q20/50 stood up to the pressures better than the lighter duty oils made by other manufacturers. Garage mechanics soon spotted this, and started to recommend Duckham oil to Mini owners. Duckham exploited this windfall well, and aimed its effort strongly against the do-

* Information from Doina Thomas, 'Duckham's Biggest Oil Change' (*Management Today*, December 1967).

it-yourself enthusiast, which included many garage mechanics. In this way it developed a deserved reputation for being a tough oil which was especially suitable for cars with fast-revving engines.

The development of new consumer durables can often open up new market possibilities. For example, there are a number of products in the USA—like pop-up breakfast tarts—which are specifically designed for families with toasters. One reason for the failure of Kellog's Pop Tarts in the UK was the low establishment of electric toasters there.

5. *Differences in Desired Product Benefits*

Every product offers a number of benefits, either real or imagined, and consumers differ in the importance they attach to these.

In the hand cream market, some people prefer a heavy and rather greasy product, like Atrixo, while others like a lighter cream which is easily absorbed into the hands, like Nulon.

In the motor car market, different consumers attach varying importance to performance, economy, styling and status, and each group of needs constitutes a separate segment. The Volkswagen is successfully exploiting the market segment which places economy and reliability at the top of its list of needs, and is less interested in styling or in the status that a car can give.

The cosmetics and toiletries markets are segmented by various types of psychological appeals. The slimming category is split by those who wish to lose a great deal of weight, those who would like to shed a little, and those who merely want to prevent themselves gaining weight. In each case the consumer need is different, and the products or appeals necessary to satisfy them vary.

6. *Differences in Outside Interests or Habits*

Manufacturers are naturally most interested in consumer habits in relation to their own markets. Coca-Cola obviously sees consumers primarily as purchasers of soft drinks, and Ford views them mainly as buyers of motor cars. But companies can sometimes discover new ways of segmenting markets by looking at the habits and interests of consumers outside the categories in which they are immediately concerned. Carreras has done this successfully with Green Shield stamps.

As already pointed out, segmentation of the cigarette market by price group is very well developed, and there seem to be no new pricing segments to exploit. Successful entry with a new brand has therefore become increasingly difficult, because the vast majority of consumers are at any point in time collecting coupons from one particular cigarette so as to obtain some gift. The incentive necessary to make smokers stop collecting for a gift, towards which they have already accumulated a number of coupons, has to be very strong.

Carreras faced this problem in planning a new entry to the recently developed intermediate filter sector of the market (22–24p). They decided to introduce their brand Cambridge with Green Shield stamps. The reasoning was that many smokers already collected these stamps from their grocers and petrol stations, and the addition of a cigarette brand would enable them to collect their gifts much more quickly. The other advantage was that this scheme would be exclusive to Carreras, among cigarette companies. The snags were that the anti-trading stamp supermarket groups might refuse to stock the brand, and that the small tobacconists could be offended by the association of trading stamps with the larger retailing groups.

In the event, some of the anti-stamp grocery companies refused to stock Cambridge, but tobacconists welcomed the brand because it enabled them to compete in a small way with the large groups which offered stamps. Cambridge is now a well established middle priced cigarette brand.

One interesting little brand of toothpaste in America has carved out a highly profitable segment of the market by making a product specially for smokers.

Plus White was launched in 1965, and its advertising spending in that and the following year was only £800 000, which is low for a new toothpaste in the American market. It tasted of liquorice, and offered better whiteness and removal of stains to smokers. Plus White's retail price was 50% higher than any of the major brands, but it passed some of this on to the trade in extra margin (trade profit was 44%) as a means of gaining long-term distribution. Despite, or perhaps because of its unpleasant taste, Plus White was a financial success, gaining a 4% share of the market, which is equivalent to a turnover of about £5 million.

SEGMENTATION IS AN OFFENSIVE TECHNIQUE

A company with a clear understanding of the main segmenting factors in its markets can use the knowledge offensively in a variety of ways. As we have now seen, in markets which are already over-crowded, such a company may succeed in introducing a new product which appeals strongly to one particular segment. Its understanding of the market may lead it to reposition or reformulate some of its existing brands, so that they attack identifiable segments and there-fore offer unique benefits to at least part of the market. In addition, it will be able to position its existing and new brands in such a way that they do not compete head-on—this reduces cannibalization, especially on the introduction of new products. And finally, a well segmented market is more difficult for competitive brands to enter, whether they be private label or from other manufacturers. Perhaps one of the most highly segmented grocery categories is breakfast cereals, and it is no coincidence that very few new cereal brands have succeeded in the past ten years.

TECHNIQUES FOR EFFECTIVE MARKET SEGMENTATION

How does one go about discovering the key factors which segment a particular market? The golden rule is to start by keeping an open mind as to the possible segmentation modes which might apply. Undoubtedly there will be a number of different market segments and some of them will interlock. Segmentation is quite simply a technique for discovering needs within needs, and all the previous research which a company has done can help uncover these. Past product tests, attitude studies, advertising concept tests and quali-tative interviews should all be scoured for new meanings and hypo-theses.

It may well be possible to build up a clear picture of the various market segments from existing research but, if not, a specially devised piece of segmentation research can be set up. There are a number of different techniques for doing this, but most of them follow a similar sequence. First, a number of depth interviews are carried out and, on the basis of these, an exhaustive list of the possible market segments is drawn up. This list is then whittled down to a manageable number and a larger sample of consumers is asked to rate 'ideal' brands according to a list of attributes selected from the earlier depth interviews. Finally, a technique like factor or cluster analysis★ is used to split consumers into groups with similar sets of attitudes or interests. The object is to identify the various segments and to measure their relative importance.

Segmentation research does not work as simply as it has been described. It does not present the marketing man with a neatly packaged register of the key segments and their importance. More often the segments can only be broadly spotted and their relative sizes are difficult to estimate. What is more, merely knowing of the existence of a particular segment is a long way from successfully exploiting it.

PITFALLS TO AVOID

The distance between successful segmentation and wasteful fragmentation is short. Fragmentation consists of breaking a market down into so many sub-segments that consumers become confused, retail distribution is difficult to maintain and large diseconomies of marketing and production are incurred.

Fragmentation often occurs when companies seek to repeat the results they or their competitors achieved by early segmentation. But they tend to focus on very fine differences, which are frequently of little importance to any group of consumers. The American shampoo category is an example of a market which has become fragmented. There is a choice between a range of product forms— lotions, liquids, cream gels and concentrates. Different products are available for dry, oily or normal hair, for blonde, brunette or grey-haired people. The packaging comes in jars, glass or plastic bottles, tubes or aerosol cans. There are cosmetic and anti-dandruff products. And many of these varieties come in four or five different sizes. Breck alone has more than nineteen different offerings. And all this in a market worth less than £100 million at manufacturer selling prices!

The other major pitfall to avoid is the 'majority fallacy'.† The fact that a prospective new product loses on blind test against the market leader does not mean that it will be unsuccessful, as long as it is distinctive and appeals strongly to a worthwhile segment of

---

★ For an excellent discussion of segmentation from the market research standpoint, see *The Effective Use of Market Research* edited by Johan Aucamp (Staples Press, 1971).

† Covered fully in Kuehn and Day, 'Strategy of Product Quality' (*Harvard Business Review*, November–December 1962).

consumers. So if two very different products are being compared on blind test, strength of preference should be checked and carefully evaluated. For example, in America Macleans toothpaste lost blind tests against virtually all its competitors before it was introduced in 1965. Its very sharp flavour and higher abrasive level were not widely popular, but had particular appeal to the minority of the market on which MacLeans successfully built a 9% share.

SUMMARY

Market segmentation is based on the fact that consumers have different needs, and that companies can achieve success by catering for the specialized requirements of smaller groups. Its aim should be to uncover segments which are sufficiently large to be profitable —constant bisecting of sub-segments results in market fragmentation, which is to be avoided.

The standard modes of segmentation are by demographics, value and level of usage. However, the segmentation repertoire is very large, and among other modes are purpose of use, occasion of use, personal characteristics of consumers, characteristics of related products, differences in desired product benefits, and differences in outside interests or habits.

Segmentation is an offensive technique, which can be used to locate new product needs, to position existing brands more effectively, to reduce profit cannibalization and to make a market more difficult for a new competitor to enter.

18: The Marketing Approach
to Acquisitions*

'Too many acquisitions are based on an attractive looking balance sheet and earnings statement plus a quick trip to the plant. The buyer is impatient to act quickly, lest somebody else grab up the prize, and he makes the deal with "details to be ironed out later".

'Later, unfortunately, may be too late.'†

Of all the activities in which a company becomes concerned, acquisitions involve the highest risks, the least accountability and the greatest glamour. They are the one aspect of business that excites popular interest, and in the past, take-over kings have been as well known as leading show-business people. However, despite the aura of secrecy and excitement that surrounds them, acquisitions are merely an alternative to new product development and should always be seen as such. And although financial and legal issues are important in most acquisitions, many of the major questions are marketing ones—the strength of a company's consumer franchise is at least as relevant as its past balance sheet performance. This chapter takes a look at the current acquisition scene, and then outlines how the offensive marketing approach can best be applied to the business of buying and selling companies.

A. ACQUISITIONS TODAY—THE CULT OF THE AMATEUR

Types of Acquisition

The word 'acquisition' is now used interchangeably with 'merger' and 'take-over'. There are three main types of acquisition—vertical, horizontal and conglomerate.

An acquisition is vertical when a company buys another which is

---

* Freely adapted from my article, 'Marketing Aspects of Mergers and Take-overs' (*Marketing*, January 1971).

† By Leighton and Tod, 'After the acquisition—continuing challenge' (*Harvard Business Review*, March–April 1969).

concerned with the making or selling of its products. A paper company which buys into timber is vertically integrating towards its source of supply, whereas a food manufacturer purchasing a chain of grocery stores is vertically integrating forwards towards its point of sale. Vertical acquisitions are a small percentage of the total in both the UK and the USA.

A horizontal acquisition is one where a company buys out a competitor, who is operating in the same line of business. The purchase of Duckham by BP was a horizontal take-over. The vast majority of acquisitions in the UK are of the horizontal type but they are in the minority in America because of the strict anti-trust laws there.

About three-quarters of the acquisitions in the USA are of the conglomerate type, where one company buys another in a different business. Had they gone through, the proposed mergers of Unilever and Allied Breweries, and Rank and De la Rue in the UK would have been conglomerate. But only a minority of UK acquisitions are of this type at present.

A Sale or a Marriage?

In cold blood, buying a company is not very different from buying a suit. You see one you like and, if the price seems right, you purchase it. But many of the best write-ups on the subject see acquisitions and mergers more as marriages than as straightforward commercial transactions. They are replete with phrases like 'the courtship', 'the wedding', and 'the adaptations necessary to a new relationship'. The analogy is coy but true, because when you acquire a company you are taking over people, and your action affects their prestige, security and careers. Many non-commercial factors enter into an acquisition, and these are especially important to understand if you wish to retain the existing management of an acquired company. Understanding the needs and motivations of the key personnel is as essential to a successful acquisition as a firm grasp of consumer needs is to an effective new product development programme.

The High Failure Rate of Acquisitions

The failure rate of acquisitions is quite high but, as in the case of new products, no one has an accurate figure. It is difficult to arrive at because the success or failure of an acquisition is often only known to those who made it, and some companies make elaborate efforts to disguise the fact that a particular acquisition did not meet expectations. However, based on various studies in the USA, the failure rate probably lies between 30% and 50% on the basis that a successful acquisition is one that increases real earnings per share in the long run. Any estimate for the UK would have to be a guess, but the failure rate here must also be quite high.

In the USA 'de-merging' has become a big business, as companies divest themselves of past mistakes. According to W. T. Grimm, a firm of Chicago financial consultants, corporate divestitures in 1970 were up 75% compared with 1969, whereas mergers of independent companies were down by 30% as follows:

	1969	*1970*	% *change*
Divestitures★	801	1401	+75
Mergers	5306	3751	−29

The cost of a failed acquisition is high, both in human and financial terms, and in most cases greatly exceeds the cost of an unsuccessful new product. In the UK, the majority of cash or paper changing hands through mergers is accounted for by deals worth £10 million or more. And unlike new products, acquisitions cannot be tested in the market place before they are expanded nationally, as a means of limiting risk. An acquisition is essentially a commitment to buy a number of national brands, new to the acquiring company, at a single moment in time.

Why Acquisitions Fail

Many acquisitions fail because they were made by amateurs in the art, and this contrasts with the increasing professionalism being applied to new product development. New products are now frequently handled by people with exclusive responsibility and sound qualifications for the task. But in the majority of UK and continental companies, acquisition is a haphazard and stop-go exercise, rather than a continuous programme and there is rarely a qualified executive with full-time responsibility for acquisitions. Many organizations approach acquisitions with no more knowledge or sophistication than the typical purchaser of a second-hand car.

There seem to be four common weaknesses in approach to acquisitions, which account for many of the failures:

(1) Acquisitions are seen in isolation, rather than as part of an overall corporate strategy for growth within which new products and acquisitions are viewed as alternatives.

★ Transactions involving sale of a subsidiary, a division or part of a division by US companies.

(2) Too much attention is paid to a candidate company's past record and present value, while much less thought is given to its *future potential*.

(3) The motivations of the seller are not fully understood.

(4) There is insufficient prior discussion and agreement as to how the acquired company will be operated after the acquisition is completed.

So you think 2 + 2 = 5?

Acquisitions are a fashionable subject. And 'synergy' is a fashionable piece of business jargon. The basic idea it expresses is that the sum of two companies together will be more profitable than each on its own, due to the benefits of combination—in other words, 2 + 2 = 5. However, synergy is usually deceptive. It sounds better in theory than it appears in practice. And it always looks easiest to achieve at a distance and becomes less promising the closer you get.

Some revealing insights on synergy are contained in a study carried out in the USA in 1960–65, by John Kitching,* who has spent most of his business career in the UK. He investigated the merger activities of 22 organizations which acquired 181 companies over the five-year period, and audited the detailed results of 69 acquisitions 2–7 years after the event. Key executives were asked to list the main synergies achieved, giving a score of 100 to the function where the greatest benefits were obtained through acquisitions, and the scores came out as follows:

Major synergies achieved through acquisition	
Financial	100
Marketing	74
Technological (including R & D)	33
Production	36

Financial synergies were almost invariably achieved because the larger business unit resulting from the acquisition increased corporate borrowing powers and sometimes reduced the cost of capital. The marketing synergies were obtained through economies in selling, distribution and advertising. But the technological and production synergies were harder to come by, contrary to the belief of many optimistic acquirers.

* John Kitching, 'Why do Mergers Miscarry?' (*Harvard Business Review*, November–December 1967).

B. THE OFFENSIVE MARKETING APPROACH TO ACQUISITIONS

One can take a 'golf course' approach to acquisitions, where the most likely candidates emerge on the nineteenth tee, or one can take a planned marketing approach to them. I happen to think that the latter is more effective and so does John Kitching, who found that 'successful companies formulate a set of acquisition criteria, which are consistent with overall strategy, then rigorously apply them'.

Of course, one must be careful not to make one's criteria too demanding, because the company seeking the perfect bride is likely to remain a bachelor for ever. And although it is vital not to be hustled in an acquisition bid, time is usually important, and companies who make elaborate studies of possible candidates, lasting months or even years, may often find that the lady has bestowed her favours elsewhere.

The four elements of the offensive approach, outlined below, are common marketing sense, and it is surprising that they are not more widely applied.

The Right Organization

The advantages of a diversification group, responsible for new product development (as opposed to line extensions) and acquisitions, have already been expounded in Chapter 4. It would be headed by a diversification director and consist of hand-picked marketing and financial personnel. Because of its joint responsibility for new products and acquisitions, such a group would regard the two modes as alternatives, and carry out 'make or buy' analyses as a matter of course before embarking on a new acquisition. For example, if Bristol-Myers were considering an entry into the UK toilet soap market, it would be wise to compare the cost and profitability of buying out Cussons (Imperial Leather soap and 1001 carpet cleaner) compared with developing and launching a new brand internally. The attractiveness of the two alternatives, discounted over a ten-year period, could then be weighed. Such calculations will obviously be rough and speculative but, for all their crudity, they can often provide guidance as to the attractiveness of an acquisition.

If it is proposed to integrate the acquired company into the parent company organization, another golden rule is to involve the person who will be responsible for running the subsidiary company in the acquisition negotiations, and to give him a major say in the final decision. This will pay dividends later because the executive's agreement to the acquisition decision will give him a greater stimulus to run it effectively (and no excuses for not doing so !).

Develop an Acquisition Strategy

The second requirement in a successful acquisition programme is to have a clear acquisition strategy. This will stem from the total corporate strategy and plan which, as we have already seen, spells out growth objectives, and from a short list of possible new markets for entry.

Let us take an example. The acquisition strategy for a typical consumer goods company could well read as follows.

POSSIBLE ACQUISITION STRATEGY

The acquired company should have:
(1) minimum turnover of £2 million;
(2) minimum growth of 7% compound in sales and profit estimated during next five years;
(3) at least one point of superiority not possessed by its competitors (e.g. strong brand name, superior products, strong patent position, better sales force, lower cost production, etc.);
(4) management which is sound, and capable of running the business at current levels—it must be retained after acquisition;
(5) terms—primarily seeking companies which can be acquired for stock;
(6) price—maximum price to be paid will be the estimated ten-year future cash flow attributable to the acquisition of the company discounted by 12% cost of capital.

It is important to specify a minimum turnover, because the problems of a small subsidiary can absorb just as much of the parent company's time as those of a large one. In his American study, Kitching found that a high proportion of failed acquisitions accounted for less than 2% of the parent company's turnover—they were not important enough to gain the share of the parent company's time which their problems required.

The strategy of this particular (imaginary) company also requires that the management of any acquisition be sound because, like most organizations, it does not have an excess of high calibre and versatile people whom it can send out to turn around lagging subsidiaries. However, if it happened, for example, to have a number of spare marketing men of high quality, it could move to a totally new strategy. Instead of seeking well managed companies with a growth trend, it could search for businesses which were rather run-down on the sales and marketing side, that could be purchased for a bargain price.

The main advantage of an acquisition strategy is that it forces the top management of a company to some common agreement on the type of company being sought. This makes it possible to eliminate unsuitable prospects either immediately or quite quickly, and to focus on those that look promising.

Evaluate Swiftly but in Depth*

When you acquire a company, you are buying a long-term commit-ment which will haunt or delight your shareholders ten years ahead. If you pay too much for it, your chances of making it viable are much reduced. So how does the offensive marketing company work out the value of an acquisition? For a start, it looks beyond the balance sheet, which is a useful (though often misleading) recorder of history, and focuses on future potential rather than past performance. Secondly, it recognizes that any acquisition has a different value to any other company, depending on the degree of synergy expected.

Applying this marketing/financial approach, the evaluation of an acquisition prospect can be divided into three steps. First of all, an estimate of sales and profits of the prospect company for the next ten years should be made—and this is where the marketing people come in, because you can't make a ten-year forecast by looking at balance sheets and plant. Then the synergies stemming from the acquisition should be worked out, and an estimate made as to their financial effect. And finally, based on these estimates, the financial group should work out the maximum price worth paying for the acquisition prospect.†

* See J. H. Davidson, 'Marketing Aspects of Mergers and Take-Overs' (*Marketing*, January 1971), for more detailed treatment of this.

† The financial group would take the final ten-year sales, profit and capital expenditure forecast, and translate it into a cash flow plan, discounted at the acquiring firm's cost of capital. This final figure would represent the funda-mental worth of the acquisition to the acquiring company over the next ten years.

The main contribution of marketing people to this process would be the ten-year forecast, and the example below shows the type of questions which would be examined.

EXAMINATION OF PROSPECT'S MARKET STRENGTHS

All questions applied to prospective acquisition:

(1) What are the growth prospects of the markets the company is operating in? Is the company well represented in the fastest growing segments? For example, one would like a beer company acquisition to be particularly strong in the keg ale and lager segments.

(2) What is the strength of the company's brands in the market? Did they gain or lose share in the past five years? How far will the factors influencing their success or failure in the past five years be repeated in the next ten? How far did the company's performance over the past five years deviate from its own forecasts and why?

(3) What are the critical skills required for success in these markets and how far does this company possess them? What are the key company strengths and how effectively has it been exploiting them? Does it have any unique strengths or weaknesses versus competition in product performance, packaging, advertising, promotions, production costs, selling or distribution, or R & D? How long are the strengths likely to remain unique and how easily can the weaknesses be eliminated?

(4) What is the company's record of innovation? How well are its current test market products doing, how likely are they to go national, and when will they start to contribute to profit?

(5) What is the likelihood of a major new competitive entry to this market? What is the trend of private label?

(6) What is the retail price elasticity of the company's major brands?

(7) How far does it rely on raw materials with a history of volatile and unpredictable pricing?

(8) What is the estimated gross and net margin for the company's major brands?

Even in an 'arm's length' situation, where there is no access to the acquisition prospect's books, an experienced marketing executive

or consultant could usually put together a workable ten-year forecast in 3–6 weeks, based on trade interviews, published sources and
personal contacts.

Treat the Vendor like a Consumer

Once a company has decided to make a formal approach to an
acquisition prospect, a marketing job should be done on the vendor,
to enhance his willingness to sell and to ensure that he is well
motivated to continue in management after the acquisition.

The first task is to identify the key individual or individuals in
the prospect company, and to approach them either directly or
through a trusted intermediary. One man, perhaps the chairman
or the major stock-holder, is often the major influence on whether
the prospect will sell. If he wishes to sell, one should try to understand his motivations and tailor the offer to meet these. He may be
selling because his company lacks sufficient capital for expansion.
He may be worried about the success of a major new competitor,
or he may have lost interest in the business and want to retire. And
what are his worries about an acquisition? He may be concerned
at his loss of prestige or autonomy, about the future of his employees
or about the way the business will be run.

All these are clear needs, which the acquiring company should
explore before making a formal offer. If it wishes to retain the
services of the prospect company's top management after acquisition,
it should also investigate their needs, and discuss how the company
will be run after acquisition—covering reporting relationships,
control systems, degree of integration with the parent company,
management incentives and future profit objectives. It all comes
back to the boomerang sequence of investigation, design and sale,
though in a new context. An acquiring company following these
steps improves its chance of persuading the prospect to sell at a fair
price, and increases the likelihood that it will be run effectively
by a well motivated management after the acquisition is completed.

C. CASE STUDY—THE GENERAL MILLS STORY

This is a case of a company which at first innovated successfully,
then found that its basic business of flour milling was becoming
increasingly unattractive in the years after the Second World War.
Its diversification programme in the 1940s and 1950s was an almost
unqualified failure, but under new management it diversified
successfully in the 1960s. General Mills failed to take the marketing

approach to acquisitions in the 1940s and 1950s but did so most effectively in the 1960s.

General Mills was founded in 1928, through a merger of four of America's largest mills. At its inception, it was the world's largest flour miller, a position voluntarily relinquished in 1965. The driving force in the early days of GM was James Ford Bell, who launched Betty Crocker cake-mixes and Wheaties, one of the leading American breakfast cereal brands, in the 1920s. However, he held on too long, and even though he retired as chairman in 1947, he continued to hold sway on some of the company's most powerful committees until his death in 1961 at the age of eighty-one.

His son, Charles H. Bell, was made President of GM in 1952, but he had by no means a free hand, due to his father's influence and the presence of many old-timers on the Board. The need to diversify the business, in order to spread the company's interests beyond an almost exclusive reliance on flour milling, had been recognized quite early on, but the new areas chosen to compete in were too often outside the company's range of experience. As a result, new ventures did not meet with success, and the pre-occupation of management with these meant that GM was vulnerable to attacks on its traditional business of flour, cereals and cake-mixes.

Consequently, the 1950s were an unhappy period for GM. After-tax profits in 1960 were no better than in 1951, despite an increase in sales from $436 million to $538 million. In 1954 GM had withdrawn from the consumer electrical appliance market— an unsuccessful attempt at diversification which aimed to exploit the metalworking facilities built up by the company in the Second World War. The Electronics Division, an outgrowth of wartime defence work, was doing poorly, and by 1961 the Feedstuffs Division was losing over $5 million per year on sales which barely exceeded $50 million. Worse still, GM was not flourishing in the food business. In 1959 Procter & Gamble displaced Betty Crocker as the leading American cake-mix with its Duncan Hines brand, while in the cereal market, GM was only Number Three behind Kellogg's and General Foods. The poor co-ordination betweeen R & D and the operating divisions had led to slowness in new product introductions plus a high failure rate.

Recognizing the need for fresh ideas and new management, Charles Bell brought in an old air force friend, General E. W. Rawlings, as Vice-President of Finance in 1959. Rawlings had spent thirty years in the air force, fourteen of them as a General, and for the past few years had headed up Air Material Command. He had been sent by the air force to Harvard Business School in 1937, where he graduated *cum laude*. Air Material Command was responsible for an inventory of over a million items across the world, and Rawlings had applied modern management techniques to this task, including an intensive use of computers, which were used widely outside their traditional application to inventory control.

Rawlings became President of GM in late 1961, and held this position until his retirement in September 1968. Charles Bell moved up to Chairman. Over the previous two years, the company had been undertaking a thorough-going review of its business. GM's problems were that it relied overmuch on one-step conversions of basic commodities like flour or feedstuffs into standard products, where there was little opportunity to build in product performance differences and a tendency for competition to be based on price alone. The flour industry was also a declining one, and it suffered from excess capacity. Other problems were that GM's current mix of businesses had no clear connecting link and no real rationale. A corollary of this was that many of the company's attempts at diversification had failed and, although it had an uninterrupted record of dividend payment, its profit record was unimpressive.

But GM also had clear strengths, and it was on these that Rawlings and Bell decided to build. The company had skills in the marketing of fast moving consumer goods to women and children. Its reputation with the grocery trade was good and GM had a number of strong brand names—Betty Crocker in particular. In addition, it had particular strength in R & D in foods and chemicals although, due to poor co-ordination in the past, it had not exploited this skill well.

The crux of the new corporate strategy agreed upon was to reshape GM from a commodity to a consumer products company, and to aim for growth, as measured by earnings per share. The company would follow a policy of concentration on areas which fitted corporate strengths and had clear profit potential, and would divest itself of any businesses inconsistent with this.

In the early 1960s, the company pursued this offensive strategy by concurrently divesting itself of unwanted businesses and expanding into new ones. In 1962 GM discontinued its Feed Division. The following year, it sold the main elements of its Electronics Division to Litton Industries, the Champion Spark Plug Company and McGraw Edison. One of the companies disposed of by GM—

the Magnavox Corporation which marketed materials and equipment testing systems—was very profitable, but was sold because it did not fit the company's new concept of its business.

Also in 1963, the company decided to discontinue its UK food operation—which mainly consisted of an abortive and very unprofitable attempt to launch the Betty Crocker range of cakemixes. And in 1964 GM made the decision to cut back heavily on its sales of flour to bakers, and to concentrate increasingly on making packaged flour for the consumer, which was more profitable. Consequently, it cut back its flour capacity by 50%.

On the expansion side, the company strengthened its position in existing markets, and decided to concentrate its food business on packaged products with a convenience advantage. Convenience foods were growing, GM already had a position in this market with its cake-mixes and cereals, and convenience products fitted its strengths of consumer marketing and outstanding R & D in food and chemicals. There were some false starts. GM entered the refrigerated foods market in a big way in the early 1960s, but later withdrew. It unsuccessfully introduced a new petfood brand called Speak! in 1963–64 and in the same year it bought Morton Foods, a snack product company, but resold it in the late 1960s.

Its first major breakthrough came in the snack market, when in about 1965 GM introduced Whistles and Bugles, cereal based snack products packed in large cardboard cartons. These were unique products and achieved large volume. They were also probably successful from a profit standpoint.

In the second half of the 1960s, GM built up the second largest craft and toy company in the world, through acquisitions. GM reasoned that its skills in marketing branded products to women and children could be exploited in the toy market. To gain technology, it acquired a number of companies with complementary product ranges. Rainbow Crafts, which specializes in pre-school products, including Playdoh, was bought in 1965 and Kenner Products, another Cincinnatti firm, in 1967. In the same year Craft Master, a leader in the 'painting by numbers' market, was acquired and GM's largest toy acquisition was made in 1968 when Parker Brothers, the makers of Monopoly, the world's leading game, was taken over. To round out the range, Model Products, which caters for teenage boys, was bought in 1969. By 1970, the Craft, Game and Toy Division had sales of $104 million.

Meanwhile, GM was expanding on four other new fronts, all related to the new corporate direction determined upon in the early

1960s. For many years, GM had possessed expertise in soy bean technology. Until the early 1960s, this was used to convert soy beans into oils and meals, but profit margins were poor and this activity was discontinued. From about 1963 GM, using its licence to the Boyer process, concentrated on producing textured protein foods, with the taste and consistency of meat, from soy bean. One of these products—Bac O's—which looks and tastes like chips of bacon, is available to the consumer in grocery stores. But most will be marketed to the institutional food sector only—to cafés, canteens, hospitals and suchlike. The most promising of these protein specialities is Bontrae, which consists of granules, cubes or chips of beef or ham or chicken flavour, that can be added to soups, stews or pies.

A quite different category entered by GM in the past two years is the fashion industry. According to GM's definition, this includes the higher priced segments of the apparel and fashion accessory businesses. This fitted GM's criteria for new markets because it was large, growing, very profitable in certain segments and provided an opportunity to apply GM's skills in marketing branded products to women. GM sought companies with branded lines, and good management, in market segments not susceptible to the risks of high fashion. Following this strategy it purchased David Crystal, a manufacturer of better priced casual dresses, children's wear and adult sportswear in 1969, and also acquired Mooncraft Products Co., a leading manufacturer of high priced jewellery for women, during the same year.

The remaining areas into which GM is expanding are away-from-home eating and direct marketing. The rationale for away-from-home eating was that this is the fastest growing sector of the food market, and GM's strengths of consumer marketing and food technology were thought to be relevant to it. Red Lobster Inns were acquired in 1970 and tests of Betty Crocker Restaurants and Betty Crocker Ice Cream Parlours are being carried out. Direct marketing is also a large and expanding category in the USA, and is becoming strongly geared to EDP techniques. GM now counts EDP among its special strengths, an expertise developed from the early 1960s under the influence of General Rawlings. To gain a foothold in the direct marketing business GM acquired Dexter Thread Mills, which published fifteen million catalogues offering a range of needlework and home decoration items in 1969.

As a result of this offensive expansion programme, combined with the sale or discontinuance of activities which did not fit the planned pattern, the GM of today is a very different company from the staid milling company of 1960. Its growth and profit figures also show a great improvement, as the table below demonstrates:

	1951	1961	1965	1970
Sales revenue ($ million)	436	575	559	1022
Net profit after tax (before extraordinary items) ($ million)	11·5	12·8	20·4	40·6
Net earnings per share of common stock ($)*	N/A	0·82	1·31	1·88

GM is by no means a company without problems. Its percentage profit on sales, while much improved in recent years, is still low. The profits of the Game and Craft Division received a setback in 1970. And England continues to be a *bête noire* for GM, since its acquisition of Smiths Foods in 1967 has proved a poor one so far, influenced at least in part by the unexpected imposition of 22% purchase tax on crisps in 1970.

However, GM is now represented in a wide spread of businesses, most of them offering good prospects for growth and improved profits in the 1970s, and all linked to the company's strengths. It seems well poised for continued expansion in the decade ahead— a dramatic contrast to its unpromising situation at the beginning of the 1960s.

Sources Used for General Mills Case Study

Annual Reports 1960 to 1970.

'General Mills: The General and Betty Crocker' (*Forbes*, 1 October 1963).

'Youth Sets the Style at General Mills' (*Business Week*, 17 May, 1969).

Presentation by General Rawlings to New York Society of Security Analysts, 15 November 1962.

Speech by L. F. Polk Jr to Cincinnatti Society of Financial Analysts, January 1964.

Speech by General Rawlings to Harvard Business School Club of Twin Cities, October 1966.

Speech by J. P. McFarland to New York Society of Security Analysts, 10 October 1968.

Speech by J. P. McFarland (Rawlings' successor as President of GM), 9 October 1970.

* Adjusted for stock splits,

SUMMARY

The failure rate of acquisitions is probably between one-third and one-half. Major reasons for failure are the tendency to view acquisitions in isolation, too great a preoccupation with a company's past record and insufficient consideration of its future potential, and lack of sensitivity to the seller's needs both before and after the acquisition. It is easy to over-estimate the degree of synergy in an acquisition. Synergies seem to be most often achieved in finance and marketing.

The offensive marketing approach to acquisitions calls for the right organization, a clear strategy for acquisitions stemming from the corporate plan, an evaluation system which takes account of marketing as well as financial factors, and an offer which is tailored to the needs and motivations of the seller.

The General Mills case history illustrates in one company the difference between the planned marketing approach, which led to success in the 1960s and the *ad hoc* style which was unsuccessful in the 1950s.

A: Ten-year Record of 20 Large UK Companies with a Reputation for 'Marketing'

	% INCREASE, 1960–69		% ratio (a)/(b)
	(a) Pre-tax profit	(b) Net capital employed	
1. LOW GROWTH, OR GAIN IN PROFIT LOWER THAN INCREASE IN CAPITAL EMPLOYED			
Gallaher	+57	+45	127
Imperial Tobacco	+100	+131	76
Unilever	+53	+71	75
Rowntree Mackintosh	+73	+100	73
Assoc. British Foods	+170	+243	70
Reckitt & Colman	+80	+131	61
Ranks Hovis McDougall	+97	+195	50
United Biscuits	+120	+302	40
J. Lyons	+37	+179	21
Hoover	+2	+94	2
2. GOOD TO HIGH GROWTH, OR GAIN IN PROFIT IN LINE WITH INCREASE IN CAPITAL EMPLOYED			
British-American Tobacco	+117	+102	115
Cadbury Schweppes	+186	+170	109
Beecham Group	+231	+237	98
Spillers	+96	+105	91
Arthur Guinness	+76	+85	89
Brooke Bond Liebig	+161	+184	88
3. OUTSTANDING PERFORMERS			
Rank Organization	+1207	+212	569
Carreras	+342	+132	259
Thorn Electrical	+1126	+526	214
Smith & Nephew	+173	+105	165

Source: Robert Heller, 'British Business Growth League '70' (*Management Today*, June 1970).

B: *Alternative Organizations for New Products and Acquisitions*

New products handled by	Advantages	Disadvantages
Method 1 Managers of existing brands	(a) No problems of friction with separate group. (b) No problems of handover of new products from one group to another. (c) Responsibility of line managers for existing and new products in specific markets.	(a) Little priority given to new products because of day-to-day pressure on existing brands. (b) Unlikely to develop new products in categories well outside company's present market base. (c) Expenditure on new products may be cut to finance current problems on existing brands.
Method 2 Separate new products group under marketing director	(a) More priority given to new products. (b) Responsibility and accountability for new products vested in one group. (c) Full-time effort on new products will give group special expertise.	(a) New product group may become out of touch with markets. (b) Line marketing managers may be unenthusiastic about new brands handed to them by new products group. (c) Acquisitions handled separately.
Method 3 Diversification group handling new products and acquisitions under Board member	(a) All advantages of separate new products group above. (b) In addition, more power for new products function within company. (c) New products weighed against acquisitions as development route.	Disadvantages (a) and (b) of above separate new products group, at intensified level.

C: *New Market Selection Grid and Key for Major Food Processor*

Note: Each criterion is given a rating from +2 to −2, based on its application to the company, e.g. under the criterion 'estimated return on investment', 30% would score +2, 24% +1, 18% −1 and 12% −2.

This grid should not be looked upon as a mathematical formula, but is a useful way of setting down all the facts clearly so that a quick assessment can be made. As a further sophistication, it might be worthwhile trying to weight the criteria, putting key factors like return on investment on a wider scale than less important factors. For the purpose of illustration, we have applied the criteria to the cookie and cracker market, which appears to be unsuitable for this company (a major natural food processor).

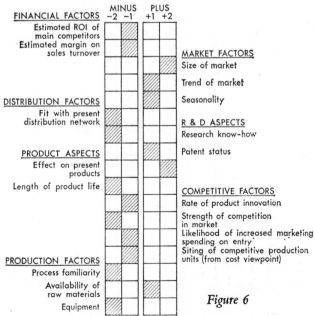

Figure 6

KEY TO NEW MARKET SELECTION GRID

FACTOR	− 2	− 1	+ 1	+ 2
Financial factors				
Estimated ROI of main competitors★	12%	18%	24%	30%
Estimated margin on sales turnover, before tax	6%	9%	12%	15%
Market factors				
Size of market	$30 million	$70 million	$130 million	$190 million or over
Trend of market	Declining	Static	Growth of under 5% annually	Growth of over 5% annually
Seasonality	30% variance in total market size, by month	20% variance	10% variance	5% or less variance
Distribution factors				
Fit with present distribution network	Requires new sales force and delivery system	Requires major modification to present sales force and delivery system	Requires additional personnel for present sales and distribution departments	Can be accommodated without change to existing sales force or distribution system
R & D aspects				
Research know-how	In a completely different field of knowledge from present know-how	Involves much new knowledge	Some experience already	Extensive previous experience
Patent status	Competition completely protected by patent	Competition partly protected, with exclusive li...	Competition partly protected, but exclusive li...	Competition unprotected by patent

Effect on present products	Major effect	Minor effect	Effect unlikely to be noticeable	No adverse effect
Length of product shelf life	Less than 3 weeks	6–8 weeks	9–14 weeks	Over 14 weeks
Competitive factors				
Rate of product innovation	Successful new products frequently introduced, and undermine existing products	Average product life of 7 years or under	Average product life of 7–10 years	Average product life of over 10 years
Strength of competition in market	Several competing products owned by aggressive marketing companies	2 or fewer products owned by aggressive marketing companies	No major national competitors	No directly competitive product
Likelihood of increased marketing spending on Heinz entry	Several competing products owned by aggressive marketing companies	2 or fewer products owned by aggressive marketing companies	No major national competitors	No directly competitive product
Siting of competitive production units	Competition sited much more economically	Competition sited slightly more economically	Company slightly better sited	Company can achieve long-term cost advantage over competition
Production factors				
Process familiarity	New process, specialized machinery	New process, machinery adaptable to other uses	Some new equipment	Utilizes existing equipment, currently under-used
Availability of raw materials	Restricted supply, from outside sources	Limited supply, produced within organization	Occasional limitation in availability	Always readily available
Equipment	Capital cost of over $20 million for national expansion	Capital cost of over $10 million for national expansion	Capital cost over $5 million	Capital cost under $5 million. Equipment for test markets can be hired

* This is taken as percentage earned on total capital before tax. Total capital is taken as equity plus long-term debt.

D: Detailed Figures behind Table 8.2

TABLE OF NEW PRODUCT NET PRE-TAX PROFIT (£000)

	1972	1973	1974	1975	1976
£5 million new brands	LAUNCH	—	700	700 LAUNCH	700
£2 million new brands		LAUNCH	— LAUNCH	280 —	280 280 LAUNCH
£1 million new brands	LAUNCH	140	140 LAUNCH	140 —	140 140†
£0·5 million new brands	LAUNCH	70 LAUNCH	70 70	70 70	70 70
Line extensions 1 at £1 million	140*	140	140	140	140
5 at £0·5 million	70* LAUNCH	70 70	70 70	70 70 LAUNCH LAUNCH	70 70 70 —† LAUNCH
Annual profit cum. total profit Cum. profit gap (as per page 136)	210 210 200	490 700 700	1260 1960 1700	1540 3500 3300	2030 5530 5500
Difference	+ 10	—	+ 260	+ 200	+ 30

* *Note:* These two line extensions were launched early in 1971, our current year.

Assumptions

(1) Net pre-tax profit on sales for new brands is 14% of sales. For a
£5 million brand, annual profit would be £700 000; for a £2
million brand, £280 000, and so on.
(2) Payout of two years for larger new brands with £2–5 million
volume. No profit from these brands until two years after
launch completed. Payout of one year for most medium or
smaller brands of £0·5–1·0 million volume.

Comments

(1) This profit plan depends greatly on the success of the £5 million
new brand to be launched in 1972. For the purpose of this
illustration, we have assumed that the brand has been test-
marketed with flying colours in 1970–71 and is ready to go
national early in 1972.
(2) The five new launches in 1975 and 1976 bring in virtually no
profit during the five-year period we are looking at. They will
only become profitable in 1977 and 1978.
(3) We have assumed a two-year payout for the brands marked †,
in order to be conservative.

E: *Principles of Blind Testing*

The correct way to run a blind test for fast-moving packaged products follows simple basic *principles*. The detailed *technique* used will, of course, depend on the particular circumstances.

(1) The test should occur at the place of usage or consumption. This is usually in the home.

(2) If the product and its major competitor do *not* have distinguishing physical characteristics, which would enable consumers to recognize them even though they were in unmarked packets, the technique used should be paired comparison. This means that consumers should be given samples of *each* product in blind packets, and be asked to use them on separate occasions, and to compare their performance. If the product is easily recognizable—like Signal toothpaste, for instance—it should be tested by consumers on its own, and compared with the product they normally purchase for the occasion. This is called the *single placement* technique.

(3) The order in which consumers are given the products, and the identifying letters or numbers used to mark the blank packets, should be statistically rotated.

(4) Consumers should not be told *how* to use the product, since that would reduce the representative nature of the test. They should be asked to use the product in the way that is normal to them. For example, some mothers taste babyfood before feeding it to the child and others don't.

(5) If the product is purchased by one group of people and consumed by another, it is usually worthwhile conducting blind tests with both groups. In the case of dogfoods, for instance, the owner judges the product by appearance, smell, nourishment value and colour, as well as dog reaction. Dogs presumably are most influenced by taste, and their attitude to a product can be assessed by speed of eating and amount consumed.

(6) The voluntary, unprompted preference of consumers is of most value in blind tests, as in other research. The most important

questions to ask are 'Which product did you prefer most?' and 'Why did you prefer it?' These will elicit overall consumer preference, and produce an automatic weighting of the product aspects considered most important by consumers. It is wrong to start off a blind test interview by asking which product the consumer preferred for texture, then crispness, taste, and so on, because this gives no indication as to how much importance the consumer places on each of these characteristics. Indeed, he/she may not even be questioned about the one considered most crucial and since voluntary comments have not been sought, this fact will not come to light.

(7) The products tested must have had a comparable life. This means that they should be picked off the shelf in a representative sample of retail stores, since it is impossible to obtain factory-fresh production from a competitor. Furthermore, the consumer purchases products from the store, not from the factory. The manufacturing or R & D department should *not* have the opportunity to examine the product picked up, or to reject it if it is not regarded as typical of normal production. Assuming the sample of stores used for the pick-up is representative, the production *will* be typical, and anyway, the competitive R & D department has no opportunity to examine its blind test product for typicality.

A company started to use the market pick-up system of acquiring blind test product for the first time. The R & D department was rather apprehensive, and gained the right to examine the company products picked up, and to reject them if they represented 'untypical' production. The R & D department rejected the first three pick-ups conducted by the market research group, as containing 'untypical' production. As a result, it took nine months to set up this product test and, when it was eventually completed, the marketing department was somewhat sceptical of the results.

F: Common Techniques for Setting Advertising Budgets

(1) *The task approach:* This method involves setting certain marketing objectives, deriving from these the task advertising has to fulfil, and allocating an advertising budget accordingly. The objectives may be set in terms of revenue and profit, in which case the translation to an advertising budget is necessarily rather vague. Or they may be more sophisticated and spelt out in terms of the number of advertising messages necessary to achieve desired changes in attitude. Many subjective judgements on inadequate data may nevertheless have to be made.

(2) *The historical approach:* Some companies base their determination of advertising budgets on the level spent in the previous year.

(3) *The percentage of turnover (or 'case rate') approach:* This consists of allocating a fixed percentage of a product's turnover to advertising. When the brand's volume grows, spending will increase, while if it falls, spending will decline. Opponents of this approach claim that it favours brands which are growing, and cumulatively kills those which are declining. This is one of its major strengths, since it tends to feed potential, and starve problems. The method has to be used with discretion, and exceptions should be recognized, since there can sometimes be justification for pouring more money into a declining brand (e.g. it may be relaunched with a major performance improvement). However, the big weakness of this approach is that the percentage to be allocated to advertising is usually arrived at arbitrarily—why should the figure be 2% rather than 1% or 5%?

(4) *The share of market approach:* This involves estimating the amount of future advertising spending for the market being served, and relating a brand's share of this spending to its target share of the market. An example is given below:

Estimated total market advertising
spending in 1971   £10m
Target brand share for 1971   10%

Planned advertising budget for brand
in 1971   £1m (10% of £10m)

This method is weak because all the figures being estimated are very speculative, and there is no evidence to indicate the most profitable relationship between share of category advertising and share of market sales.

(5) *The 'match competition' approach:* This is the worst available method. It is both speculative and defensive.

G: 50 New Product Successes and 50 Failures Used for _____ Analysis (1960-70)

Categories included in analysis (38 in all)

Aluminium foil
Biscuits
Breakfast cereal
Butter
Cake mix
Car polish
Chocolate confectionery
Cigarettes, cigars
Deodorants
Desserts
Dishwashing liquids
Fabric softeners
Floor cleaners
Fruit drink, squash
Furniture polish
Hair colouring
Hair dressing
Hair spray
Hand cream

Household cloths
Instant coffee
Instant milk
Instant potato
Motor oil
Nappy liners
Oven cleaner
Packet meals
Petfood
Razors and blades
Rice
Shampoos
Snack products
Spaghetti
Tea
Toilet soap
Toothpaste
Washing powder
Yogourt

50 NEW PRODUCT SUCCESSES USED FOR ANALYSIS (1960–70)

Brand	Company	Category
After Eight	Rowntree Mackintosh	
Matchmakers	,, ,,	Chocolate
Marathon	Mars	confectionery
Revels	,,	
Counters	,,	
Albany	Gallaher	
Player's No. 6	Imperial Tobacco	
Embassy	,, ,,	Cigarettes
Embassy Regal	,, ,,	
Player's No. 10	,, ,,	
Sovereign	Gallaher	
Hamlet	,,	Cigars
Choosy	Spillers	
Mick	Petfoods	Petfood
Chunky	Quaker Oats	
Tuc	United Biscuits	Biscuits
McVitie's Butter Crumble	,, ,,	
Cadbury's Smash	Cadbury Schweppes	Instant potato
Wondermash	Dornay Foods	
Nappy liners	Johnson & Johnson	Nappy liners
J-Cloths	,, ,,	Household cloths
Wilkinson Sword	Wilkinson	Razor blades
Gillette Techmatic	Gillette	Razors & blades
Ariel	Procter & Gamble	Washing powder
Supersoft hair spray	Reckitt & Colman	Hair spray
Sunsilk ,, ,,	Gibbs	
Ultra Brite	Colgate-Palmolive	Toothpaste
Signal	Gibbs	
Polycolor	Warner-Lambert	Hair colouring
Quavers	Smith's Foods	Snack products
Chipitos	,, ,,	
Pledge	S. C. Johnson	Furniture polish
Right Guard	Gillette	Deodorant
Kerrygold	Irish Dairy Prod. Board	Butter
Turtle Wax	Lloyd's Industries	Car polish
Dual	Unilever	Floor cleaners
Ajax Liquid	Colgate-Palmolive	
Ski	Express Dairy	Yogourt
Fairy toilet soap	Procter & Gamble	Toilet soap
C & B spaghetti rings	Nestlé	Spaghetti
Gold Blend	Nestlé	Instant coffee
Bird's Dream Topping	General Foods	Desserts
Bird's Angel Delight	,, ,,	
Bird's Trifle	,, ,,	
Baco foil		Aluminium foil
Viota Economix	Viota Foods	Cake mix
Duckham's Q20–50	BP	Motor oil
Cadbury's Marvel	Cadbury Schweppes	Instant milk
Vesta	Bachelors	Packet meals
Shift	Phillips Scott & Turner Co.	Oven cleaner

50 NEW PRODUCT FAILURES USED FOR ANALYSIS (1960–70)

Brand	Company	Category
Trice	General Foods	Rice
Maxim	,, ,,	Instant coffee
Persil Liquid	Unilever	Dishwashing liquid
Dreft Liquid	Procter & Gamble	
Gay	,, ,,	
Wisk	Unilever	Dishwashing cloth
Jergens hand cream	Jergens	Hand cream
Dermafresh	Alberto-Culver	
Clearway	Cheesebrough-Ponds	Hair gel
Aztec	Cadbury Schweppes	Chocolate confectionery
Summit	Mars	
Royal Mint	Cadbury Schweppes	
Puffa Puffa Rice	Kellogg	Breakfast cereal
Corn Crisps	Nabisco	
Krispbred	United Biscuits	Biscuits
Goldfish/starlets	,, ,,	
Tropical Creams	,, ,,	
Golden Glen shortcake	,, ,,	
Lyril	Unilever	Toilet soap
Dial	Armour	
Dawn	Procter & Gamble	
Dove	Unilever	
Crest	Procter & Gamble	Toothpaste
Gibbs Fluoride	Gibbs	
New Dawn	Alberto-Culver	Hair colouring
Belle Color	L'Oréal	
Jacks, Freds, Alberts	Van den Berghs	Snack product
Downy	Procter & Gamble	Fabric softener
Vim floor cleaner	Unilever	Floor cleaners
Mr Clean	Procter & Gamble	
Tempo	Procter & Gamble	Deodorant
Head & Shoulders	,, ,,	Shampoo
Spic	,, ,,	
Cheer	,, ,,	
Presto	Unilever	Washing powder
Bold	Procter & Gamble	
Skip	Unilever	
Diplomat	Carreras	
Cameron	Carreras	Cigarettes
Embassy Kings	Imperial Tobacco	
Betty Crocker cake mix	General Mills	Cake mix
Spree	Van den Berghs	Fruit squash
Swiss Delight	Cadbury Schweppes	Dessert
Nestea (came out before 1960)	Nestlé	Instant tea
Top C	General Foods	Fruit drink
Cerola	Ranks Hovis McDougall	Packet meals
Heinz-Erin foods	Heinz-Erin	
Knorr	Corn Products	
Buster	Petfoods	Petfood
Faithful	Petfoods	

Index